CHRONOLOGY OF THE
ANCIENT WORLD

ASPECTS OF GREEK
AND ROMAN LIFE
General Editor: H. H. Scullard

CHRONOLOGY OF THE ANCIENT WORLD

E. J. Bickerman

Second Edition

CORNELL UNIVERSITY PRESS
ITHACA, NEW YORK

First published 1968 by Cornell University Press
Second printing 1969
Third printing 1974

Second edition 1980

Library of Congress Cataloging in Publication Data
Bickerman, Elias Joseph, 1897–
  Chronology of the ancient world.

  (Aspects of Greek and Roman life)
  Includes bibliographical references and index.
  1. History, Ancient—Chronology. I. Title. II. Series
D54. 5. B5 1978   529'.32   78–58899
ISBN 0–8014–1282–X

Printed in Great Britain

CONTENTS

CONTENTS

NOTES 96

LIST OF FIGURES

PREFACE

THIS BOOK was originally written at the suggestion of Eduard Norden. I was young at that time, and did not realize the difficulty of my task: knowledge is required to prepare a work of scholarship, but only ignorance gives the courage to publish it.

Nevertheless, my very imperfect work seems to have been of some use: it has appeared twice in German, also in Italian, and most recently in Russian. Its aim is to answer a simple question: how are we able to date the events of ancient history? For instance, we say that Caesar was assassinated on 15 March 44 BC. How do we know it? To answer this kind of question, we have to understand the calendar systems used by the ancients and their time reckoning.

The English edition was undertaken at the invitation of Professor H. H. Scullard. At his wish a supplement containing various chronological tables has been added. The text itself has been completely revised and often changed to make it clearer or to adapt it to my present views. On this occasion many slips of previous editions have been tacitly corrected. It is a pity that the reviewers of my book preferred to praise it instead of pointing to its faults. A book and its author profit from blame and not from approval. We all owe a never-to-be-repaid debt of gratitude to Jeanne and Louis Robert for their censorious *Bulletin épigraphique*.

Professor L. Bonfante (New York University) competently rendered my Italian text into English; my students Mr Albert Baumgarten, Mr D. Graves and Mr Alan Koenigsberg checked references to sources and made the index. Professors O. Neugebauer and R. A. Parker kindly answered questions of the author, who was also privileged to use the typescript of Professor

Neugebauer's lectures on Astronomical Chronology delivered at Brown University in 1941-2.

I am writing this preface at the end of my last year as Professor of Ancient History at Columbia University. It seems fitting to dedicate the English edition of my book to the memory of William Linn Westermann, my dear friend and predecessor in the same Chair, and to Morton Smith, my dear friend and successor: *et, quasi cursores, vitai lampada tradunt.*

Columbia University,   E. J. B.
March 1966

INTRODUCTION

TIME IS THE PROPER DIMENSION OF HISTORY. A fact is historical when it has to be defined not only in space but also in time. A fact is placed in the fourth dimension, that of Time, by measuring its distance from the present. Chronology, an auxiliary of history, enables us to state this time-interval between a historical fact and ourselves by converting the chronological indications of our sources into units of our own time reckoning.

If, for example, it is said that Horace 'died on the fifth day before the Kalends of December when C. Marcius Censorinus and C. Asinius Gallus were consuls' (*decessit V Kal. Dec. C. Marcio Censorino et C. Asinio Gallo consulibus*: Suet. *De viris ill.* 40) chronology translates this Roman date into one of our dating system: 27 November 8 BC, and thus expresses our time-distance from Horace's death.

We count by year-units (1967, 1968, and so on) which do not recur, and by months and days, which recur every year. Each complete date, therefore, consists of two parts, the calendar date, which repeats itself periodically (*i.e.* 27 November), and the chronographic date, which occurs only once (*i.e.* 8 BC).

Such is the division of this volume, which is meant to be neither a shortened handbook nor merely a guide for converting dates, but rather an introduction to the basic elements and problems of ancient chronology. The plan of the book is therefore to explain the structure of the ancient calendar, the principles followed in antiquity in computing the years, and the rules which we can derive from these principles in relating ancient dates to our own time reckoning.

Our time reckoning uses three standard units: the day, the year and the month. A (solar) day is the time taken by the earth to revolve once on its own axis. A (tropical) year is the length of the period which the earth takes to complete its revolution around the sun. This solar year equals 365 days, 5 hours, 48 minutes and almost 46 seconds. Our month, on the other hand, does not depend on natural phenomena. It consists of a varying number of days (28 and 29, 30, 31), the sum of which amounts to 365 and, thus, equals the number of days in the year. This irrational arrangement is a relic of the Roman calendar which our calendar continues with only one modification.

For practical reasons, a calendar year must be made up of integral days. In reforming the traditional Roman calendar, C. Julius Caesar established a year of 365 days with an added 'bissextile' day (now 29 February) every four years to account for the difference between the solar and the common civil year. Thus, four Julian years equal 1,461 solar days. Therefore, the Julian calendar advances by c. 44 minutes every four years with reference to the sun. At the end of the sixteenth century AD the accumulated difference between the Julian calendar and the solar year amounted to about ten days. Accordingly, Pope Gregory XIII omitted ten days in the year 1582 (so that 5 October became 15 October) and suggested that three intercalary days be omitted every four hundred years, so that the years 1600 and 2000, but not 1700, 1800 and 1900, are leap years. Except for this correction, our 'Gregorian' calendar is still the Roman calendar as reformed by Caesar (see p. 47). This is why historians use the Julian calendar for the dates before AD 1582. A year contains 365 days and begins on 1 January; an additional day (29 February) is added every four years (1, 5, 9, etc. BC; AD 4, 8, 12, etc.).

The purpose of chronology is therefore to convert the chronological references of our sources into the Julian dates of our era (BC, or AD). The device of counting backward from the (supposed) date of the birth of Christ was first used by D. Petavius (in 1627) and has been in regular use from the end of the eighteenth century.[1]

We should remember, however, to use the true (Gregorian) reckoning in calculating the dates of seasonal events for remote periods such as the barley harvest in Babylonia c. 1700 BC (cf. S. Langdon and J. K. Fotheringham, *The Venus Tablets of*

Ammizaduga (1928), 69) or the inundation of the Nile. For instance, *c.* 4200 BC the Julian dates would have been 34 days in advance of the Gregorian calendar (and of the sun): the solstice 24 June (Greg.)=28 July (Jul.). *Cf.* Ed. Meyer, *APA* 1904, 43.

This volume deals with the dates furnished by the ancients themselves. We do not take into consideration the methods of relative dating developed in archaeology nor the methods of direct dating established by modern science.

The typological method of archaeologists, for example, dates a Greek vase according to its style, that is, finds its relative position within a certain stylistic development. The typological evolution must then be related to some ancient time-scale in order to obtain an absolute date. The relative dating of archaic Greek vases is based on finds made in Italy and depends on the dates of the Greek colonies in Italy. The relative chronology of these colonies is given by Thucydides (VI, 1): Gela was founded forty-five years after Syracuse, and so on. Thucydides' relative chronology, in turn, is related to our reckoning with the help of the tables of Eusebius (see p. 88), where, for instance, the founding of Syracuse is recorded under a date which corresponds to 733 BC.[2]

On the other hand, methods of natural science allow us, in certain circumstances, to determine the age of artifacts directly. For instance, the remains of ancient organic matter, such as wood, wool and bones, that once was alive, can be dated by the Carbon-14 technique; trees, by tree-rings; magnetic measurements and the thermoluminescence technique serve for dating pottery, and so on. Of course, the historian must use his own judgment in evaluating the information furnished by a laboratory. For instance the age of a log given by its tree-rings or by the radio-carbon method refers to the time when the tree was cut down. The log in question may have been used in a building a long time after the construction of the latter, for instance for repair.[3]

CHAPTER I

THE CALENDAR

OUR CALENDAR takes into account the revolution of the sun, which produces the 'day' and the 'year'. Our 'month' is a conventional unit. Ancient peoples, however, with the exception of the Egyptians and the Romans, based the civil calendar on the phases of the moon as well as on the movement of the sun.[4]

THE DAY

The regular alternation of day and night constitutes the first measure of time. The Celts and the Germans counted by 'nights' (Caes. *B.G.* VI, 18; Tac. *Germ.* 11); Homer reckoned time according to 'dawns'.

The working day, in practice, coincided with the daylight hours because of the insufficiency of artificial means of lighting. The period of darkness did not count. The word ἡμέρα (*hemera*: 'day') is used in two senses: (1) for the time from the sun's rising to its setting; (2) for the time from the sun's rising to its rising again (Geminus, *Elementa astronomiae* 6).[5] The same is true for the Latin word *dies*, for our word 'day', and so on. (The composite word νυχθήμερον for 'a night and a day', used, *e.g.*, in Paul 2 *Cor.* 11, 25, is not attested before the first century AD.) Thus, the day was everywhere considered to begin in the morning. This was true in Greece and Rome, in Babylonia and Egypt, as it is true for our own usage. Pliny (*N.H.* II, 188) wrote: 'the actual period of a day has been kept differently by different people . . . by the common people everywhere from dawn to dark' (*ipsum diem alii aliter observare . . . vulgus omne a luce ad tenebras*).

On the other hand, the complete day, for the purpose of the calendar, is generally reckoned in conformity with the respective calendar systems. The peoples who use lunations as the basic time-measurement (p. 16), for instance the Athenians (Varro, *ap.*

Gell. *Noct. Att.* III, 2), the Gauls (Caes. *B.G.* VI, 18), the Germans (Tac. *Germ.* 11), the Hebrews, and others, counted the complete, twenty-four hour, day from evening to evening. We, too, still speak of a 'fortnight'. Where, as in Egypt, the calendar disregarded the moon, the official day began at dawn. The Zoroastrians, who condemned the lunar reckoning as false, insisted that the day was a period between two sunrises (*cf.* H. S. Nyberg, Texte zum Mazdayanischen Kalender, *Uppsala Univ. Årsskrift* 1934, 11). Again, the Babylonian astronomers used the midnight epoch for lunar computations (O. Neugebauer, *PAPhS* 107 (1963), 529).

For some reason, which was already unknown to the Romans themselves, the Roman *dies civilis* (*cf.* *Thes. Ling. Lat.* III, 1214, 60) also began at midnight (Plut. *Quaest. Rom.* 84).

The different periods of the natural day were distinguished according to the movement of the sun (*e.g.* 'morning') and to man's use of the day-time (*e.g.* 'dinner-time'). The corresponding Greek expressions are collected in Pollux 1, 68; the Latin in Censorinus 24 (*cf.* W. Sontheimer, *RE* IV A, 2011). The requirements of war led to the division of day and night into watches (φυλακαί, *vigiliae*). The Babylonians, the Old Testament and Homer (*Il.* X, 253; *Od.* XII, 312) had three watches during the day and three more during the night, while the Greeks and the Romans later adopted the Egyptian system of four watches (Eurip. *Rhes.* 5), which was also widely used in civil life to indicate parts of the night (*cf. e.g.* Asclep. *Anth. Pal.* V, 150).

The division into hours is first attested in Egypt. As early as *c.* 2100 BC, the Egyptian priests were using the system of twenty-four hours: ten daylight hours, two twilight hours, and twelve night hours. This arrangement, based on the decimal method of counting, gave way *c.* 1300 BC to a simpler system which allotted 12 hours to the day and 12 hours to the night. The Babylonians similarly divided the day and the night by 12. The Greeks, according to Herodotus (II, 109), learned this arrangement from the Babylonians. The Greek term ὥρα, from which, via Latin *hora*, we get our word 'hour', originally referred to a season, then to the fitting or appointed time (*e.g.* Arist. *Ath. Pol.* 30, 6;

Sappho, *ap.* Hephaest. *De re metr.* 11, 3=D. L. Page, *Poetae Melici Graeci* (1962) *fr.* 976, for a lovers' assignation). The sense of 'hour' is first attested in the second half of the fourth century BC (Pytheas in Geminus, *Elem. Astro.* 6, 9; Arist. *fr.* 161). At the same time the expression a 'half-hour' appears in our sources (Menander).

The hour of the ancients, however, was not, as it is for us, $\frac{1}{24}$ part of the whole (astronomical) day, but $\frac{1}{12}$ part of the actual length of the time from sunrise to sundown and, again, from sundown to sunrise. Thus, the length of an hour varied according to the latitude and the season.[6] These seasonal hours equalled between $\frac{3}{4}$ and $\frac{5}{4}$ of our hour (for a table of correspondences see Ginzel II, 166; Kubitschek, 182). The hours were reckoned from the rising of the sun or, at night, from the coming of darkness. Thus, the seventh hour roughly corresponded to our midday (or midnight)[7] and marked the end of business hours. Ἓξ ὧραι μόχθοις ἱκανώταταί, αἱ δὲ μετ᾽ αὐτὰς γράμμασι δεικνύμεναι ΖΗΘΙ λέγουσι βροτοῖς (*Anth. Pal. X*, 43). 'Six hours are most suitable for toil, and the four that come after, when shown in letters, say to men "Live".' (The Greeks used letters of the alphabet as figures: thus 7, 8, 9 and 10=ΖΗΘΙ=Live.) The ninth hour, dinner-time in Imperial Rome (Mart. IV, 8), varied from 1.30 to 2.30 p.m. (Ideler, *Lehrbuch*, 260).

As Xenophon (*Mem.* IV, 3, 4) says, the sun during the day, the stars during the night, showed the time. The length of a man's shadow indicated the progress of the day (Aristoph. *Eccles.* 652).[8] Very primitive hand-tables gave the approximate relation between the length of the human shadow and the (seasonal) hour of the day. For the nightly offices in the temples, Egyptian priests as early as *c.* 1800 BC used the so-called star-clock. (The apparition of a certain star in the proper decade of a month signalled the hour.) Sundials and water-clocks made possible a more precise measurement of time.[9] The earliest preserved water-clock (*c.* 1600) and shadow-clock (*c.* 1450) have been found in Egypt. According to Herodotus (II, 109) the Greeks learned to use the sundial from the Babylonians. A later tradition (Favorinus, *ap.* Diog. L. II, 1) ascribed the construction of the first Greek sundial to Anaximander of Miletus (*c.* 550) or to Anaximenes, his disciple (Plin. *N.H.* II, 187). In Rome, the first sundial was constructed in 293 BC (Plin. *N.H.* VII, 213).

Our hours of equal and constant length were invented and used by savants such as astronomers and writers on cosmography (*cf.* Strabo II, 5, 36, p. 133). There were two systems of counting, which divided the complete day into twelve equal parts, as the Babylonian priests did, or into twenty-four constant units, as the Egyptian priests reckoned. The Hellenistic astronomers adopted the Egyptian division of the calendar day but, following the Babylonian counting system, they divided the Egyptian hour into sixty equal parts. They used water-clocks in which a predetermined quantity of water would always pass in the same period of time. Medieval astronomers followed the same arrangement, and mechanical time-keepers were scaled accordingly, so that we still count sixty minutes to one hour. The use of the variable hour, however, was retained in everyday life, and persisted in some parts of the Mediterranean world well into the nineteenth century.[10]

THE MOON AND THE MONTH

As constant as the alternation of day and night is the waxing and waning of the moon which is repeated (on the average) every 29·53 days. The moon has no light of its own, but 'the sun places the brightness in the moon', as Anaxagoras said (Plut. *De facie* 929 b), to whom Plato (*Cratyl.* 409 A) attributed the discovery that the moon receives its light from the sun. Because its period of rotation on its axis is about the same as the period of its circling the earth, the same side of the moon always comes into our view. But when the moon, the sun and the earth are in a line so that the moon comes between the sun and the observer on the earth, the sun illuminates the back of the moon, and the satellite is invisible to us (*conjunctio, synodos*). As the moon continues to move eastward (that is counter-clockwise) from the sun, it reappears from one to three days later at twilight, in the western sky, as the new crescent. The illuminated (right) part of the lunar hemisphere waxes every night. About fourteen days later, when the

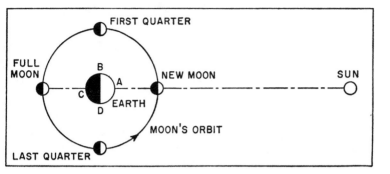

Fig. 1. The lunar cycle

moon is in opposition to the sun, so that the observer is between the two celestial bodies, the whole face turned toward us is illuminated in the light of the full moon (*dichomenia*). Afterwards, the moon again approaches the sun; only the left side of the lunar hemisphere shines, then the moon disappears at dawn in the eastern sky, and the lunar cycle begins anew (Fig. 1).

Almost every people of the earth have used the lunar phases for measuring time: *luna regit menses* (Ovid, *Fasti* III, 883). The Greek word μήν (*men*) and our term 'month' equally point to the moon. The same is true for the terminology of the Semitic languages. For instance, in Hebrew the word *yerah* means 'moon' and 'month', and the other word for 'month', *hodesh*, properly signifies the 'new' crescent.

As a matter of fact, almost all the peoples of the Mediterranean world, the Celts (Plin. *N.H.* xvi, 44), the Germans (Tac. *Germ.* 11), as well as the Hebrews and the Babylonians, began the month at the apparition of the young crescent, as the Islamic peoples still do today for their religious calendar: the new moon signals the longed-for end of the fast month (Ramadan). The beginning of the month was sometimes publicly announced (for Greece *cf.* Nilsson, *Kalender* 29). In early Rome, the *pontifex minor* observed the sky and announced the new moon and, consequently, the new month to the king (Macr. *Sat.* I, 15, 9). Not even the rationalization of the Greek calendar (see below, p. 19) could separate the beginning of the month from the new moon: 'Do you not see, how a slender-horned moon in the western sky marks the beginning of the new month?' (Arat. *Phaen.* 733).

In principle the lunar months of all the ancient peoples run parallel. 'The (Doric) month Karneios is what the Athenians call Metageitnion' (Plut. *Nic.* 28). The Athenian Pyanepsion, the Macedonian Dios, the Babylonian Tashritu, and so on, were different labels of the same lunation.

Figure 2 shows the correspondence of names of the month in several calendars. Yet the observation of the crescent could be hampered by the local atmospheric conditions, and the beginning of the new month at a given place could be accordingly delayed. For instance, Ashurbanipal (668–626) received a report as follows: 'On the 29th we made an observation. On account of the appearance of clouds we did not see the moon.'[11]

On the other hand, neither is the length of the lunation constant (it varies from 29·26 to 29·80 days) nor is the interval between the conjunction and the visibility of the new crescent always the same. Several variable factors, such as the distance of the moon from the sun at the time of conjunction, determine the visibility of the new moon, and the computation of these factors became the main problem of Babylonian astronomy in the Hellenistic age. Last but not least: sighting the new crescent also depends on the longitude and latitude of the observer. Points in the west have a later sunset than points in the east. On the other hand, if the interval between the conjunction and the apparent new moon varies between 16 hours 30 minutes (in March) and 42 hours (September) in Babylon (latitude 32·5°, longitude 45°) it oscillates between 23 and 69 hours in Athens (latitude 38°, longitude 23°).[12] For Greece, Geminus (9, 14) gives a general rule: 'The new moon is visible at the earliest one day, at the latest three days after the conjunction.' Therefore, as based on the sighting of the new moon, two or three months of 30 days (or of 29 days) could occur in a row.[13] On the other hand, the government sometimes antedated the beginning of the month. A court astronomer could write to Esarhaddon (681–668): 'On the thirtieth I saw the moon, it was in a high position for the thirtieth day. The king should wait for the report from the city of Ashur, and then may determine the first day of the month.'[14]

As long as the beginning of the month was determined by observation of the new crescent, the months of all Mediterranean peoples ran parallel. But the lunation is an awkward instrument for measuring time. It is the movement of the sun which determines the succession of seasons and, thus, the rhythm of man's life. The lunation, however, is not an even divisor of the solar year. The earth makes a complete circle around the sun in $365\frac{1}{4}$ days. Therefore, the solar year is longer than twelve lunations by about 11 days ($29\frac{1}{2} \times 12 = 354$) and about 18 days shorter than 13 lunar months. Each lunar month falls behind 11 days in the twelve-month solar year and, within the cycle of $32\frac{1}{2}$ years, passes through all the four seasons. This is what happens in the Mohammedan calendar. Therefore, as Geminus (8) says, the ancients had before them the problem of reckoning the months by the moon, but the years by the sun. The evolution of the calendar, thus, follows three logically and also historically successive stages: 1. Separation of the beginning of the month from the sighting of the new moon. 2. The empirical adjustment of the lunar count to the course of seasons, that is, practically to the solar year. 3. The cyclic calculation of lunar months. The first stage is reached by most peoples. Though the Mohammedan month in principle begins with the crescent, the beginning of the fast month Ramadan was fixed in Turkey by calculation from the date of the latest observed new moon (cf. Ideler, *Lehrbuch*, p. 501). The Greeks never went and never wanted to go beyond the second stage. The Babylonians mastered the third problem. The Egyptian official calendar did not take the moon into account; and the Romans, in historical time at least, disregarded lunation as a time-measure. Accordingly, we have to deal separately with the Greeks, the Babylonians, whose time-reckoning was followed in the whole Levant, the Egyptians, and the Romans, who, in the end, created our own calendar system.

Athens	Delos	Miletus	Delphi
1. Ἑκατομβαιών	Ἑκατομβαιών	Πάνημος	1. Ἀπελλαῖος
Μεταγειτνιών	Μεταγειτνιών	Μεταγειτνιών	Βουκάτιος
Βοηδρομιών	Βουφονιών	Βοηδρομιών	Βοάθοος
Πυανεψιών	Ἀπατουριών	Πυανοψιών	Ἡραῖος
Μαιμακτηριών	Ἀρησιών	Ἀπατουριών	Δᾳδοφόριος
Ποσειδεών[1]	Ποσειδεών	Ποσειδεών	Ποιτρόπιος[1]
Γαμηλιών	1. Ληναιών	Ληναιών	Ἀμάλιος
Ἀνθεστηριών	Ἱερός	Ἀνθεστηριών	Βύσιος
Ἐλαφηβολιών	Γαλαξιών	1. Ἀρτεμισιών	Θεοξένιος
Μουνυχιών	Ἀρτεμισιών	Ταυρεών	Ἐνδυσποιτρόπιος
Θαργηλιών	Θαργηλιών	Θαργηλιών	Ἡρακλεῖος
Σκιροφοριών	Πάναμος[1]	Καλαμαιών	Ἰλαῖος

Aetolia	Thessaly	Boeotia	Rhodes
Λαφραῖος	Φυλλικός	Ἱπποδρόμιος	Πάναμος
Πάναμος	1. Ἰτώνιος	Πάναμος	Καρνεῖος
1. Προκόκλιος	Πάνημος	Παμβοιώτιος	Δάλιος
Ἀθαναῖος	Θεμίστιος	Δαμάτριος	1. Θεσμοφόριος
Βουκάτιος	Ἀγαγύλιος	Ἀλαλκομένιος[1]	Διόσθυος
Δῖος[1]	Ἑρμαῖος	1. Βουκάτιος	Θευδαίσιος
Εὔσαιος	Ἀπολλώνιος[1]	Ἑρμαῖος	Πεδαγείτνιος
Ὁμολώιος	Λεσχανόριος	Προστατήριος	Βαδρόμιος
Ἑρμαῖος	Ἄφριος	Ἀγριώνιος	Σμίνθιος
Διονύσιος	Θυῖος	Θιούιος	Ἀρταμίτιος
Ἀγύηος	Ὁμολιός	Ὁμολώιος	Ἀγριάνιος
Ἱπποδρόμιος	Ἱπποδρόμιος	Θειλούθιος	Ὑακίνθιος

Epidauros	Cos	Macedonia	Babylonia (Jews)[2]
1. Ἀζόσιος	Πάναμος	Λώιος	Duzu (Tammuz)
Καρνεῖος	Δάλιος	Γορπαῖος	Abu (Ab)
Προράτιος	Ἀλσεῖος	Ὑπερβερεταῖος	Ululu (Elul)[1]
Ἑρμαῖος	1. Καρνεῖος	1. Δῖος	Tashritu (Tishri)
Γάμος	Θευδαίσιος	Ἀπελλαῖος	Arahsamnu (Marheshvan)
Τέλεος	Πεταγείτνυος	Αὐδναῖος	Kislimu (Kislev)
Ποσιδαῦος	Καφίσιος	Περίτιος	Tebetu (Tebeth)
Ἀρταμίτιος	Βαδρόμιος	Δύστρος	Shabatu (Shebat)
Ἀγριάνιος	Γεράστιος	Ξανδικός	Addaru (Adar)[1]
Πάναμος	Ἀρταμίτιος	Ἀρτεμίσιος	1. Nisanu (Nisan)
Κύκλιος	Ἀγριάνιος	Δαίσιος	Aiaru (Iyyar)
Ἀπελλαῖος	Ὑακίνθιος	Πάνεμος	Simanu (Sivan)

Fig. 2. List of months

NOTE

1   They are the normal leap months, though other months could also be intercalated. For Athens *cf.* W. K. Pritchett, *CPh* 1968, 53. The order of the months in this Table follows the Attic calendar, in which Hekatombaion usually fell in high summer. The succession of the months in other calendars, however, is not always certain, and the correlation with the Athenian calendar is often hypothetical.

Our knowledge of Greek calendars is very limited. For instance, we do not know all the months of Argos and Sparta, and cannot fill up the gaps by conjecture (*cf.* W. K. Pritchett, *AJA* 1946, 358). The calendar of the Thessalian League was not followed, for example, in the Thessalian city of Scotussa (*cf.* J. Pouilloux, *BCH* 1952, 449). The Greek months were generally named after festivals, and the festivals of the same name could be celebrated at different times in different cities. The same name could also be pronounced differently in another city: the Macedonian month Loos was called Olaios in the (Macedonian) city of Thessalonike and in the East of Parthia (*cf.* L. Robert, *RPh* 1974, 193, n. 7). Again, a festival and a month name could be peculiar to a specific city, *e.g.* Bosporius to Byzantium (*cf.* L. Robert, *RPh* 1959, 230). Furthermore, the months' names were changed for political reasons—for instance, to honour a king (*cf.* K. Scott, *YCS* 1931, 199; L. Robert, in *Melanges Isidore Lévy* (1953), 560, and in *Monnaies antiques en Troade* (1966), 15.

On Greek calendars see Samuel ch. III (and Index of months, 284) with the indispensable *addenda* and *corrigenda* of Robert (1973), 77. For Istros *cf.* D. M. Pippidoi, *Epigraphische Beiträge zur Geschichte Istrias* (1962), 57; for Samothrace *cf.* L. Robert, *Gnomon* 1962, 56. Foreign groups in the Hellenistic Age sometimes used the native calendar: see *e.g.* P. Roussel, *Les Égyptiens à Délos* (1916), 204.

2   For the Sumerian months see Y. Rosengarten, *Le concept sumérien de consommation* (1960), 408, and A. Falkenstein, *Festschrift für J. Friedrich* (1959), 148. On calendars in Ebla in the third millennium BC *cf.* G. Pettinato, *Oriens Antiquus* (1977), 157. The names of the Babylonian months given above originated in Nippur and became widespread after *c.* 2000 BC (S. Langdon, *Babylonian Menologies* (1935)). On Babylonian months before the introduction of the Nippur calendar *cf.* D. O. Edzard, *ABA* 72 (1970), 140. Calendar of Mari: J. R. Kupper, in *Symbola . . . F. M. Th. de Liagre Böhl dedicatae* (1973), 260. Babylonian month names at Ugarit: Ch. Virolleaud, *Le palais royal d'Ugarit*, II (1957), no. 162. The Hebrews adopted the Babylonian calendar after 587 BC under Babylonian dominion.

THE LUNISOLAR YEAR

Experience shows that on the average a lunation lasts no more than thirty days. This makes it possible to regulate the length of a month, without abandoning its relation to the moon. The Sumerians, then the Babylonians, and the peoples following the Babylonian system, e.g. the Assyrians, limited the length of a month to a maximum of thirty days. The first appearance of the new crescent on the eve of the thirtieth day of a month marked the beginning of a new month. If, however, the new crescent, for whatever reason, was invisible, the next month began anyway, on the eve of the thirty-first day of the current month. Months of 29 and 30 days therefore alternated in irregular sequence.[15] The adjustment of the lunations to the solar year was more difficult. As a matter of fact, many primitive peoples paid no attention to this problem. They did not care how many lunar months followed one another between two crops.

The fiscal needs of the government, however, demanded a certain stability in the calendar. For instance, it was convenient for the central administration that a certain tax should be paid in a certain month in the whole territory of the state. The Sumerian bureaucracy, as early as c. 2500, advanced to the practice of exact and detailed daily, monthly and yearly accounting (cf. M. Lambert, RH 1960, 23). The lunisolar year, that is, the agricultural year of twelve lunations, was probably an accounting device. Sumerian records from c. 2400 give evidence for the practice of inserting months from time to time in order to keep the traditional month of the barley harvest, the Nisanu of the Babylonians, in the harvest season.

The intercalation was ordered by the government. For instance, the Babylonian king Hammurabi, c. 1700 BC, decreed:[16] 'Since the year has a deficiency, let the month which is beginning be known as the second Ululu, but the tribute due in Babylon on the 25th of the month Tashritu, let it arrive in Babylon on the 25th day of Ululu II.' In other words, the month following Ululu, which usually was called Tashritu, was to be Ululu II, so that the month of Tashritu was moved ahead thirty days. By means of such additional months which were inserted irregularly, on occasion two or three times during an agricultural year, and at varying intervals, the Babylonians and the peoples of Western Asia generally regulated their calendar down to the sixth century BC. Trade in agricultural commodities, as early as *c.* 1900 and as late as *c.* 525, was often stipulated in terms of the ideal calendar. The dates were to be delivered in the month of 'Tishri', though in a given year the time of picking dates could fall in a month with a different name according to the official calendar.[17] It is probable that the farmer and the merchant relied on the stellar calendar (p. 51) which was independent of the vagaries of the official time-reckoning.

Ptolemy (*Almag.* III, 7 p. 254, ed. Heiberg) tells us that the ancient observations of heavenly phenomena were preserved almost completely from the reign of the Assyrian king Nabonassar (747–733) onwards. Some reports of court astronomers dating from the first half of the seventh century BC have been discovered. The lunar eclipses were systematically observed and recorded from *c.* 730 (*cf.* A. J. Sachs, *Late Babylonian Astronomical Texts* (1955) p. xxxi). The numerical relation between the length of lunar months and that of solar years could have been established as early as the seventh century. Yet, as late as the third quarter of the sixth century, and perhaps for a long time afterwards, official letters continued to inform the local officials that the current year should be embolismic. On the other hand, cuneiform documents show that from *c.* 600 the intercalations followed certain norms. Between 611 and 387, that is, for 224 years, we know of 78 leap-years.[18] Since the quality of many years is still unknown, it is possible that the court astronomers followed the simple rule of 3 intercalations for each 8 years. It is also possible that from the second part of the sixth century on, they followed the schema of 7 intercalations for every 19 years, though the choice of inter-calated years may have been decided from case to case. As Geminus put it: 'It is a matter of indifference if, while preserving the same disposition of intercalary months, you put them in other years.' In any case, the Babylonian astronomers succeeded in limiting the variations of the New Year's date. Thus, under Cyrus, between 538 and 520, 1 Nisanu never fell before 12 March or later than 18 April. (Easter now falls between 22 March and 26 April.) In other words the first month always coincided with the early spring season, while the beginning of every month agreed with the course of the moon.

The prestige of the Babylonian civilization was such that its lunisolar calendar, imperfect as it was at that time, was adopted c. 1100 by the Assyrians.[19] Later the Babylonian kings, like the Egyptians before them (O. Tufnell, *Lachish* (1958), 133), propagated their reckoning system in the conquered territories (*cf.* E. Dhorme, *RAss* 1928, 54), as in the case of the Jews.

The pre-Babylonian time reckoning of the Hebrews is virtually unknown. It is certain that the calendar was lunisolar. The names of some months are known and seem to refer to agricultural seasons. For instance 'Abib' (*Ex.* 13, 4) is the time of ripening barley. The months were also numbered. In 586, after the annexation of Jerusalem by Nebuchadnezzar, the Jews began to reckon by the regnal years of the kings of Babylon (*e.g.* II *Kings* 24, 12) and to use the imperial calendar. As the ancient Rabbis already noted, the Jews had also adopted the Babylonian month names: Nisan is Nisanu, and so on.[20]

The Persian kings, after the conquest of Babylon in 539, adopted the Babylonian calendar. In the reign of Artaxerxes II (c. 380) the court astronomers switched definitely to the 19-year cycle, which became standardized in 367: from now on, the month Addaru II was intercalated in the years 3, 6, 8, 11, 14 and 19, and the month Ululu II in the year 17 of every cycle. In this way, the variations of 1 Nisanu were reduced to 27 days and the difference between the 19 solar years and 235 lunar months brought down to c. 2 hours. As a result, the corresponding years of each cycle were practically identical: in 367, in 348, in 329, and so on, 1 Nisanu coincided with 21 March.

Like their predecessors on the throne of Babylon, the Achaemenids made the Babylonian calendar official in the whole Persian empire. This is shown by the documents found at Elephantine in Egypt. Since these records happen to come from a Jewish military colony, modern scholars erroneously speak of a 'Jewish' calendar at Elephantine.[21] Newly discovered papyri prove that this calendar was used by Gentiles and that it was the official calendar of the Persian empire to the end of the Achaemenids (cf. E. J. Bickerman, ArchOr 1967, 205).

After the fall of the Persian empire, Seleucus I continued the practice of the Achaemenids. He ordered that the 'Syrian' (Babylonian) months receive Macedonian names (Malalas, p. 257, Oxon.). For the Seleucid court and the Greek settlers Nisanu became Artemisios, and so on. Later, the Parthian kings followed the Seleucid arrangement.[22]

We do not know whether the Seleucids regulated the intercalation in the calendars of the subject cities. When the Greek cities became independent, they were free to rearrange their time reckoning as they wished. As a result, at the time when the Roman emperors imposed the use of the Julian calendar (e.g. see p. 50), 1 Dios of Ascalon corresponded to 1 Apellaios of nearby Gaza, and fell nine days behind 1 Dios of Tyre (cf. Fig. 3). On the other hand, two horoscopes from Dura-Europos, coins minted at Seleucia on the Tigris, the usage of Josephus, who equates Nisan with Xanthikos, Dios with Marchesvah (Bab. Arah-samna) and so on, and last but not least the fact that in the Julian calendar of Antioch the first month of the year was Hyperberetaios which corresponded to October—all this evidence proves that from the first century AD on, the Macedonian months were one month behind the Babylonian calendar: Dios now corresponded to the eighth and not to the seventh month of the Babylonian reckoning. We do not know when, how, and for what reason this happened. In the Parthian empire the change occurred between AD 17 and 31, as it seems. A single excessive intercalation, ordered, for whatever reason, by the Parthian king, would suffice to disturb the series of Macedonian months. But neither the Jews in Palestine nor the city of Antioch in Syria were subjects of the Arsacids.[23]

The aforementioned vagaries of local calendars were sometimes caused by arbitrary intercalations. But the fasti were also a part of the given religious system. For instance, the Mosaic law bound the beginning of the new month to the new crescent and the liturgical year of Jerusalem depended on the time of barley ripening (*Lev.* 23, 10; *cf. Ex.* 12, 2). The arbitrary or precalculated calendation of Babylon must have disagreed again and again with the sighting of the new moon in Jerusalem and the growth of crops in Judaea. Thus, the religious calendar of Jerusalem became separated from civil reckoning. Months and days (*cf.* S. Gandz, *JQR* 1949, 264) were inserted at convenience, though the science of the 'calculators of the calendar' was not disregarded. As late as the second century AD the Jewish authorities ordered the intercalation when the need arose. 'The doves being still young, the lambs still weak, and the (barley) grain not yet ripened . . . I have decided to add thirty days to the year.'

We do not know when and how the new system was established. The schismatics of the Dead Sea Scrolls community refused to accept it, and used their own schematic calendar for 'the proper reckoning of the time' of festivals.[24] Thus, the manipulated, 'pontifical' calendar of the Temple was already in use in the first century BC. Therefore, it is impossible to deduce the date of Christ's last Passover and of the Crucifixion from any scheme of fixed calendars (in fact, there is no calendar date—day and month, or even just a month name—in the whole New Testament). Later, but not before the fourth century, the Jewish authorities accepted the principle of precalculated calendation for the liturgical year and, for this purpose, adopted the same Babylonian cyclical scheme which regulated the civil calendar.[25]

Thus, the Jewish religious calendar of today, with its Babylonian month names and the Babylonian arrangement of intercalations, is still the Babylonian 19-year scheme, albeit with some minor modifications. The great 'elegance' of this reckoning was praised by J. Scaliger, the founder of chronology as science (*De emend. tempor.* (1583), 294). For similar religious reasons, the lunisolar calendar continued to be in use in the Orient despite the introduction of the Julian calendar (see p. 50). In fact, it was not the solar year of the Caesars but the Islamic, purely lunar, calendar which ended the use of the cyclical (Babylonian, Seleucid) time-measurement in the Near East.

GREEK CALENDARS

The Greeks went their own way. The early history of the Greek calendar is virtually unknown. The reading of some month names in Mycenaean and Knossos texts, written before *c.* 1200 BC, is uncertain, and, were it certain, would not help the chronologist much. The word *meno* would indicate, it seems, that these months were lunar. Homer is reticent about any calendar. We learn from him that the apparition of the new moon (*Od.* XIX, 306) was a festive occasion (*Od.* XX, 156), but he mentions no month names, and does not number the months within the year, though he counts months (lunations) of pregnancy (*Il.* XIX, 117. *Cf. Hymn. Merc.* 11). A Homeric year seems to be seasonal: the year goes wheeling around and the same seasons return (*Od.* XI, 294; *cf.* Hes. *Th.* 58; *Op.* 561). The Homeric Hymns and Hesiod speak of the same primitive calendar. Hesiod numbers the days in the period of a 'waxing' and of a 'waning' month, but he can also number the days consecutively through (the '29': τρισεινάδα, *Op.*, 814), and he speaks of the 'middle' days of the month.[26]

When and how the later calendar system of a lunisolar year began, with months named after festivals and divided into decades, we do not know. The hypothesis[27] that the reform originated at Delphi in the eighth (?) century cannot be either disproved or proved. Its force is weakened by the observation that the sources do not mention this activity of the Delphic oracle.

The names of the months were generally derived from a festival which was celebrated in the given month. For instance, Lenaeon was the month in which the Dionysiac festival of the Lenaea was held, and so on. The months within the year and the days within the month were not counted, except for some Hellenistic calendars (*cf., e.g.,* L. Robert, *La Carie* II (1954), 194; E. L. Hicks, W. K. Paton, *Inscriptions of Cos* (1891) Index V; P. Herrmann, *DWA* 80 (1962) 8).

A month was rather divided into three decades, and the days were then counted within the decade.[28] The origin of this tripartite division, which was already used by Hesiod, is unknown (*cf.* Ginzel II, 319; E. Gjerstad, *Opuscula Atheniensia* I (1953), 187).

The problem of the irregular length of the visible lunation was solved in Greece as follows: 'For business and social life' (πρὸς τὴν πολιτικὴν ἀγωγήν) the length of the monthly period was rounded off to 29½ days, so that two months came to 59 days. For this reason the civil months (οἱ κατὰ πόλιν) were considered alternately full (πλῆρες), consisting that is of 30 days, and hollow (κοῖλοι), of 29 days (Geminus, 8, 3). The synchronization with the moon was therefore lost, so that the Greeks had to distinguish between the civil 'new moon' (νουμηνία), that is, the first day of the month, and the actual new moon, νουμηνία κατὰ σελήνην (cf. Thuc. II, 28). Nothing illustrates the religion of the *polis* better than the fact that the festivals of gods were celebrated according to the civil calendar (cf. p. 36). But the Greeks had no priestly caste which could have opposed this rationalization of the *fasti*. We do not know when the Greeks limited the length of the year to twelve lunations. Homer, of course, knows that there is a sun year (*e.g. Od.* XIX, 306), but neither he nor Hesiod indicates whether a fixed number of months corresponded to the sun's course. Again, we do not know whether the Greeks originally used the haphazard intercalation of the Babylonians (cf. p. 23). The earliest method of intercalation known to Geminus (8, 6) is very primitive, yet it is already rational: 'The ancients added the intercalated month every other year.'[29] This parallels the alternation of full and hollow months. Two lunisolar years of this kind contain 25 months, that is, *c.* 737 days as against the 730½ days of two solar years. Nevertheless, Greek cities (Herod. II, 4; Censor. 18) and the Romans as well (see p. 43) were satisfied with this device. The Macedonians brought the same biennial scheme into Egypt, and held to it in the age of Eratosthenes and Archimedes (p. 38).

After speaking of the biennial cycle in Greece Geminus (8) continues: 'As the days and the months did not agree with the moon, nor did the years keep pace with the sun, they sought for a period which should, as regards the years, agree with the sun, and, as regards the months and the days, with the moon.' In fact, both the lunar months and the solar year are reducible to the same time unit: the day. A given intercalary cycle attempts to make the number of days the same for the sun years and for the lunar months within a given period of time. The proportion is easy to calculate: $365 \cdot 25 : 29 \cdot 30 = 1 : 12$; $2 : 25$; $3 : 37$; $8 : 99$; $11 : 136$; $19 : 235$. As Geminus tells us: 'The first period they constructed was the *octaeteris* (or eight-year cycle) which contains 2,922 days, 99 months (of which the years 3, 5 and 8 are intercalary), and 8 years.' Yet, as Geminus (8) again informs us, while the eight years contain 2,922 days, 99 lunar months contain $2,923\frac{1}{2}$ days. Thus, in 16 years, the *octaeteris* will be behind by 3 days in comparison with the moon. Accordingly, a new schema was put forward: a 19-year cycle of 235 months, including seven embolismic months, and 6,940 days. The 19-year cycle was proposed in 432 BC by the mathematician Meton, lampooned by Aristophanes (*Aves*, 995). The scheme then was improved by Callippus in 330 and by Hipparchus about 125 BC. The astronomers used these cycles for their calculations (B. L. van der Waerden, *JHS* 1960, 169), and Meton's cycle was of great practical importance for the construction of popular almanacs which offered weather forecasts. When Aratus (750) refers to Meton, he says nothing about the calendar use of Meton's cycle, but speaks of the true message which the stars beam to men, particularly to mariners, with regard to weather-changes. In this sense, as Diodorus (XII, 36) says, to his own day a great number of the Greeks used Meton's period (*cf.* Samuel II).

Influenced by Geminus' report of the progress of cyclic systems, and by the parallel account of Censorinus, modern scholars for a long time believed, and some of them continue to believe, that Greek cities docilely and steadily followed the rules of intercalation which were put forward by astronomers. But Geminus, who elsewhere speaks of a 'civil' calendar, nowhere says that 8-year, 16-year and other such cycles were used by the cities. The simple fact that the Greeks often lengthened the year by adding fractions of a month, day or days, and sometimes shortened the year in the same way (p. 31), excludes the idea that the *polis* ever adopted any astronomical system of intercalation. The magistrates charged with bringing the lunar months into approximate correspondence with the seasons may have used the cycles devised by astronomers as standards by which the calendar variations could be adjusted.

As late as the middle of the third century AD the rather primitive *octaeteris* was normal for the Greeks, the Jews and the Church (Africanus *ap.* Hieron. *Ad Daniel.* 9, 24=*PL* XXV, 524; Eus. *H.E.* VII, 20; M. Richard, *Muséon* 1974, 307). The Alexandrian church *c.* 277 adopted the 19-year cycle. Accepted by Rome in 525, the latter has remained in force until today for calculation of Easter dates (*cf.* Ed. Schwartz, *ZNTW* 1906, 64). *Cf.* also A. Strobel, *Ursprung und Geschichte des frühchristlichen Osterkalenders* (1977).

With or without astronomical advice, the magistrates of Greek cities, just as did their counterparts in Rome (p. 45) or Babylon (p. 22), ordered intercalations according to the need of the moment. In the third century BC, at Samos, a year had four 'embolismic' months (Ch. Michel, *Recueil d'inscr. grecques* (1899) no. 899). Censorinus, writing in 238, when the Julian time-reckoning had already been accepted by the majority of Greek cities, explains the disarray of pre-Julian lunisolar calendars by the uncertainty concerning the actual duration of the solar year. In fact Hipparchus (*c.* 125 BC) still had to oppose the opinion of those astronomers who believed that the length of time in which the sun passes from a solstice to the same solstice again is exactly $365\frac{1}{4}$ days (Ptol. *Almag.* III, 3). Hipparchus himself was able to give the almost exact value of the length of the year ($365\frac{1}{4}-\frac{1}{300}$ of a whole day) which is less than 7 minutes in excess over the true mean year (*cf.* T. Heath, *Aristarchus of Samos* (1913), 297). Yet he acknowledges the possibility of error in the observations, which according to him could amount up to $\frac{3}{4}$ day for the time of a solstice and up to 6 hours for the time of an equinox. Thus too Ptolemaeus, who quotes Hipparchus, was not so sure of ascertaining the length of the solar year (Ptol. *Almag.* III, 1, 1), and the astrologer Vettius Valens (IX, 11) *c.* AD 155 (*cf.* O. Neugebauer, *HTR* 1954, 65) still quoted several values exceeding $365\frac{1}{4}$ days (*cf.* O. Neugebauer, *Rivista degli studi orientali* 1949, 92).

Igitur cum tanta inter viros doctissimos fuerit dissensio, quid mirum si anni civiles, quos diversae civitates rudes etiam tum sibi quaequae statuebant, tam inter se discrepent quam cum illo naturali non congruant (Censor. 19, 4). In consequence, as Censorinus says, the relationship between what were in principle the same months of different cities was disturbed by haphazard intercalations and by the renaming of months which are often attested (*e.g.*, at Argos: Thuc. V, 54; Xen. *Hell.* IV, 7, 2; V, 1, 29; at Sparta: Plut. *Agis*, 16; in Macedonia: Plut. *Alex.* 16). The absence of a fixed calendar is also evidenced by the contract clause: 'if a month should be intercalated', *e.g.*, *IGRR* IV, 949 (Chios), *ABSA* XXII (1916–18) 196 (Mylasa) (*cf.* also W. K. Pritchett, *CPh* 1947, 235; *BCH* 1957, 277). The Thessalian month of Thyos at one time coincided with the Delphic Enduspottropios (*GDI*, 17200), at another time with the Delphic Bysios (*Fouilles de Delphes*, G. Colin, *Inscr. du trésor des Atheniens*, no. 213). In a document (forged in the Hellenistic period) in Dem. XVIII, 157, the Macedonian month of Loos is equated with the Athenian Boedromion, though, in principle, it corresponded to the Hekatombaion.

On the other hand, as Censorinus states, the calendar often did not keep pace with the natural year. Twelve lunations are longer than twelve Greek months (which comprised $6 \times 30 + 6 \times 29 = 354$ days) by $0 \cdot 36707$ days, so that, in order to have the lunar months in agreement with the moon's phases, it was necessary to insert three days every eight years. This in turn disturbed the agreement of the calendar with the sun.

According to Cicero 'it is the custom of the Sicilians and all Greeks, since they wish their days and months to agree with the movements of the sun and moon, to remove an occasional discrepancy by shortening a month by one day or at most two days . . . they also sometimes lengthen a month by one day or two'. *Est consuetudo Siculorum ceterorumque Graecorum, quod suos dies mensesque congruere volunt cum solis lunaeque ratione, ut non numquam, si quid discrepet, eximant unum aliquem diem aut summum biduum ex mense . . . item non numquam uno die longiorem mensem faciunt aut biduo* (Cic. *Verr.* II, 2, 129).

The resulting confusion can be illustrated by some statements of Greek authors. Aristoxenus, a disciple of Aristotle, in order to explain the disagreement of theoreticians concerning the musical scales, compares it to the state of Greek calendars: 'The tenth day of the month for the Corinthians is the fifth for the Athenians, and the eighth somewhere else' (*Elem. harm.* II, 37). Three centuries later, Diodorus (I, 50) explains to his readers that the Thebans in Egypt do not intercalate months or suppress days in the year as most of the Greeks do. Two centuries afterwards, Plutarch (*Arist.* 19) observes that the beginning and the end of months in various Greek cities did not coincide. A wit could say that in Abdera, the proverbial city of fools, every one had his own crier proclaiming a new moon for his master alone (Athen. VIII, 41, p. 349 b., *cf. Corpus Paraemiogr. Graec.* I, App. 2, no. 61, and Crates, *ap.* Athen. III, 117 b (on Ceos)).

The actual sequence of the calendar in different Greek cities remains unknown. Authors, naturally, mention only exceptional facts (*e.g.* Alexander set back the calendar by one day: Plut. *Alex.* 25), and the double dates come down to us by chance and in a haphazard manner. The Boeotian month of Panamos in principle corresponded to the Athenian Metageitnion. The battle of Plataea (479 BC) took place on 27 Panamos according to the Boeotian calendar, but on 4 Boedromion according to the Athenian calendar; at that time the beginning of the Athenian month came seven days later than the Boeotian (Plut. *Arist.* 19; *Camill.* 19; *cf.* M. P. Nilsson, *De Dionysiis Atticis*, Diss. Lund 1900, 7). In 423 BC, 14 Elaphebolion, in Athens, corresponded to 12 Gerastios in Sparta; in 421 BC 25 Elaphebolion corresponded to 27 Artamitios, which preceded Gerastios (Thuc. IV, 119; V, 19). A Spartan month could be nine days behind the moon (Herod. VI, 106; *cf.* Pritchett, *BCH* 1957, 278). It happened, rarely, that two cities agreed to begin the months on the same day (Knossos and Tylissus *c.* 450; Tod I, no. 33). The confusion remained the same in the Hellenistic period. In the collection of letters ascribed to Themistocles (*Ep.* 7, 1) it is said that the last day of the Athenian Boedromion 'is the same day' as 10 Panemos in Corinth; there is, therefore, a difference of ten days. In the second century BC, in Tanagra, the first day of the month of

Thiouios, was, in the lunar calendar, κατὰ δὲ τὸν θεόν, the eleventh day of the following month, Homoloios (*IG* VII, 517). A law of Stymphalia dating from the third century BC sets a final possible date for a trial 'until the tenth day (of the month) according to the moon (κατὰ σελ [άναν])' (*IG* V, 2, 357). Each of the cities of the Euboean league, around 290 BC, had its own calendar (*e.g.*: μηνὸς Ληναιῶνος ὡς Χαλκιδεῖς ἄγουσι). The League decided that the months should be of equal length, but at the same time it allowed each city to add as many as three days (*IG* XII, 9, 207, *Suppl.*, 178). In the Cretan confederacy, the 20th at Knossos once corresponded to the 4th in Gortyna (*IG* XII, 3, 254). On the other hand, the months ran parallel at Knossos, Latona and Olus in 116 BC (*Syll.* 712). The same was true for Ephesus and Smyrna *c.* 100 BC (*OGIS* 438, 90). The calendar difference between Miletus and Magnesia in 196 BC was of one day only (*Syll.* 588). The confusion of the Greek calendar appears strange to us; but a calendar is a conventional device just like weights and measures. Each *polis* had its own mode of time reckoning as it had its own month names and numerals. For instance, the Athenians preserved the acrophonic notation (where Δ was 10) until *c.* 100 BC (*cf.* M. N. Tod, *ABSA* 1950, 126). There was no more reason for an Athenian to get worried about the disagreement of his calendar with that, say, of Sparta, than for a Frenchman to be preoccupied with the fact that the clocks everywhere in France indicate the hour of Paris, which (since 1911) has been Greenwich Mean Time: so that, for instance, in Besançon on 1 November the legal time is 40 minutes behind the sun (*cf.* P. Couderc, *Le Calendrier* (1961), 125).

Moses (*Gen.* 1, 14) and Plato (*Timaeus* 38 c) were in agreement that God placed the luminaries in the firmament as measures of time. Accordingly, as Geminus (8) says, the principle that the sacrifices should be offered after the manner of the forefathers was understood by all Greeks as meaning that 'they should keep the years in agreement with the sun, and the days and months with the moon'. In this way, the same sacrifices will be offered from year to year in the same season when they fall due. The Greeks (Plato, *Leg.* VII, 809 d) and Jews agreed on this point.

THE ATHENIAN CALENDAR

The functioning of the Athenian calendar in the Classical age is rather better known to us than the time-measurements in the other Greek cities.[30] Firstly, the documentary evidence is more abundant. Secondly, the list of archons makes it possible to determine the Julian year of documents. Thirdly, the Athenians used two official dating systems simultaneously: the civil lunisolar calendar and the schematic Prytany reckoning. The *Prytanis* was the working committee of the Council (*Boule*) which governed Athens for a certain fraction of the year. 'The Council of Five Hundred is elected by lot, fifty from each tribe. The members from each tribe function as the *prytanis* in turn, the order being determined by lot. The first four serve for thirty-six days each, the last six for thirty-five. [This makes 354 days for ten prytanies.] For they reckon the yearly period [of the Council] according to the moon.' This statement of Aristotle (*Ath. Pol.* 43, 2) is valid for his time and for the period after *c.* 408 (Meritt, 215; *cf.* W. K. Pritchett, *BCH* 1964, 473). The length of service of the Council before this date is uncertain. From an accounting record (*IG* I, 324 = Tod I, 64) it was inferred that in 426/5–423/2 four prytany years amounted to 1,464 days (*cf. IG* I², 155; Ginzel II, 80), but some figures are not preserved on the stone, and the restorations are doubtful.[31]

The *Boule* probably took office, together with the archon, on 1 Hekatombaion, but in 411 its mandate ended on 13 Skirophorion (Arist. *Ath. Pol.* 32), that is, some fifteen days before the term of the archon's year 412/411.

After Aristotle's time, from 307/6 to 224/3 there were twelve tribes. During this period prytanies and the months of the civil year probably run parallel (*cf.* Pollux VIII, 115; Meritt, 135). There were thirteen tribes from 223/2 to 202/1, eleven in 201/1, and again twelve from 200 BC until the time of Hadrian.

In Classical Athens the count of prytanies served as the working calendar of the government. For instance, the armistice of 423 was accepted by the popular assembly when the tribe of Acmantis held the prytany (Thuc. IV, 119). The revalidation of the extant laws had to be voted by the popular assembly on the 11th day of the first prytany (Dem. 24, 25), and so on. The financial records of the government (Arist. *Ath. Pol.* 47), including mining leases (M. Crosby, *Hesp.* 1950, 192), were reckoned on the same time-standard. A public debtor who had not paid by the ninth prytany lost his civic rights (Dem. 24, 87). The civil calendar, the twelve months of the archon's year, was used for general indications of time. Thus, for instance, a marriage was concluded when Polyzelus was archon (367 BC) in Skirophorion, and the divorce document written when Timocrates was archon (364 BC) in Poseideon (Dem. 30, 15).[32]

The extant evidence shows that the Athenians did not use Meton's cycle or some other regular system of intercalation for adjusting the official calendar,[33] though as Petavius supposed (Ideler I, 318), the cyclic calculation might help the magistrates in adjusting the calendar to the course of the sun (*cf.* p. 30). In Athens, as in Sicily (p. 31), months were added as needed. For instance, *c.* 420, the people decreed that the archon of the coming year should intercalate the month of Hekatombaion (*IG* I, 76). As late as the second century BC the intercalation was handled so haphazardly that two successive years could have extra months (Margaret Thompson, *The New Style Silver Coinage of Athens* (1961), 612). The Athenians may have adopted the principle of alternating full and hollow months (p. 28, and *cf.* Meritt, 84). In practice, days could be suppressed (*cf.* W. K. Pritchett, *BCH* 1964, 460, 473) or inserted (W. K. Pritchett, *BCH* 1957, 276) at will. The essential reason for such adjustment was that the dates of most religious acts were fixed in the official calendar. The temple of Dionysus in Limnae could be opened only once in a year, namely on 12 Anthesterion (Dem. 30, 15), and so on. The *fasti*, first published by Solon (Plut. *Solon*, 25; Nilsson, *Kalender*, 68), were inscribed on stones. Thus, everyone could read that, for instance, the sacrifice to the Kourotrophos which was to be offered by the *deme* of Erchia had to be offered on 3 Skirophorion.[34]

It would have been an offence against the gods if these fixed dates were disregarded. But it was possible to change the position of the given fixed date in respect to the movement of the heavenly bodies. For instance, the theatrical representation at the Great Dionysia was to be held on 10 Elaphebolion (*cf.* L. Deubner, *Attische Feste* (1932), 142). In 270, for some reason, the performance was to be postponed. Accordingly, the four days following 9 Elaphebolion were counted as the second, third and fourth 'inserted' 9 Elaphebolion. Ἐλαφηβολιῶνο[ς] [ἐ]νάτει ἱσταμένου τετάρτει ἐμβολίμωι (W. B. Dinsmoor, *Hesp.* 1954, 299). Again, the Athenians could rename the month Mounichion first Anthesterion and then Boedromion, to allow Demetrius Poliorcetes to be initiated in the lesser mysteries of Eleusis (celebrated in Anthesterion) and in the greater (celebrated in Boedromion) during his short stay in their city (Plut. *Demetr.* 26). On the other hand, as the popular assembly did not meet on feasts and unlucky days (Busolt-Swoboda, II, 988), this tampering with the calendar could also play into the hands of the politicians. If the gods, as Aristophanes supposed, lived according to the true time, the Athenian calendar often made them 'go to bed without their supper' (*Nubes*, 618).

Therefore, the length of a given civil year or month must be established empirically, and the proposed schemes of the Athenian civil year can only be tentative. The prytany year sometimes can help in this respect. Athenian documents often bear double dates: the date of the civil and of the prytany calendar. The prytanies were numbered from 394, and the day within the prytany was stated from 346 on. For instance, a decree gives the equation: 23rd day of the IX Prytany = 11 Thargelion (*Syll.* 287). In this way we can find out whether the given civil year was intercalated. (The length of each prytany in the intercalated year was extended.) For instance, in 333/2 the 29th day of the I Prytany fell on the 9th day of the second month (Metageitnion) of the civil year. Thus, the first prytany had a length of 39 days (at least), and the year 333/2 was intercalary (*IG* II, 338). On the other hand, in 332/1, the 19th Elaphebolion, that is to say, the 255th day of the standard civil year, corresponded to the 7th day of the VIII Prytany (*IG* II, 345). Thus, the Prytanies I–VII contained 248 days, and the whole year included (248:7) × 10 = 354 (or 355) days. In other words, the year 332/1 was a common year. Of course one of the double dates may be lost, or even not recorded at all on stone (*cf.*, *e.g.*, *IG* II, 337 of 333/2). Though in the fourth century the prytany year and the archon's year were coterminous, we do not know the Julian dates for 1 Hekatombaion. The hypothesis, deduced from Plato, *Leg.* VI, 767 and Arist. *H. Anim.* 543 b (Ginzel II, 380; Samuel, 64), and repeated by recent scholars, that the beginning of the year coincided with the summer solstice moon remains unproven and improbable. It postulates that the Athenians tried to balance the number of inserted and suppressed days in every official year. They were probably more casual. The *parapegma* (p. 58) made it easy to overlook the vagaries of the official time-measurement. The equation of an Athenian with a Julian date is possible only in exceptional cases (*cf.* W. K. Pritchett, *CPh.* 1947, 235). This is true even for astronomical dates (*e.g.* Ptol. *Almag.* IV, 11: the eclipse of 23 December 383 occurred when Phanostratus was archon, in the month of Poseideon), since the astronomers used the Athenian calendar names for their theoretical calendar of mean lunations[35] (*cf.* B. L. van der Waerden, *Museum Helveticum* 1958, 106). As to the prytanies, their lengths may have been tampered with, but no evidence of this practice has yet been found. The, at least relative, stability of the prytany calendar may depend on its use in financial records. The use of a schematic year of 12×30 days months in business (A. Mommsen, *Chronologie* (1883), 48; Sontheimer, *RE* XVI, 16) again palliated the inconvenience of the civil year.

The most important corrective was furnished by the direct observation of the moon. Neglecting the official reckoning, the man in the street started to count the days of the new month at sighting of the new crescent. As Aristophanes (*Nubes*, 626) sententiously advises Athenian politicians to regulate days of their life according to the moon: κατὰ σελήνην ὡς ἄγειν χρὴ τοῦ βίου τὰς ἡμέρας, from the beginning of the second century the official dating included the reference to the true course of the moon. The date within the year was given 'according to the archon' and 'according to the deity', *i.e.* Selene, the Moon (*cf.*, *e.g.*, *IG*

II, 967: Ἐλαφηβολιῶνος ἐνάτει μετ᾿ εἰκάδας κατ᾿ ἄρχοντα κατὰ θεὸν δὲ Μουνιχιῶνος δωδεκάτει). Hence, in this year of Achaios' archonship, when the official calendar recorded the date as 19 Elaphebolion, the moon was already in the 12th day of the following lunation (Mounichion). But in the year of Euergetes, 19 Elaphebolion of the archon was only two days behind the moon (cf. B. D. Meritt, Hesp. 1957, 73; Pritchett–Neugebauer, 15; Pritchett, 330; J. Pouilloux, REA 1964, 211).

THE MACEDONIAN CALENDAR IN EGYPT

Alexander the Great brought the Macedonian lunisolar calendar to Egypt, and the Ptolemies held to it for a long time. The months had 29 and 30 days, the days of the month were numbered successively, and the '29' was omitted in a hollow month (P. Cornell, 1) so that the last day of the month was always counted as '30'. A month was intercalated from time to time (Plut. Alex, 16; FrGrH 257 a, 3; cf. P. Oxyr. XVII, 2082). How the calendar was handled outside Egypt remains unknown. For the Seleucids (cf. p. 25) Alexander the Great died on 29 Airu of the Babylonians, that is, in the evening of 10 June 323 (A. E. Samuel, Ptolemaic Chronology (1962), 47). According to Alexander's Ephemerids the king died on the last day of the month Daisios (Plut. Alex. 75–76). Thus, at this time, the Macedonian calendar agreed with the moon. (Or did Alexander, as later Seleucus I, use the Babylonian cyclic system?) The date of Alexander's death in Pseudo-Callisthenes (Historia Alexandri Magni 146, ed. G. Kroll: 13 Pharmuthi = 13 June) is erroneous.

The Greek documents of Ptolemaic Egypt offer numerous equations between the Macedonian and the Egyptian dates. The latter are easily converted into Julian dates (see p. 40). The evidence shows that until c. 240 the Macedonian months agreed with the moon. It appears that the calendar was regulated by the Egyptian 25-year cycle. As in the old Macedonian calendar, an intercalary month was inserted every other year (cf. p. 28), though the cycle required only nine intercalations (1,309 lunar months = 25 Egyptian years = 9,125 days). But because the calendar was regulated by the solar year, it did not become confused by superfluous intercalations. Only the order of the names of the months in the solar year was affected.

The Macedonian calendar survived in Egypt chiefly for cult purposes. Even the feasts of the Egyptian gods were set up by the Alexandrian court according to the Macedonian calendar. The relationship of months to seasons, however, was affected by the adjustment to the solar year and by the extra intercalations. The 1st of Dios varied in position from 25 August in the beginning, to 15 January at the end of the reign of Ptolemy II. On the other hand the Egyptian calendar, which was simpler, was more convenient for everyday affairs (see a list of Egyptian months on a stone in Samos, a Ptolemaic possession: L. Robert, *Etudes épigraphiques* (1938), 118 and *cf.* P. Roussel, *Les cultes égyptiens à Délos* (1916), 204). Already in the middle of the third century BC, the Greeks in Egypt calculated according to the Egyptian calendar; so that, for example, a Greek in 257 BC asked on what Egyptian date of that year the birthday of the king would fall—the king's birthday was fixed according to the Macedonian calendar (*P. Cair. Zen.* IV, 59541). The Macedonian calendar was used for all official acts. So in Morocco today, the solar calendar is used in business life, while officially, the dating system runs according to the Islamic lunar year (*cf.* E. Westermarck, *Ritual and Belief in Morocco* II (1926), 150). But the Egyptian year, in turn, being mobile, the Greeks consulted the stellar calendar (see p. 54) arranged according to the course of the Egyptian year. In this way, the festivals could be celebrated year after year at the same time of the true solar year (*P. Hibeh*, 27; *P. Paris*, 1; F. Blass, *Ars Eudoxi*, 1887).

Under the rule of Ptolemy III the synchronization of the Macedonian calendar with the moon was neglected. For example, 1 Gorpiaios in 232 BC fell five days after the full moon. At the end of the third century BC (*cf.* P. *Tebt.* III, 820) the Macedonian calendar was adjusted to agree with the Egyptian, so that the names of the Macedonian months were only different denominations for the Egyptian months. At first the equation was Dystros = Thot, and so on. Ptolemy VII Philometor then re-established the Macedonian calendar in 163 BC (U. Wilcken, *Urkunden*

Ptolemäerzeit I (1927), 496), but his action was repealed after his death in 145 BC. A new equation of Macedonian and Egyptian months (this time Dios=Thot) came into use later (the first evidence is in 199 BC), although the preceding system existed until the end of the second century AD. As in the area ruled by the Seleucids, in Egypt, too, the Greek calendar was replaced by the local calendar. However, while in the case of the Seleucids the lunisolar calendar was merely corrected, the Ptolemies in effect completely abolished the lunisolar reckoning of time.[36]

THE EGYPTIAN YEAR

'The Egyptians, alone and always, had a year of definite length. Other peoples varied it by different but equally erroneous reckonings' (Macrob. *Sat.* I, 12, 2). The Egyptians had *anni certus modus* because their year was composed of days only. These 365 days were schematically grouped into four seasons, and twelve months of thirty days plus five supplementary days (ἐπαγόμεναι).[37] The days within the month were counted successively. The months were counted, from the first to the fourth, within each of the three agricultural seasons: 'Inundation' (when the Nile overflowed the fields), 'Going out' (from the Nile waters; time of agricultural work) and 'Deficiency' (the season of low water). In later popular usage, the Egyptian months were named after festivals. We transcribe these names (inherited by the Copts) according to their Greek form: Thot, Phaophi, Athyr, Choiak, Tybi, Mecheir, Phanemoth, Pharmuthi, Pachon, Payni, Epeiph, Mesore (plus five epagomenal days). *Cf.* T. G. H. James, *The Hekanakhte Papers* (1962), 3.

The resulting year, which was $\frac{1}{4}$ day shorter than the actual solar year, could have been corrected by means of intercalation, but this was not done in Egypt. Therefore every four years the beginning of the year (1st of Thot) was delayed by one day in respect to the solar year. Every month—in the course of the cycle of 1,461 Egyptian years (=1,460 Julian)—thus rotated through all seasons of the solar year. (*Cf.* Sethe, *GGN* 1920, 30; R. A. Parker, *Revue d'Egyptologie* 1957, 85.) It should be noted, however, that the length of a Sirius cycle is somewhat variable (*cf.* M. F. Ingham, *JEA* 1969, 36).

The decree of Canopus (*OGIS*, 56) says: 'It came about that the festivals which were celebrated in winter fell in the summer, and that those celebrated in summer were instead in the winter.' The priests, however, blocked the reform proposed in 238 BC by Ptolemy III to correct the *annus vagus*.

In effect, alongside the official year, there was the popular lunar calendar of alternating months of 29 and 30 days which is attested from *c.* 1900 on. It was basic in everyday life and used for cult purposes (*cf.* D. Bonneau, *Revue d'Egyptologie* 1971, 57). At some time (before 235 BC), the Egyptians devised a 25-year cycle of 309 months which indicated the dates of the civil calendar on which the lunar months were to begin (*cf.* R. A. Parker, *JNES* 1957, 39; 1970, 217; Neugebauer, 90). The Egyptian lunar month began in the early morning (*cf.* R. A. Parker, *JNES* 1970, 217).

The Egyptian mobile year was independent of both sun and moon, but, as often among primitive peoples (M. P. Nilsson, *Acta Orientalia* 1941, 1 = *Opusc. Selecta* II, 54), it was related to a fixed star. The sighting of Sirius in the east horizon at sunrise, on 19 July, after the star had been invisible for about 70 days, fell close to the beginning of the flood of the Nile, and thus to the Egyptian New Year, the first day of the first month of the Inundation season, that is, 1 Thot. The Egyptians praised the star as 'the Bringer of the Nile' and 'the Renewer of the Year' (Plut. *De Isid.* 38; *cf.* Th. Hopfner, *Plutarch über Isis und Osiris* II (1941), 174). The sighting of the star was officially announced: 'Sirius rises on 16 Pharmuthi', and so on (see p. 83). The Sirius year, however, corresponds to the solar year (which is by *c.* 12 minutes shorter). Thus, the rising of Sirius fell on 1 Thot once every 1,460 Julian years. Censorinus tells us that it happened on 21 July (in fact 20 July), AD 139.

In agreement with his contemporaries—coins were issued at Alexandria representing the fabulous bird, the phoenix, the symbol of renewal, with the legend *AION* (J. Vogt, *Die Alexandrinischen Münzen* (1924), 115)—Censorinus spoke of the return of *annus canicularis* (Sirius being also called *Canis maior*). From his words modern scholars inferred, without any warrant, that the Egyptian *annus vagus* must have started on the day when the heliac rising of Sirius fell on 1 Thot. From Fréret (1758) on, they hesitated between 1322 and 2782 as the starting years of the Egyptian calendar (Ideler I, 126). Ed. Meyer went back to 4241. But the dispute is futile. A calendar is a tool which cannot be justified by either logic or astronomy. The Egyptian calendar took account of the Nile and not of Sirius[38] (O. Neugebauer, *Acta Orientalia* 1938, 169; *JNES* 1942, 396). Furthermore, there is no inherent necessity to start a new calendar on its first day. England changed from the Julian calendar and the year beginning on 25 March, to the Gregorian style and the adoption of 1 January as the New Year, on 2 September 1752.

In fact originally the Egyptians, together with many primitive peoples, did not count by years, but by agricultural seasons (Diod. I, 26, 5). All conjectures about the date of the introduction of the *annus vagus* are premature. We can only state that there is evidence of the use of the variable year from the V Dynasty on, that the rising of Sirius was observed as early as *c.* 1900, and that the celebration of this event was, from the Middle Kingdom, a changeable date in the civil year.

The 'day' and the (lunar) 'month', as their hieroglyphic signs show, were related to the sun and the moon respectively (K. Sethe, *Vom Bilde zum Buchstaben* (1939), 23). The Egyptian word for 'year' does not have any astronomical connotation; it means 'renewal' and each year was a beginning (E. Edel, *Altaegyptische Grammatik* (1955), 179; id. *JNES* 1949, 35; *cf.* Gardiner, 70).

The variable year probably was introduced for administrative purposes. The Egyptians had the schematic financial year of $12 \times 30 = 360$ days. The *annus vagus* originated when the financial year, by the addition of five epagomenal days, was equated with the mean agricultural year, which in Egypt happened to have the same length as the solar year: the regularity of the flood of the Nile was conditioned by the snow thaw in mountains of Ethiopia (*cf.* D. Bonneau, *La crue du Nil* (1964), 29).

The divergence of the Egyptian year from the course of the sun is almost imperceptible in one lifetime: the difference in forty years amounts only to ten days. For Herodotus (II, 4) the Egyptian year agreed with the cycle of the seasons. The advantages of the Egyptian calendar—its simplicity and regularity—are so obvious that astronomers, from Hellenistic times to Copernicus, used it.

For the same practical reason, the schematic year of 12 × 30 + 5 days, probably based on the Babylonian business year of 12 × 30 days (*cf.* O. Neugebauer, *JNES* 1942, 400), became the official system of time-reckoning in Persia under the Sassanids as well as in Armenia and Cappadocia.[39] (According to Arabian astronomers the Sassanian year was adjusted to the succession of seasons by the intercalation of one month every 120 years.) *Cf.* A. Christensen, *L'Iran des Sassanides* (1944), 168; E. S. Kennedy and B. L. van der Waerden, *JAOS* 1963, 315; E. J. Bickerman, *ArchOr* 1967, 197; id. in *Cambridge History of Iran* III.

THE ROMAN CALENDAR

The Roman calendar, at the time of Caesar, consisted of 12 months; 4 of 31 days (Martius, Maius, Quintilis = July, October), 7 of 29 (Ianuarius, Aprilis, Iunius, Sextilis = August, September, November, December) and 1 of 28 (Februarius), totalling 355 days in a year.[40]

Every other year (in the even years BC) 22 or 23 days were intercalated. The intercalation took place in February, after the feast of *Terminalia* (23 February); while the 5 remaining days of February were added at the end of the intercalary month (*Intercalaris*), so that this month consisted of 27 or 28 days.

The first day of the month was called *Kalendae*, the 5th (or the 7th in a month of 31 days) *Nonae*, the 13th (or the 15th of the months which contained 31 days) *Idus*. Counting backwards from these established dates, one calculated the days of the month. The calculation was inclusive; that is to say, the day from which one counted and the day to be designated were both included. Thus 2 January was: *ante diem IV Non. Jan.*; 2 March: *ante diem VI Non. Mart.* The day before the last day to be counted was called *pridie* (Table IV, p. 125). The last days of February, after the Ides, were counted in the intercalary year back from the beginning of the inserted month: *ante (diem) V Kal. Intercalaris*

=20 February (Cic. *Pro Quinct.* 79). Sometimes as late as 14 February it was unknown whether the *pontifices* would intercalate a month: in this case 14 February became *ante diem X Terminalia* (Dessau, 6302=Degrassi, 719).

Counting the days in succession, although possible, appears rarely (A. Gagner, in *Festskrift Per Persson* (1922), 202).[41]

No account of the moon was taken in this system; on the contrary, the biennial insertion of 22 (23) days must have destroyed all agreement with the lunations. Yet the days within the month were numbered from the coming moon phases backwards. A *pontifex* announced the new crescent (p. 17) and according to its form and position told how many days were to be counted until the Nones, that is, the first quarter. At the Nones it was again proclaimed how many days there were until the Ides (the full moon), and on which days the festivals were to be celebrated (Ginzel II, 173).

The Roman calendar, however, with its many peculiar features (the length of the months, the intercalation system) was rather a conscious effort at 'synchronizing the civil and solar years' (Censor. 20, 6). Yet, the Roman quadrennial cycle consisted of 355+378+355+377 days. It looks as if its author tried to adjust the lunar year to the path of the sun, that is, to the agrarian year. (The months of 29, 30, and 31 days also occur in Greek meteorological calendars.) But the Roman 4-year cycle amounted to 1,465 days, that is, it was four days longer than four solar years. Thus the calendar was behind four days every quadrennium in respect to the seasons. In fact, it was not easy to establish the true length of the solar year (p. 30). Herodotus (I, 32) erred in this respect; the great engineer Harpalus (*c.* 480) believed that the revolution of the sun takes 365 days and 13 hours and, as late as *c.* 190, Ennius spoke of 366 days of the solar year. We cannot be surprised at the mistakes made by the Roman peasants *c.* 500: 'Your knowledge, Romulus, of weapons was better than of stars' (*Scilicet arma magis quam sidera, Romule, noras,* Ovid, *Fasti* I, 28).

The Roman pseudo-solar cycle was probably a modification of the 'year of Romulus', that is, of the purely agricultural ten-month year which ran from March to December, the 'tenth' month. Primitive peoples often take into account only the period of agricultural activity and neglect the rest of the natural year. The whole annual period, from one spring to the next, is divided into fractions of irregular length. Such 'months', up to 39 days each, are attested for the Romulean year (Plut. *Numa* 18; Lydus, *De mens.* I, 16) and for ancient Italy generally (Censor. 22, 6; 19, 6). The month names from Martius to Junius seem to refer to the stages of growth of crops and cattle (*cf.* J. G. Frazer, *The Fasti of Ovid* II (1929), 8; J. Bayet, *Histoire de la religion romaine* (1957), 89). The ancients usually attributed the introduction of this calendar to Numa (and its defects to later changes. *Cf.* Cic. *De leg.* II, 12, 29). Modern authors mostly attribute the system to the Decemviri (mid-fifth century BC). But the latter formulated, rather, an intercalation law (Macrob. I, 13, 21). On the other hand, the calendar presupposes the Capitoline cult: the Kalends are dedicated to Juno, and the Ides to Jupiter.[42]

The divergence of this calendar from the sun's course was so patent that *c.* 450 the Decemviri already tried to correct the system. There was also an intercalation law of M'. Acilius Glabrio, in 191 BC. But these reforms did not help. Many other projects for adjusting the calendar to the solar year were made (Macrob. I, 13; Liv. I, 19; *cf.* Ideler II, 69; Ginzel II, 253) but apparently never accepted by the Romans (Mommsen, 44). Rather, at some unknown time, they abandoned the rule of schematic intercalation and, just like Athens and other Greek cities (see p. 31), practised intercalation according to their needs. From the Second Punic War to Caesar's reform in 45 BC, the *pontifices* adjusted the calendar at will. As in Greece the standard was, or was to be, that the same sacrifices should be performed at the same seasons (*Quod ad tempus ut sacrificiorum libamenta serventur fetusque pecum . . . diligenter habenda ratio intercalandi est*, Cic. *De leg.* II, 121, 29). In fact intercalation became a tool of politicians in their struggles for power, and it was often handled arbitrarily and without regard to the seasons.

The result of such arbitrary intercalation was that the formula of the contracts in Cato (*De agr.* 150) contained the clause *si intercalatum erit.* In 50 BC Cicero, on 13 February, still did not know whether or not there would be an intercalation on the 23rd (*Ad Att.* V, 21, 14), and in 70 BC he had explained to his listeners as a peculiarity of the Greeks their preoccupation with making their calendar correspond to the sun (*Verr.* II, 2, 129). In fact the Roman calendar did not correspond to either the sun or the moon, but '*ging vielmehr gänzlich ins Wilde*' (Mommsen).

It follows that all the attempts to establish fixed intercalary cycles for this calendar are in vain (*cf.* Ideler, *Lehrbuch*, 309 and Mommsen, 44). The incidental documentation in our hands, as already mentioned, allows us only to draw the general conclusion that the Roman calendar, from the beginning of the First Punic War (264 BC) until the beginning of the Second (218 BC), corresponded more or less to the Julian calendar, perhaps running behind the latter by a few weeks; that during the Hannibalic War intercalation was neglected so that in 190 BC the Roman calendar was ahead by 117 days; and that this difference had declined to 72 days in 168 BC, so that in the intervening 22 years the calendar must have been intercalated 12 times. It can be supposed that the calendar at the time of the Gracchi was almost in correspondence with the seasons, as is shown by the dates for military campaigns during the period approximately from 140 to 70 BC. In Caesar's time, however, intercalation was again abandoned: in 46 BC there was a lag of 90 days.

The above summary of the use of the Roman calendar in the second century BC follows G. De Sanctis.[43] We must emphasize that our information is insufficient for generalizations. There are only two astronomical equations: the solar eclipse of 14 March, 190 was sighted in Rome on 11 July (Roman) (Liv. XXXVII, 4, 4), and the lunar eclipse of 21 June, 168 was seen on 4 September (Roman) (Liv. XLIV, 37, 8). On the other hand, under the terms of some contracts of the same period (Cato, *De agr.* 146) the grain and the olives are harvested in the due months, at the end of May and in November respectively. The contracts probably indicated the 'ideal' month, which was independent of the vagaries of the official calendar (*cf.* p. 23). But the battle of the Campi Raudii, near Vercelli, on 30 (Roman) July, 101 BC actually was fought in midsummer (Plut. *Marius* 26). The numerous dates which have come down to us from the time of Caesar cannot be converted into Julian dates with certainty (*cf.* Ginzel II, 273; J. Carcopino, *César* (1936), 696). See now J. Beaujeu, in *Mélanges offerts à J. Heurgon* (1976), 13.

THE JULIAN YEAR

Caesar did not reform the Roman calendar, but abandoned it and instituted the solar calendar of $365\frac{1}{4}$ days which was stable and agreed with the seasons. He could well have said, with reference to Greek calendar schemes: 'the Julian year shall not be outdone by the calendar of Eudoxus' (*Nec meus Eudoxi vincetur fastibus annus*, Lucan X, 187). First it was necessary to insert 90 days in 46 BC in order to bring the months back to their right seasons (*cf.* A. Rehm, *RE* III A, *c.* 1153). From 1 January 45 (T. Rice Holmes, *Roman Republic* I (1923), 339) a common year of 365 days, and the months of their present length were in use. The ten extra days over the former 355-day year were placed at the end of different months so that the usual dates of feasts remained undisturbed (*cf.* A. Rehm, in *Epitymbion für H. Swoboda* (1927), 225). For instance, the feast which was celebrated on 21 December was not moved, though the notation of its day changed from X Kal. Jan. to XII Kal. Jan. since the month now had 31 and no longer 29 days.

Every fourth year an extra day was inserted after VI Kal. Mart. (= 24 February), and this added day was called *bis sextum Kal. Mart.* In late imperial times, the intercalary year was accordingly called *annus bissextus*, from which comes our 'bissextile'.

After Caesar's death, the *pontifices* erroneously inserted the extra day every three years, so that Augustus in 9 BC had to omit the intercalation for 16 years. Only from AD 8 on did the Julian calendar function with regularity (Macrob. *Sat.* I, 14, 4; *cf.* M. Hoffmann, *Caesars Kalender* (1934); G. Radke, *RhM* 1960, 178; J. Beaujeu, *Mélanges . . . J. Heurgon* (1976), 13.

In the West the Julian year was introduced without modification, but in the Eastern provinces, where Greek was the official language of Roman administration, the new reckoning was

Antioch		Lycia & Sidon	Tyre[2,3]	
Hyperberetaios[2]	= Oct.	= Loos[2,4]	1 Dios	= 18.11(=Nov)[3]
Dios	= Nov.	= Gorpaios	1 Apellaios	= 18.12
Apellaios	= Dec.	= Hyperberetaios	1 Audynaios	= 17.1
Audynaios	= Jan.	= Dios	1 Peritios	= 16.2
Peritios	= Feb.	= Apellaios	1 Dystros	= 18.3
Dystros	= Mar.	= Audynaios	1 Xanthikos	= 18.4
Xanthikos	= Apr.	= Peritios	1 Artemisios	= 19.5
Artemisios	= May	= Dystros	1 Daisios	= 19.6
Daisios	= June	= Xanthikos	1 Panemos	= 20.7
Panemos	= July	= Artemisios	1 Loos	= 19.8
Loos	= Aug.	= Daisios	1 Gorpaios	= 17.9
Gorpaios	= Sept.	= Panemos	1 Hyperberetaios	= 19.10

	Alexandria[5]	Gaza[5]	Ascalon[5]
29. 8 = 1 Thot		= 1 Gorpaios	= 1 Loos
28. 9 = 1 Phaophi		= 1 Hyperberetaios	= 1 Gorpaios
28.10 = 1 Hathyr		= 1 Dios[2]	= 1 Hyperberetaios
27.11 = 1 Choiak		= 1 Apellaios	= 1 Dios
27.12 = 1 Tybi		= 1 Audynaios	= 1 Apellaios
26. 1 = 1 Mecheir		= 1 Peritios	= 1 Audynaios
25. 2 = 1 Phamenoth		= 1 Dystros	= 1 Peritios
27. 3 = 1 Pharmuthi		= 1 Xanthikos	= 1 Dystros
26. 4 = 1 Pachon		= 1 Artemisios	= 1 Xanthikos
26. 5 = 1 Payni		= 1 Daisios	= 1 Artemisios
25. 6 = 1 Epeiph		= 1 Panemos	= 1 Daisios
25. 7 = 1 Mesore		= 1 Loos	= 1 Panemos
24. 8–28.8: 5 Epagomenai			

		Asia	Smyrna[6]	Bithynia	Paphos[7]
31	Days	23. 9 = 1 Kaisarios	= 1 Kaisarios	= 1 Heraios	= 1 Aphrodisios[8]
30		24.10 = 1 Apellaios	= 1 Tiberios	= 1 Hermaios	= 1 Apogonikos
31		23.11 = 1 Audynaios	= 1 Apaturios	= 1 Metroos	= 1 Alnikeios
31		24.12 = 1 Peritios	= 1 Poseidon	= 1 Dionysios	= 1 Julios
28		24. 1 = 1 Dystros	= 1 Lenaios	= 1 Herakleios	= 1 Kaisarios
31		21. 2 = 1 Xanthikos	= 1 Hierosebastos	= 1 Dios	= 1 Sebastos
30		24. 3 = 1 Artemisios	= 1 Artemisios	= 1 Bendidaios	= 1 Autokratikos
31		23. 4 = 1 Daisios	= 1 Euangelios	= 1 Stratios	= 1 Demarchexasios
30		24. 5 = 1 Panemos	= 1 Stratonikos	= 1 Periepios	= 1 Pleisthypatos
31		23. 6 = 1 Loos	= 1 Hekatombaios	= 1 Areios	= 1 Archierios
31		24. 7 = 1 Gorpaios	= 1 Antiocheios	= 1 Aphrodisios	= 1 Hestios
30		23. 8 = 1 Hyper-beretaios	= 1 Laodikos	= 1 Demetrios	= 1 Loos

Fig. 3. Some local Julian calendars[1]

generally adapted to local taste, as to the beginning of the year and the names and lengths of months. For example, 6 January in Rome was equated elsewhere with 11 Tybi, 6 Audnaios, 14 Julos, and so on (Epiphan. *Panar.* 51, 24; *cf.* Mommsen, *RStR* III, 755).

The imperial government introduced the solar year slowly and, as it seems, in agreement with the local authorities. Salamis (Cyprus) was, probably, the first Greek city to accept Caesar's reform in 46 BC (*cf.* G. Jerphanion, *L'Antiq. class.* 1932, 21). In Egypt, Augustus, in 26 BC, reformed the Egyptian variable year by adding the sixth epagomenal day every four years (AD 3, 7, 11, and so on). From this time on, the 'Alexandrian' year, as it was called, always began on 29 August. In the province of Asia the Julian year was adopted *c.* 9 BC and the New Year was to coincide with Augustus' birthday on 23 September (D. Magie, *Roman Rule in Asia Minor* (1950), 1343; U. Laffi, *SCO* 1966, 1). The non-Julian calendars, however, partly survived in the West (Kubitschek, 136) and in many parts of the East. The Roman government

NOTE

1 Local forms of the Julian calendar have been preserved in three medieval manuscripts which give synchronistic tables, day for day, for the calendars of eighteen provinces and cities. W. Kubitschek, *DWA* LVII, 3 (1915). Nine of these hemerologia are reprinted in H. Lietzmann, *Zeitrechnung ... für die Jahre 1–2000 nach Christus* (1934), 106. Samuel, 173 gives a (updated) list of months for sixteen provincial forms of the Julian year. The indigenous population sometimes used old names for Julian months, *e.g.* the Julian Hyperberetaios (18 Sept.–17 Oct.) was also called *Thesre* (*Tishri*) in Roman Arabia (F. Preisigke–E. Kiessling, *Sammelbuch griechischen Urkunden aus Ägypten* X, 10288).

2 *New Year.* Between AD 458 and 483 the New Year day of Antioch was shifted to 1 September (E. Honigmann, *Byzantion* 1945, 338, and *cf.* Grumel, 195). The New Year day of the Lycian calendar is uncertain.

3 *Cf.* E. Schwartz, *GGN* 1906, 343. The calendar of Caesarea (Palestine) was of the same type: *cf.* J.-P. Rey-Coquais, *Analecta Bollandiana* (1978), 55.

4 In some cities, the first day of the month was called 'Sebaste', and the second day numbered as the 'first'. *Cf.* W. Kubitschek, ib. 81.

5 Calendars of Alexandrian type; all months have 30 days.

6 *Cf.* L. Robert, *REA* 1936, 23.

7 *Cf.* K. Scott, *YCS* 1931, 214; C. Bosh, *Kleinasiatische Münzen der römischen Kaiserzeit* II, 1 (1935), 132.

8 New Year on the birthday of Augustus.

did not impose the official calendar in the provinces. Galen c. 160 has to explain the Julian year to his readers and states that numerous Greek cities 'and the inhabitants of Palestine' continued to use the time-reckoning 'according to the moon' (*In Hippocr. Epid.* XVIII, 1, p. 23, ed. Kuhn). Such cities as Ephesus and Miletus still clung to the old calendar in the age of the Antonines (*cf.* Magie, ib. 1343, n. 40), and Rhodes as late as AD 244–48 (*cf.* J Oates, *JEA* 1969, 206). At Sardis in AD 459 a document was dated: V Kal. Mai (27 IV), 4 Daisios (*cf.* Samuel, 187). Such double dating was also used in Macedonia (*cf.* Robert, 400). For centuries after the introduction of the Julian (Alexandrian) year in Egypt, people continued to date according to the 'old style' ($\kappa\alpha\tau$᾿ ἀρχαίους), that is, according to the variable calendar (*cf. e.g.* U. Wilcken, *Chrestomathie* (1912) no. 497). A late sixth- or seventh-century papyrus gives the approximate equations between Roman (Julian) and Alexandrian (Julian) months: September = Thot, and so on (H. Gundel, *APF* 1956, 13). Nicopolis ad Istrum, a Roman *municipium* in Bulgaria, followed the Julian calendar (*cf.* G. Mihailov, *Inscr. Graecae in Bulgaria repertae* II (1958), 669). The free city of Thessalonica also used the Julian year (Ginzel III, 7), but Odessus (Varna), a provincial city of Moesia Inferior, as late as January 215, held to the lunisolar calendar which, at this date at least, was in accord with the moon (L. Robert, *RPh* 1959, 210). Nor was the Julian calendar adopted in the Bosporan kingdom (*cf. Corp. Inscr. Regni Bosporani* (1965), 845). In most cities, however, the moon calendar was disarranged. For instance, at Tyras, on the northern shore of the Black Sea, 30 Artemision corresponded to 27 April in 182 (the conjunction fell on 1 May), and 8 Lenaios corresponded to 17 February in 201 (conjunction: 22 January) (*Inscr. Ponti Euxini* I (1916), nos. 2 and 4). At Gerasa (Palestine) the Macedonian lunisolar year was also in confusion (C. B. Welles in C. Kraeling, *Gerasa* (1938), 476). Sometimes the disagreement with the sun year is so wide that it becomes puzzling. In a Palestinian document of 124, 19 October is given as the equivalent of 15 Dystros. Yet Dystros should have approximated to the Julian March (*cf.* P. Benoit in *Discoveries in Judean Desert* II (1961), no. 115).

A history of the diffusion of the Julian year has not yet been written, but the solar year made the cult of the sun popular (M. P. Nilsson, *ARW* 1932, 166=id. *Opuscula* I, 462; S. Weinstock, *JRS* 1948, 37). The importance of this religion in the later Roman Empire is evidenced by the fact that the Church transferred the date of Christ's birth to the birthday of the unconquered sun (*dies natalis solis invicti*: cf. B. Botte, *Les origines de la Noël* (1932)). On the representations of Julian months in the arts, cf. H. Stern, *Journal des savants* 1965, 122.

THE NATURAL YEAR

All the ancient calendars before the Julian year (except for the late Babylonian 19-year cycle) were inadequate. They diverged from the sun, disagreed with the moon, and always differed one from another. But the heavens and the earth offered standards of time-reckoning which were independent of the official calendars and common to all: the succession of seasons and the changing aspects of stars.

The geocentric path of the sun ('ecliptic') is a circle, the plane of which is inclined to the plane of earth's equator at an angle of about 23° 27'. This tilt causes the change of seasons. All life on the earth depends on the sun, and the amount of light and heat received from the sun mainly depends on the angle at which its rays fall on the earth's surface. There are four 'turning points' (*tropai*) of the sun: two solstices when it reaches its farthest positions from the earth in the ecliptic, and two 'equinoctial' points at the intersection of the ecliptic and the equator of the earth. When the sun, moving on its inclined orbit northwards, arrives at the equinoctial point, it equally irradiates the north and south poles, and the duration of day and night at this time is equal and the same over the whole globe. Crossing the equatorial line from south to north (vernal equinox), the sun irradiates more and more the northern atmosphere: the length of the day and the intensity of the sun's rays, which fall more directly on the surface of the northern hemisphere, increase and reach maximum at solstice, when the sun stands directly over the tropic of Cancer (23° 5' N).

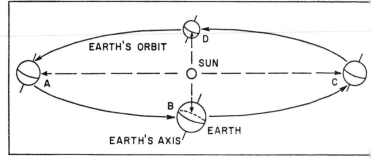

Fig. 4. The earth's orbit

Afterwards, the sun begins its southward movement, crosses the
equator again at the autumnal equinox point, days get shorter
and shorter, and the rays striking our hemisphere are more and
more slanted and thus less and less efficacious. The minimum is
reached at the winter solstice, after which the sun begins its
northward course again. At the latitude of Rome (41° 54′ N),
the insolation at summer solstice is more than three times greater
than the amount of irradiation at winter solstice. (The maximal
changes in the distance of the earth and sun during the yearly
revolution of the sun are insignificant, about 1 per cent of the
mean distance in each direction, and thus they do not influence
our climate.) The sun's revolution in the sky determines the
repetition of the same seasons at about the same time, and, therefore, the rhythm of vegetation, and of animal and human life.
This is the natural year (Figs 4, 5).

Local conditions fit the main periods of the natural year: for
instance, inundation, sowing and harvesting time after the inundation, and the period of low water were the three seasons in
the Nile Valley. For the Sumerians, the winds divided the year
into a hot and a cold period (B. Landsberger, *JNES* 1949, 248).
Similarly, the Greek and the Roman natural year was originally
subdivided into two parts. Four seasons are first mentioned by
Alcman (*apud* Athen. X, 416 d), and their limits remained
fluctuating. What counted in the farmer's (or mariner's, soldier's
etc.) year were not these abstract concepts, but the phenomena of
the natural year. The departure of the cranes signalled the time

to sow (Aristoph. *Aves* 709); the coming of the twittering swallow announced that the spring had begun (Hesiod, *Op.* 566). When the tender branch of the fig tree put forth leaves, men realized that the summer was near (*St Matth.* 24, 32). Χειμών, *hiems*, for military historians included autumn, that is, the whole bad season (*cf.* M. Holleaux, *REA* 1923, 352). Ὀπώρα is the height of the summer, but also the time of gathering the fruit.

The stars, however, are more reliable than the fig-tree in marking the progress of the year. From time immemorial man had observed that fixed stars (which retain the same position with respect to one another) change nightly in the sky. The light of these self-luminous bodies is effaced in the overwhelming brightness of the sun, and a given star is visible only when it is sufficiently remote from the sun. The sun advances among the stars on its annual eastward course along the ecliptic. The celestial dome, however, performs its diurnal motion in a contrary direction: both sun and stars rise in the east and sink below the western horizon. Therefore, the sun, which reaches the same point of ecliptic every 365 days, must travel $1:365$ portion of its path to come back to the same fixed star. As $24 \times 60 = 1,440$

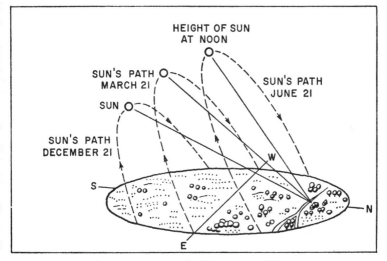

Fig. 5. The (geocentric) path of the sun in different seasons

minutes: 365 gives the quotient 4, the sun lags about 4 minutes behind the stars in its daily course. The true and uniform period of the earth's rotation with respect to stars is c. 23 hours 56 minutes. The (mean) solar day is 24 hours. When the sun progresses far enough from a given star, the latter appears above the eastern horizon just before sunrise (the 'heliacal' rising). From now on the star gains about 4 minutes daily on the sun and rises earlier and earlier every night until it catches up with the evening sun and is again lost in its proximity. The schedule for the setting of the same star in the west is similar. These four epochs (the first and the last apparition in the east; and the first, before the sunrise, and the last, just after sunset, descent under the western horizon) occur only once during a solar year, and, for a given latitude, on the same dates, which can be regarded as constant for historical purposes. For instance, the respective dates for Sirius in Athens (38° N) in 43 BC were: the heliacal rising: 28 July; the last visible ascent: 31 December; settings, on 5 May and 26 November. Thus, the star was invisible between 5 May and 28 July (cf. F. Boll, RE VI, 2427; Gundel, ib. IIIA, 339).

As early as the beginning of the second millennium the Egyptian priests computed the daily delay of stars. In the Hellenistic age, Greek navigators used a sort of computing instrument for the same purpose (Fig. 6).[44]

A natural and reliable standard of time-measurement, the stars appear in the farmer's almanac of Hesiod, besides the voice of the crane (Op. 448), to point the propitious time for agricultural work: harvest when 'the Pleiads, daughters of Atlas' rise, and sow when they set (Op. 383; cf. Aratus, 266). The shepherds in Sophocles' Oedipus Tyrannus (1137) describe the period of pasturage as six lunations 'from spring to Arcturus'. The ancient mariners depended on the stars for navigation and time-measurements: 'then the sailor numbered the stars and gave them names' (navita tum stellis numeros et nomina fecit, Virg. Georg. I, 137). In Athenian contracts of bottomry, the charged interest went up from 22·5 per cent to 30 per cent after Arcturus (Dem. 35, 10). Scholars (e.g. Hippocrates) again used time references of the natural year (K. Deichgraeber, APA 1933, 29). For Aristotle

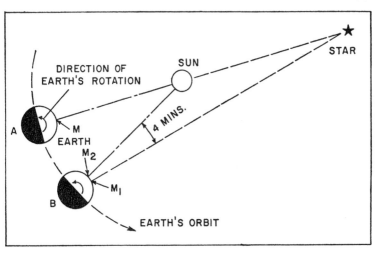

Fig. 6. The solar and sidereal day

(*Hist. Anim.* VI, 569 b) the rising of Arcturus ends the summer, and the migration of cuckoos occurs between the rising of Sirius and the spring (ib. IX, 633 a). Thucydides' 'divisions of time' (V, 20: κατὰ τοὺς χρόνους) were again seasons: 'summer', that is, the period of military operations, and 'winter'. His readers probably knew the chronological meaning of these terms (*cf.* W. K. Pritchett, B. L. van der Waerden, *BCH* 1961, 29). Within the season, Thucydides used the subdivisions of the farmer's year: 'when the grain comes into ear' (IV, 1), 'before the grain was ripe' (IV, 2) and so on, and sometimes celestial phenomena, such as winter solstices (VII, 16, 2; VIII, 39, 1; *cf.* A. W. Gomme, *Commentary on Thucydides* III (1956) 699, 716). He regarded his chronological system as more exact than the reckoning in civil years (V, 20). Four centuries after Thucydides, in Diodorus' annalistic work, the years are named after the Athenian archons, but within the year the time is indicated in seasonal terms: thus, for instance, Agathocles of Syracuse began his African campaign in the fruiting season (XIX, 65) and returned to Sicily 'at the time of the setting of the Pleiads' (XX, 69).

The art of reading the signs written in the sky, those of the night, of the month and year (Xen. *Mem.* IV, 7), this gift of

Prometheus (Aesch. *Prom.* 457), before the Imperial age was a part of basic education. This fact explains the great success of the didactic book in verse about the stars written by Aratus (died in 240 BC). In Rome too, daily conversation included the morning rising of the Lyre just as today we talk of the weather (Plut. *Caes.* 59), and the aspects of the stars constituted the basis for meteorological forecasting (Cic. *Verr.* II, V, 27). So Polybius (IX, 14) claimed that generals too should be able to tell the length of the day and night by the stars, as well as recognize the solstices and equinoxes, and be capable of constant observation of celestial bodies. As Copernicus (paraphrasing Plato, *Epin.* 987a) once said: 'the ancients were favoured with a clear sky, because the Nile, so they say, never gave off vapours like those of the Vistula'.[45]

Of course, neither the given agricultural work nor the setting of the Pleiads occurs everywhere and always at the same Julian date. The setting of the Pleiads happened for Agathocles on 6 April and in Diodorus' time on 8 April. But the stellar or agricultural reference gave a universal and undisputed, though approximate, indication of time within the year. The situation changed only with the introduction of the Julian year. When he wrote (*c.* 36 BC) his treatise on agriculture, Varro could refer to the Julian dates of the agricultural calendar, *ad dies civiles nostros qui nunc sunt* (*De re rust.* I, 28, 1). Nevertheless farmers' calendars continued to juxtapose the stellar and the Julian dates, since the stars were regarded as harbingers and even as originators of weather changes (*cf.* G. Boll, *Griechische Kalender*, SBHA 1910, 1911, 1913, 1914, 1920; A. Rehm *RE*, *Suppl.* VII, 175). For Virgil (*Georg.* I, 218) and for Petronius (55) the spring began not on 22 April, but under the sign of Taurus, and it was indicated by the arrival of the stork, *titulus tepidi temporis*. A mosaic of St Romain-en-Gal (Museum of St Germain-en-Laye) well ill-ustrates this popular climatology (*cf.* G. Lafaye, *RA* 1892, 322).

THE ZODIAC

The accord of the natural calendar, regulated by the stars, with the sun and with the civil reckoning was established by dividing the yearly path of the sun through the fixed stars into twelve equal sections, according to the number of lunations in a solar year. This is the Zodiac. The Babylonians were, probably, the first to trace it and divide it in signs of 30 degrees each. The twelve signs were named after relevant constellations which, however, as Geminus (1) warns his reader, do not exactly fit the allotted portions of the sky.

> *Signifer inde subest, bis sex et sidera complent*
> *Hunc: Aries, Taurus, Gemini, Cancer, Leo, Virgo,*
> *Libra, Scorpius, Arquitenens, Capricornus et urnam*
> *Qui tenet et Pisces . . .*

(*Poetae Latin. Minor*. ed. W. Baehrens V (1883), 352). The Zodiacal year began with Aries, that is, the sign of the vernal equinox. When the sun entered the sign of Cancer, it was summer; Libra corresponded to the autumn; and Capricorn marked the winter. Thus, the position of the sun in the Zodiac was of the greatest importance for the course of the seasons.

For us, the longest day (the summer solstice) is 22 June (Gregor.). For the ancients it was the time when the sun was in the first degree of the Cancer. This zodiacal clock was simpler to use than the star-clock of the natural year (p. 54). For instance, Varro dated the Roman feast of *Robigalia* as follows: 'When the sun reaches the tenth degree of Taurus' (Plin. *NH* XVIII, 286). The Babylonian astronomers, however, as early as *c.* 1100 related the official lunisolar calendar to the rising of the given stars in a given month. A Babylonian astronomical work written before 700 BC used the schematic year of 12 × 30 months to correlate the star calendar and the official time-reckoning (B. L. van der Waerden, *JNES* 1949, 6; Pritchett and van der Waerden, *BCH* 1961, 41). In Greece, Meton was probably the first who, in 432, publicly displayed the stellar calendar which, using the zodiacal division, indicated the daily progress of the sun. For instance, an almanac of this kind announced: '30 days (of Aquarius). The 1st: The sun in Aquarius. The 2nd: The Lion begins to set in the evening. Setting of Lyra. The 5th: the evening setting of the Cygnus begins,' and so on (*cf.* A. Rehm, *SPAW* 1904, 97). Now, it was easy to relate this star calendar to the official reckoning. Suppose the sun entered the sign of Aquarius on N-day of the civil calendar. The evening setting of Cygnus would, then, happen on the civil day $N + 4$, and so on. These tables were construed with regard to the astronomical cycles (p. 29) and also gave weather prognostics. An ingenious device (*parapegma*) made it possible to mark the days of the given calendar month by movable pegs inserted in holes beside the stellar references. For instance, in the almanac of Euctemus the appearance of the swallow was fixed on the 2nd day of Pisces. The *parapegma* allowed the conversion of this indication into a date of the local calendar. In a similar way, the zodiacal year was used in modern Persia. Until the introduction of the Gregorian calendar, in 1925, the Persian financial year ran from one spring equinox to the next, and its twelve months were named after the zodiacal signs (*cf.* S. H. Taqizadeh, *BSOAS* 10 (1939–42), 132).

We may note on this occasion that for the ancients the chart of the sky differed somewhat from ours. The change was determined by the phenomenon of the precession of the equinoxes, discovered by Hipparchus (O. Neugebauer, *JAOS* 1950, 1). The vernal point moves westward, along the zodiac. (The causes of this retrograde movement are a part of the general law of gravitation and the precession, in turn, confirms Newton's theory.) Consequently, the distance of the stars from the equinoctial points changes. Hipparchus could calculate that *e.g.* the distance of Spica from the autumnal equinoctial point in his own time was 6° but in the time of the astronomer Timocharis (*c.* 300 BC), 8° (Ptol. *Almag.* VII, 2); accordingly, today Aries is in the ancient sign of Taurus. In other words, today at the spring equinox the sun enters the sign of Pisces, between *c.* 1000 BC and AD 1000 the vernal point was in Aries, between 3000 and 1000 BC in Taurus, etc.[46]

THE WEEK

The Venerable Bede, that famous chronologist of the Middle Ages, said that the division of time *natura aut consuetudine aut auctoritate decurrit* (*PL*, XC, 279). The year is timed by nature,

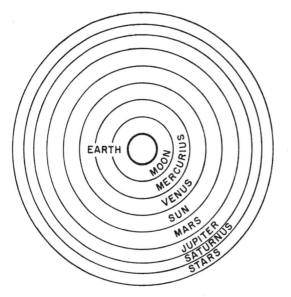

Fig. 7. The order of the planets

he unequal lengths of the months by tradition, and the week by
authority.

The artificial time-units of three, five, seven, etc., days occur
among many peoples (*cf.* Nilsson, *Time-reckoning*, 324). For
instance, a seven-day period of time is often mentioned in
Sumerian and Babylonian texts (*cf.* Langdon, *Menologies*, 89;
H. and J. Lewy, *HUCA* XVII (1942–3), 6). The Romans used the
market week (as do many primitive peoples, Nilsson, ib. 325) of
eight days, known also to the Etruscans (Macrob. *Sat.* I, 15, 13).
These *nundinae* were indicated in the calendar by the letters A to
H: seven days of work, the eighth day for the market (Macrob.
, 16, 32).

The rural population came to the city at the Nundinae (Varro,
De re rust. II, *Praef.*). Thus public auctions and the like were also
held on the Nundinae, which became a day of festivity. Varro
implies that the countryman only shaved for market-days when
he went to town. (*Quoties priscus homo ac rusticus Romanus inter
nundinum barbam radebat?* Varro *ap.* Nonius, p. 214, 28.) Our

Century	S(aeculum)	Century	S(aeculum)	Year	A(nnus) 0 1 2 3 4 5 6 7 8 9	Month	M(ensis)	
0	0	10	3	0	2 1 0 6 4 3 2 1 6 5	January	1	2
1	1	11	4	10	4 3 1 0 6 5 3 2 1 0	February	5	6
2	2	12	5	20	5 4 3 2 0 6 5 4 2 1	March	5	
3	3	13	6	30	0 6 4 3 2 1 6 5 4 3	April	2	
4	4	14	0	40	1 0 6 5 3 2 1 0 5 4	May	0	
5	5	15	1	50	3 2 0 6 5 4 2 1 0 6	June	4	
6	6	16	2	60	4 3 2 1 6 5 4 3 1 0	July	2	
7	0	17	0	70	6 5 3 2 1 0 5 4 3 2	August	6	
8	1	18	2	80	0 6 5 4 2 1 0 6 4 3	September	3	
9	2	19	4	90	2 1 6 5 4 3 1 0 6 5	October	1	
						November	5	
						December	3	

Fig. 8. The week

The Sunday is found by addition of the numbers under S(aeculum), A(nnus) and M(ensis). For seventeenth–nineteenth centuries the dates are Gregorian. For January and February in bissextile years (*cf.* p. 47) use the last column. For example, a funerary inscription is dated as follows: *post consulatum* [of Arcadius and Rufinus] *die Lunae, IX Cal. Iun.* (E. Diehl, *Inscriptiones Latinae Christianae* I, no. 582). The date corresponds to 24 May AD 393 and the day is said to be Monday. Let us check this statement. 393 = 300 + 93. According to our table, 300 corresponds to the number 3 in the column S; 93 corresponds to the figure 5 in the column A. May corresponds to the number 0 in the column M. We add: 3 + 5 + 0 = 8. Accordingly, 8 May was a Sunday in AD 393. Therefore, 22 May was also a Sunday, and 24 May was a Tuesday. 24 May was, however, Monday, in AD 392. The author of the inscription probably confused the year of the consulate of Arcadius and Rufinus (AD 392) and the year *post consulatum*, that is AD 393 (Mommsen). The figures in the example quoted here are in bold type in the table.

week, of which Bede spoke, goes back to the authority of the Bible and Jewish practice. Toward the end of the first century, Flavius Josephus could state (*Contra Apionem* II, 39, 282): 'There is no city, Greek or barbarian, not a people, to whom our custom of abstaining from work on the seventh day has not spread.' The origin of this septenary time unit (Hebrew *shabua*; *cf.* Hebrew *sheba*—'seven') is unknown. The days of the Hebrew week are counted as they still are in the Greek Orient and by the Orthodox Church (and therefore among the Slavs). In Western Europe, on the other hand, the days are named after planets: Moon, Mars, Mercury, Jupiter, Venus, Saturn, Sun. Our week, in fact, has its secondary origin in the planetary, astronomical week of the Imperial age, which gave each day its ruler, that is to say, the planet which governed the first hour of each day.

The Jewish week began on the Sunday. Thus, for instance, *St Matth.* 28:1: 'after the Sabbath, toward the dawn of the first day of the week'. In the planetary week, the sequence of days corresponded to the order of planets according to their distance from the earth (Fig. 7): Saturnus, Jupiter, Mars, Sun, Venus, Mercurius, Moon. Thus, the first day was Saturday. But the planets also ruled the 24 hours of each day. The first (and consequently the 8th, the 15th, the 22nd) hour of Saturday were allotted to Saturn, the 23rd to Jupiter, the 24th to Mars; and the first hour of the next day to the Sun, which thus ruled Sunday. Therefore, in the planetary (and our own) week, *dies Solis* follows *dies Saturni* (*cf.* F. Boll, *RE* VII, 2558). From this comes the custom, introduced in the third century AD from East to West, of indicating the most important dates according to the weekdays as well (*e.g. CIL* III, 1051: X K. *Iun. lun.* XVIII *die Iovis* = 23 May, AD 205).[47]

The planetary week, which according to Celsus (*ap.* Orig. *c. Cels.* VI, 22) was a part of 'Persian theology' (*cf.* F. Cumont, *RHR* CIII, 1931, 54), penetrated into the West under Augustus (*cf.* Tib. II, 3, 18). Constantine, in 321, sanctified the astrological week by ordering that *omnes judices . . . et artium officia cunctarum venerabili die solis quiescant* (*Codex Just.* III, 12, 2). The farmers were expressly excused from observing this ordinance.[48]

CHAPTER II

CHRONOGRAPHY

TIME-UNITS RETURN again and again and are always the same: one day is like another. Only events—birth and death, a good harvest, a bad harvest—singularize time-units by making them unequal in value and thus memorable. Chronography, the method of establishing time-intervals between events and between them and the present, is thus different from calendariography, which deals with standard elements of time measurement.

RELATIVE CHRONOLOGY

The simplest and most ancient method of dating is the relative time-reference which does not require any chronological devices (*e.g.* the Epidamnians exiled the aristocrats 'before the war': Thuc. I, 24). Except for savants, men have little interest in absolute time notations; they use, instead, relative time-references. Primitive peoples usually do not know how old a man is, but only who is the oldest in a group (Nilsson, 98).

The counting of generations is the simplest device of chronography. In order to measure the length (otherwise unknown) of the IV and V Egyptian dynasties, scholars add up life-ages of successive court officials. In the same way, the earliest Greek historians set up a chronological framework for their narratives by counting generations. The first Greek historical work by Hecataeus of Miletus was entitled 'The Genealogies'. The Alexandrian scholars used the same device in order to establish synchronisms: 'Hecataeus lived at the time of Darius I and was older than Herodotus.'

Relative chronology hinges on some known time-point. Thucydides dates events which led to the Peloponnesian War indirectly, making the attack on Plataea his reference point

(F. Jacoby, *GGN* 1928, 1). In order to establish the date of the sack of Rome by the Gauls, a date which was fundamental for his Roman chronology, Polybius (I, 6, 1) states that the event was contemporaneous with the peace of Antalcidas and the siege of Rhegium by Dionysius, and that it happened 19 years after the battle of Aegospotami and 16 years before the battle of Leuctra. With the aid of a series of such fundamental datings, which he used as points of reference, Eratosthenes (*c.* 250 BC) composed the first scientific chronology.

Every dating, however, is useful only if its distance from the present is known; each dating system must be related to the present. An inscription, known from the name of the place in which it was found as the Parian Chronicle (*Marmor Parium*), enumerates events of the past according to the distance from its own date (264/3 BC): 'From the time when Cecrops became king of Athens—1,218 years.' This device, which (in a short time) made the Parian list useless, shows the inherent inadequacy of relative chronology, which is intelligible only in connection with an absolute date.[49]

On the other hand the elements of absolute chronology are not isolated dates but uniform time-units, an uninterrupted series of which leads to the present. Absolute chronology borrows the concept of 'year' from the calendar, but the chronological year is an historical unit, that is, a link in a series of years, whether they be numbered or otherwise individualized. This labelling distinguishes the chronological year from the calendar unit.

NAMING THE YEAR

We have a uniform standard of time, our civil year. (The fiscal, the ecclesiastical, the school year, etc., serve specific purposes only.) This civil year is the Julian year, which did not exist before 45 BC. Our New Year also comes from the Julian year. The Greek language distinguished between the yearly cycle of seasons (*eniautos*) and the civil year (*etos*) (Ad. Wilhelm, *SWAW* CXLII (1900), 4). An *eniautos* lasted from any chosen time-point in the natural year to its recurrence. Greek calendars based on the natural year could begin with Aries as well as with Cancer, and so on. The *etos* was a conventional time-unit. The new moon was one of the most important Greek festivals, while the new year, or 'new new-moon' had no importance (*OGIS*, 458, 21: νέα νουμηνία). In Rome, wartime operations began at the *Kalendae Martiae*, but this day was in no way distinguished from the other first days of the months.

The Greeks celebrated birthdays every month (W. Schmidt, *RE* VII, 1136). The annual renewal of treaties was performed at the same festival, not on the same calendar date (Thuc. V, 23, 4); the treasurers rendered accounts at the Panathenaea. For Polybius a year is a variable quantity: its beginning and length change in the course of his work, according to his sources and his organization of material (*cf.*, however, P. Pedech, *La méthode historique de Polybe* (1964), 449). The fluctuating value of the *etos* came to be stabilized for administrative or religious reasons. In both Egypt and Babylonia, important festivals of the 'beginning of the Year' were celebrated from the most ancient times. The period between two consecutive New Year festivals became the earliest chronographic unit, marked by year-names such as 'year of counting of cattle', 'year of the victory over the Nubians', and so on. A series of years thus described constituted the earliest chronological tables. Such a table, written at the end of the V Egyptian dynasty, has been preserved on the 'Palermo Stone' (*cf.* note 66 and K. Sethe, *GGN* (1919), 303). Another way of defining a civil year was to begin it at the fixed date, when some major magistrate took office: Hekatombaion for the (eponymous) archon in Athens; 15 March for the consuls in Rome, from 222 to 153 BC (Mommsen *RStR* I, 599); 13 Aiaru for the 'limmu' of the city of Ashur, and so on. This eponymous year became a chronological unit (of variable length by reason of intercalation), but with a definite beginning. The office-year, however, was not the same for all magistrates. The prytany year in Athens did not have to coincide with the archon's year (p. 34); similarly, the Roman consuls took office on 15 March and (from 153 BC) on 1 January, but the tribunes began their year on 10 December. The Roman emperors numbered the years of their tribunician power, which was renewed annually. From Augustus o Trajan, the tribunician years were reckoned from the accession day; but from Trajan until the Severi, they were numbered from to December.[50]

The stability of the office-year made possible its use as a chronographic unit. The years were indicated by the name of the eponymous magistrate (archon, ephor, etc.): 'o faithful jar of wine, born with me in the consulship of Manlius' (*o nata mecum consule Manlio . . . pia testa*, Hor. *Odes* III, 21). If the eponymous magistrate served for six months, the civil year had the same length; it was ἐξάμηνος (*cf.* Busolt-Swoboda II, 457; *IG* XII, 5, 881 (Tenos); R. Herzog, *APA* 1928, 50 (Cos)). Likewise, in Babylonia the 'year' originally comprised six months as there were two 'Akitu' festivals, one in the month of Tashritu and another in the month of Nisanu (F. Thureau-Dangin, *Rituels Accadiens* (1921), 87; S. A. Pallis, *The Babylonian Akitu Festival* (1926)). In early Sumerian texts, the dating by the term of office of a magistrate corresponded to years of varying length; W. W. Hallo, *JCS* 1960, 189. *Cf.* H. Tadmor, *JCS* 1958, 26.

Thus, the calendar year was identical with the office-year of the eponymous magistrate. In a document commemorating the introduction of the Julian year in the province of Asia, the New Year was described in Latin as *tempus anni novi initiumque magistratuum*, and in Greek as 'the beginning of the term in office' (*OGIS* 458, 14). Similarly the Praenestine Fasti note under 1 January: *Annus novus incipit quia eo die magistratus ineunt*. Accordingly, the pre-Caesarian Roman calendar year already began with January since, from 153 BC on, the consuls entered office on 1 January (*cf.* Degrassi, *Fasti Antiati*, no. 9). The offering of the *strena* was similarly advanced from 1 March to 1 January (L. Deubner, *Glotta* (1912), 34). Only under the Caesars, under the influence of astrology, did the New Year as such acquire the value of a time mark, and thus gave rise to our civil year, and our New Year holiday (*cf.* M. P. Nilsson, *ARW* 1916, 66, and M. Messlin, *La fête des calendes de Janvier* (1970)).

Where the iteration of the eponymous magistracy was permissible (as in Rome), the repeated magistracies could be counted. The consul-year of 44 BC was *Caesare V et Antonio* ('Caesar for the fifth time and Antonius'). Royal years as well could be numbered. The regnal years naturally were counted from the accession day. Thus the regnal year, like the eponymous year, determined the beginning and the end of the civil year or, at least, ran independently from the latter. Such was the case of the Ptolemies in Egypt during the entire time that they used the Macedonian calendar, and of the Seleucids (cf. p. 38).

The same is true for the regnal year of other Greek and Macedonian kings. But in Egypt and Babylonia naming of year preceded the reckoning by the numbered regnal years. The latter system became standard in Babylonia only in the Kassite period, that is, from seventeenth century BC on, according to the now usually accepted chronology (see p. 84). Thus, the regnal year had to be adjusted to the standard civil calendar. The Egyptian reckoned the period from the accession to the next New Year (I Thot) as the first year of the reign. The next full calendar year was counted as the second year of reign, and so on. Only under the eighteenth through the twentieth dynasties did the regnal year run from the accession day to its anniversary. On the other hand, in Babylonia the period from the accession to the next New Year (1 Nisanu) was called 'the beginning of the reign' and the next full calendar year was numbered as the first year of the new king.[51]

The Roman emperors did not count their years of reign but their tribunates; yet dating by the regnal years of the Caesar was widely used in Palestine (cf. Luke 3, 1), Syria, Arabia, Bithynia, Pontus, Cyprus and Egypt (cf. J. Goldstein, JNES 1966, 8). The counting of Imperial years was adapted to the local style of reckoning. In Syria, for example, the second year of the new emperor began on the next 1 October after his accession, that is, at the next New Year of the calendar of Antioch (cf. C. Cichorius, ZNTW 1923, 18). In Egypt, the second regnal year began on 29 August after the accession, that is, the Alexandrian New Year (see p. 50). For Byzantine dating, see F. Doelger, Byz. Zeitschr. 1932, 275; id. SBA 1949, no. 1.

The chronographers, in order to be able to use the years of reign as chronological units, had to relate them to a standardized year in order to make them uniform. The year in which a sovereign came to the throne was accordingly attributed sometimes to his predecessor (antedating), and sometimes to his successor (dating in advance). For example, while the last year of the reign of Alexander the Great (d. 10 June 323 BC) was usually counted as the first year of Philip Arrhidaeus, in some lists the whole year was assigned to Alexander (S. Smith, *RAss* 1925, 86). For the same chronographic reason a Babylonian list attributes to Alexander only seven years of reign in order to make his years follow the reign of Darius III, which ended in 330 BC. Babylonian documents naturally count Alexander's years from his ascent to the Macedonian throne, in 336 BC (*cf.* Ed. Meyer, *Forschungen* II, 457).

THE EPONYMOUS YEAR

The main bulk of datings given in our sources from the ancient Near East, Greece, and Rome, refer to the eponymous years. Therefore, in order to understand these chronological references, we must be able to ascertain the distance of the given eponymous year from the present. First, we have to determine the relative chronology of the eponymous year in question, that is, its place in the succession of eponymous magistrates of the given city, and secondly, we must link the list of eponymous magistrates to our absolute chronology.

The latter problem can be solved as soon as we obtain a synchronism for the list in question. Thus, the whole series of the eponyms of the city of Ashur from 893 to 666 BC is dated, thanks to the mention of the solar eclipse of 15 June 763, in the year of one of these eponyms. Alexander the Great was the *stephanephoros* of Miletus, probably in 333 BC. His name in the list of these *stephanephoroi*, which begins in 525 BC, dates the whole series (A. Rehm, *Milet* III; *Delphinion* (1913), no. 122).

The establishment of the relative chronology of eponyms is rarely possible unless we have the ancient lists of them; otherwise the names float in time. The catalogue of Athenian archons from the Persian War to 302 BC has been preserved in the Books

XI–XX of Diodorus, who in his annalistic narrative mentions the
Athenian archon of each year from 480 BC on. Dionysius of
Halicarnassus (Dinarc. 9) enumerates the archons until and
including 293/2 (cf. Dinsmoor, 39). For the later period we have
only fragmentary and disconnected lists on stone. From 356/5
on (with some interruptions such as under the oligarchic regime
from 321/0 to 308/7) the annual secretaries (grammateis) followed
each other in a regular sequence according to the tribes from
which they came: the grammateus of the Erechtheis was followed
by the grammateus from the Aeges, and so on. Thus, the tribe
of the grammateus indicates the place of the corresponding archon
in the tribal cycle (W. S. Ferguson, Athenian Archons (1899)).
Yet, there were also disturbances within the cycle (cf. Pritchett
385). Thus the number of Athenian archons before 480 and after
292 whose Julian year is certain remains very small, e.g. Phainippo
in 490 (battle at Marathon). Only five archons of the third century
(after 292) are dated with certainty by synchronisms (Dinsmoor
45; Samuel, 210). On the date of the archon Arrheneides, cf
Pritchett, 288.

The case of the archon Polyeuctus, whose date is crucial for
Delphic chronology, illustrates the difficulty of dating the
Athenian archons of the Hellenistic Age. Two synchronisms show
that he exercised his functions at the time of Antigonus Gonatas
(263–240) and Seleucus II (246–225) (cf. L. Robert, REA 1936, 5)
His year in office must thus be placed between 246 and 240. His
probable date would be 246/5 (cf. G. Nachtergael, Historia 1976
62). Yet the date 251/0 (E. Manni, Fasti Ellenistici e Romani (1961)
82) or the date 249/8 is still supported by competent scholars (cf
Meritt, 234; Samuel, 214; Meritt, Historia 1977, 168).

Thus all proposed lists of the Athenian archons of the Hellenistic Age differ and all are equally uncertain (cf. Manni, op. cit.
Samuel, 212; Meritt, Historia 1977, 168).[52] On the archons
between AD 96 and 267 cf. S. Follet, Athènes au IIème et IIIème
siècles (1976).

Our reconstruction of a series of eponyms generally depends
upon the existence (and availability) of corresponding ancient
records. At some date a city decided to write down a list of its

past magistrates and to continue it each year. For instance, a list of priests at Cos which begins in 30 BC was published in 18 BC. The aforementioned list of the *stephanephoroi* of Miletus covers the period from 525/4 to 314/13 (ib. nos. 123–8 name eponyms from 313/12 to AD 2/3). The list was engraved in 334/3, and afterwards the name of the eponym was added every year. The question for the chronologist is how far back such a record is reliable. In the time of Plato (*Hipp. Maj.* 285 e), the Athenians believed that the list of archons, starting from Solon (594–3) was reliable. Yet, compilers could easily tamper with the list or simply invent the eponyms or kings of hoary antiquity. We reject as impossible the figures given in a cuneiform list for the twenty-three kings of the First Dynasty of Kish who allegedly reigned for 24,510 years. We disbelieve the list of archons for life and of decennalian archons of Athens for 1068–684 BC, but we may also question whether the first annual archon was Creon who exercised his office in 683 BC, as the *Marmor Parium* tells us.[53]

The Romans dated by consuls until AD 537 when Justinian (*Novell.* 47) introduced the dating according to the regnal years of the emperors. From 534 in the West and after 541 in the East, only the emperors held the consulship. Yet, the dating by consuls continued to be used in Egypt until 611. Accordingly, we have the complete list of consuls from Brutus and Collatinus, the founders of the Roman Republic in 509 BC, to Basilius in AD 541: 1,050 years.[54]

From *c.* 300 BC on, the *fasti* are reliable, as the Greek historical tradition and contemporary documents show. It is probable that the original list was composed by the *pontifices c.* 300 BC. The question is how far the list for 509–*c.* 300 is trustworthy. Following Mommsen, modern historians generally accept the list except for the first years of the Republic. The Julian years of early consulship, however, remain uncertain because of the disagreement among sources. The cornerstone of ancient Roman chronology was the capture of Rome by the Gauls, since this event was the earliest fact of Roman history mentioned and dated by contemporary Greek authors. The date corresponded to 387/6 BC (see p. 63; *cf.* F. W. Walbank, *Commentary on Polybius* I (1957), 46;

P. Pedech, *La méthode historique de Polybe* (1964), 438). Yet, the Roman consular list indicated 382 BC. In order to use the Greek synchronism, Diodorus twice gives the names of the same Roman eponyms, to wit, for Olymp. 96, 3–97, 3 and Ol. 98, 3–99, 3 (*cf.* Ed. Schwartz, *RE* V, 695). Livy reaches the date 387/6 by inserting a quinquennium of anarchy without the magistrates (VI, 35, 10: *solitudo magistratuum*). The *Fasti Capitolini* insert four years of dictators *sine consule* and in this way arrive at 391/0 as the date of the Gallic sack of Rome (*cf.* Mommsen, 114; id. *RStR* II, 1, 160).

As a matter of fact, before 222 there was no fixed date for taking office. A consul could start and end his consulship at any date within the seasonal year (see Mommsen, ib. I, 597). On the other hand, the length of the seasonal year was also variable (*cf.* p. 44). Thus the number of consulships was hardly the same as the number of Julian years between the foundation of the Republic and the redaction of the consular list *c.* 300 BC.[55]

What has been said concerning the eponyms is also true of the royal lists. We are able to ascertain the succession of kings and their dates only on the basis of corresponding lists compiled by ancient historians (see *e.g.* the list of the rulers of Pergamum in Strabo, 624 C; *cf.* W. Kubitschek, *RE* XI, 996). Where such lists are lacking, as for example for Parthia or Pontus, a new discovery might at any time change the accepted order of the kings and their chronology. This has already happened more than once (*cf. e.g.* Th. Reinach, *Histoire par les monnaies* (1902), 167; E. J. Bickerman, *BO* 1966, 15).

THE ERAS

The datings by eponyms or regnal years are isolated items which must be grouped in a series continued to the present. The era (that is, 'number': *cf.* A. Ernout, A. Meillet, *Dictionn. étymolog. de la langue latine*[4] (1959), s.v. *aera*) numbers the years. It is enough to know its point of departure for converting its datings into Julian years. A church council took place in Tyre on 16 September 643 of Tyrian reckoning. We know that the Tyrian era began in the autumn of 126 BC and that the Tyrian year (in the Roman period) started on 18 October. Therefore the aforementioned Tyrian date corresponds to 16 September AD 518. (Of course this conversion rule is inapplicable to purely lunar, or even lunisolar, dates, where we must also know the character of the year and month in question, *e.g.* whether the year was intercalated.)

This convenient method of dating came into public use only in the Hellenistic Age. Indeed, the era postulates a uniform year as its basic unit. Such a year (leaving out the Egyptian mobile year) was first achieved, thanks to the 19-year cycle, in Babylonia (p. 24). The first 'era' came into being there also when Seleucus I began to count his regnal years according to the Babylonian calendar and Antiochus I continued the counting of his father's years. His successors, in turn, followed his example and in this way the earliest dynastic reckoning was adopted in the whole Seleucid empire, as 'the years of the Greek domination', to use the name given to this era by the Jews and the Syrians.

The epoch from which the Seleucid years were counted was the Julian year 312/11. After reconquering Babylon in August of 312, Seleucus I, in the next royal year (the 7th year of Alexander, son of Alexander the Great), began to count his satrapal years (*cf.* S. Smith, *RAss* 1925, 190). In this he followed the example of Antigonus and other satraps in Babylon (*cf.* Ed. Meyer, *Forschungen* II, 458). According to the Babylonian calendar, the 7th year of Alexander IV began on 2 April 311. The Macedonians, however, counted the years of Alexander IV from the death of Philip Arrhidaeus in the autumn of 317. Thus, for them the 2nd year of the satrap Seleucus began in the autumn of 311, while for the Babylonians the same year began on 22 April 310. As king, Seleucus continued the reckoning of his satrapal years (E. J. Bickerman, *Berytus* 1944, 73; A. Aymard, *REA* 1955, 105). For the court, the Seleucid year began between 1 Loos and 1 Dios, that is, in the late summer or early autumn (*cf.* C. B. Welles, *Royal Correspondence in the Hellenistic Period* (1934), 18; id. *The Parchments and Papyri* (1959), 10).

The beginning of the Seleucid year could vary according to the calendar of the city. In the Julian calendar of Antioch, the year began on 1 Dios (1 October) (*cf.* p. 25). The same epoch was later used by Arab astronomers. The Arabs called the Seleucid reckoning the era of Alexander, though al Biruni recognized this error.[56]

The Seleucid era remained in use in some parts of the Near East until modern times (Ginzel I, 263), and it was imitated by several Oriental dynasties. The Arsacids in Parthia counted their years from the spring of 247 BC (Arsacid era, cf. Kugler, II, 444), though the Greek cities in the kingdom used the epoch of the autumn of 248, but they also employed 'the old style' (ὡς δὲ πρότερον) of the Seleucids.[57] The era of the kings of Pontus and Bithynia (297/6) was also used in the Bosporan kingdom (cf. R. Fruin, Acta Orientalia 1934, 29; W. H. Bennet, Historia 1961, 460). According to Syncellus the era began in 283/2 (cf. G. Vitucci, Il regno di Bitinia (1953), 17). Pharnaces I of Pontus counted the years from 337/6, the accession date of Mithridates of Cius, the founder of the dynasty, but his successor Mithridates II changed to the era of 297/6. E. Diehl, RE XIX, 1850; cf. L. Robert, Etudes anatoliennes 1937, 231.[58]

The era of Diocletian (ἔτους Διοκλητιανοῦ) can also be classed among the dynastic reckonings. Diocletian introduced into Egypt the dating according to the consular year, beginning on 1 January. The reform inconvenienced the astronomers, since all astronomical observations were noted according to the Egyptian mobile year. Thus, the astronomers continued, even after Diocletian's abdication, the fictitious numbering of the years of his reign, from 29 August 284.[59] This era appears in horoscopes (cf. O. Neugebauer and B. v. Hoesen, Memoirs of the American Philosophical Society 48 (1959)). From Egypt, the era came to the West thanks to its use for Easter calculations (cf. Ginzel I, 231; Ambrosius, PL XVI, 1050); but its more general use remained limited to Egypt from the sixth century AD. The Coptic church still uses this reckoning.

The cities which won independence from the Seleucids or other monarchs started to use their own eras, which generally commenced with the year of liberation. Thus, a list of officials of the city of Amyzon has the heading: οἱ γεγονότες ἀφ' οὗ Κᾶρες ἠλευθερώθησαν (167 BC) (cf. L. Robert, La Carie II (1954),

309). For example, in 126/5 Tyre announced to other cities her new independence (*SEG* II, 330), began her own era, and displayed her new status by issuing a new coinage. The earliest examples of such freedom eras are those of Tyre from 275/4, which probably celebrates the end of the local dynasty (W. Ruge, *RE* VIIA I. 1896), and of Aradus in 259, which refers to independence from the Seleucids (H. Seyrig, *Syria* 1951, 192). The so-called Pompeian era (64 or 63 BC) again refers to the liberation of the city in question from the Seleucids or the Maccabees. At Antioch the 'Pompeian' era began in 66 BC (H. Seyrig, *Syria* 1954, 73; 1959, 70). Sometimes cities agreed on a common era (H. Seyrig, *RN* 1964, 37). On the use of the city eras of Berytus, Sidon and Tyre in Byzantine times, see H. Seyrig, *Syria* 1962, 42. On the era of Edessa see A. Maricq, *Syria* 1955, 278.

The so-called provincial eras, such as that of Macedonia (148 BC), of Achaea (146 BC), the 'Sullan' era (85/4) in Asia Minor, etc., counted the years of Roman rule in the province or city in question: (ἔτους) ά 'Ρώμης (H. Seyrig, *Syria* 1959, 71). In Egypt, Octavian's conquest (κράτησις Καίσαρος θεοῦ υἱοῦ) marked an epoch (from 1 August 30 BC) which lasted until the first years of Tiberius (U. Wilcken, *JRS* 1937, 138; J. Bingen, *CE* 1964, 174).

Similar are the eras which are counted from the date of a victory and were used by the Greeks of Greece, Asia Minor and Syria. Thus the eras of Pharsalus (June 48 BC) and Actium (2 September 31 BC) refer to the transfer of domination from Pompey to Caesar and from Antony to Augustus, respectively. Compare for example an inscription from Lydia which says: ἔτους εἰκοστοῦ καὶ πρῶτον τῆς Καίσαρος τοῦ πρεσβυτέρου αὐτοκράτορος θεοῦ νείκης (=Pharsalus 48 BC), τετάρτου δὲ τῆς Καίσαρος τοῦ νεωτέρου αὐτοκράτορος θεοῦ υἱοῦ (=Actium 31 BC), στεφανηφόρου δε καὶ ἱερέως τῆς 'Ρώμης 'Απολλωνίδου τοῦ Αἰσχρίωνος μηνὸς Δαισίου δωδεκάτηι.[60]

All the sacred eras belong in the same category, and ultimately they all have as their model the era of Actium.

The Jewish era from the creation of the world starts on 6 October 3761 BC (*cf.* Finegan, 126). The Byzantine creation era began on 21 March 5508 BC, and later on 1 September 5509 BC.

After the attempts of Hippolytus, Clement of Alexandria and others, the so-called Alexandrian computation of the date of creation was worked out: 25 March 5493 BC. Later in the seventh century, the creation was placed in the year 5508 BC. The Eastern church avoided the use of the Christian era since the date of Christ's birth was debated in Constantinople as late as the four-teenth century (Grumel, 62).

The commemorative eras number the years from some historical event. For example, in Paphlagonia years were reckoned 'from the twelfth consulate' of Augustus, that is, 5 BC (or, as the Paphla-gonians reckoned, from 6/5 BC). Likewise, for some time the Athenians dated 'from the visit of the Emperor Hadrian' in AD 126. The Manicheans reckoned from Mani's birth (or death).[61] The Neoplatonists computed the years from the accession of Julian the Apostate (AD 361; cf. Marinus, Vita Procli). The Christian era of incarnation, invented in AD 532 (cf. p. 81) and the Islamic era from Muhammad's flight to Medina (from 15 June 622) are of the same class.

It should be noted, however, that many eras deduced by modern scholars from the dates on coins are imaginary. Though numismatists continue to develop ingenious theories about the supposed Alexander's eras in Phoenicia (cf. e.g. I. L. Merker, Americ. Numism. Soc. Notes XI (1964), 15), the dates so interpreted on the coins of Acco refer to the local rulers (E. T. Newell, The Alexander Coinage of Acco and Sidon (1916), 59; G. Kleiner, Abh. der Deutsch. Akad. Berlin (1947), 24). In Sidon and Aradus the letters of the alphabet were used to mark successive (annual?) issues of coins. After the twenty-fourth series, the counting began again. In Sidon, the legend of the series 'N' (=13) changes from 'Alexander' to 'Philip'. This change assigns this group to the year 324/323 (R. Dussaud, RN 1908, 450). In the series '18' the name 'Alexander' is substituted for that of Philip: Sidon fell into the hands of Ptolemy who did not issue coins in the name of Philip Arrhidaeus (cf. E. T. Newell, ib. 36, whose chronology of coins is, however, incorrect). Again, the numbers on coins of Tyre (for which numismatists invented imaginary eras) are misread (H. Seyrig, Syria 1957, 93). Again, numismatists imagine that the coins of Alexandria Troas bearing the dates from '137' to '235' attest a city era from the renaming of the city by Lysimachus, c. 300 BC. H. v. Fritze, Nomisma 1911, 27; A. R. Bellinger, Coins (Troy: Supplementary Monographs 2) (1961), 93. In fact, we do not know when the city received the name of Alexandria (Strabo 13, 593), and it is difficult to believe that she would count the years not from the foundation by Antigonus but from the renaming date. Anyway, an era ab urbe condita would be without any parallel in antiquity (cf. p. 77). Alexandria Troas became a part of the Seleucid empire in 280, and thus it is probable that the city continued to use the Seleucid reckoning when she became independent (cf. p. 71). On her coinage now cf. L. Robert, Monnaies antiques en Troade (1966). Similarly, an era of Eumenes II from 188 BC never existed; L. Robert, Villes de l'Asie Mineure² (1962), 253.

A third group of eras was invented by scholars and mainly used by historians. The disagreement between local calendars and eponyms made it desirable to find a method of dating which would be understandable everywhere. The periodic Panhellenic festivals offered such a common time standard (cf. Thuc. III, 8, 1; V, 49, 1; and A. W. Gomme, Commentary on Thucydides II (1956), 258).

An inscription dates the appearance of Artemis in Magnesia by reference to the Olympic year (140 Olympiad, first year), to the Pythian games and to the Athenian archon of the year (Syll. 557). Greek writers, such as Pausanias, often use the reckoning according to the Olympiads in order to date some event. This implies the existence and use of lists of Olympic victors. The first list was published by the sophist Hippias. It was then kept up to date and often re-edited. The list for the Olympiads 1–249 has been preserved in Eusebius' Chronicle (ed. J. Karst, 89). Fragments of earlier catalogues are collected in FrGrH 414 ff.

The numbering of Olympiads was introduced by Timaeus or by Eratosthenes. Other Panhellenic games, such as the Pythian, were also sometimes numbered. The trustworthiness of the earlier part of the list of Olympic victors, which begins in 776 BC, is doubtful.[62]

From Eratosthenes on, all Greek chronology was based on the

Olympiads. All other datings were synchronized with the Olympiads (*cf. e.g.* the dating of Moses in Eusebius *Pr. ev.* X, 9). The Byzantine chronographers continued to refer to the Olympiads. The documents, however, are only rarely dated according to this chronographic standard (*cf. e.g. Inschriften von Olympia* 530; A. Rehm, *Didyma* II, 214).

The counting of the years within an Olympiad goes back to Eratosthenes (*FrGrH*, Commentary II, 707), but an 'Olympic year *per se* did not exist: the games were held every four years (776, 772 BC; AD 1, 5, etc.), alternatively after 49 and 50 months in midsummer at a full month (Samuel, 191). A more precise date is not possible (*cf.* Ginzel II, 304; B. R. Sealey, *Class. Rev* 1960, 185). Chronologists equated each year of the Olympic quadrennium with the corresponding Attic year, which also began in the summer. It seems that the author of the Parian Chronicle in 264 BC already used this device (*cf. FrGrH* Commentary II, 670). No one, of course, had to count years of an Olympiad in conformity with the Athenian calendar. Many scholars used the Macedonian year which began in the autumn. It seems that following his sources Porphyry used now the Athenian, now the Macedonian year (*cf. FrGrH* ib. 855). Polybius' flexible Olympic year (p. 64) coincided roughly with the autumnal Achaean year: *cf.* F. W. Walbank, *Historical Commentary on Polybius* I (1957), 35; Samuel, 194.

The use of the Olympic years in chronography posed the problem of their equations with years expressed in some other system of datings. Thus, a Roman consular year, which from 153 BC began on 1 January, corresponds to parts of two Olympic years. Thus, Ol.180, 1 = 60/59 BC is equated in Diodorus with the consular year 59 BC, in Dionysius of Halicarnassus with the consular year 60 BC. The first method, which was also used by Polybius, gives 775 BC as the epoch of the Olympiads, while the second, which we generally follow, gives 776 BC as the starting point of the reckoning (*cf. FrGrH* II, 664; Ed. Meyer, *Klein Schriften* II (1924), 288). Again, the use of the Macedonian year leads to the epoch 777 BC (*cf.* G. Unger, *SBA* 1895, 300; Ed. Meyer, *Forschungen* II (1899), 446).

Similarly, the conversion of Athenian dates to Roman dates and vice versa could be done in two ways. Diodorus, for instance, ends his chronographic list with the consular year 59 BC (*cf.* p. 91) which for him corresponds to the archonship of Herodus in 60/59 BC. On the other hand, Castor ended his work with the year 61, yet he equated it with the archonship of Theophemus in 61/60 (*cf.* Leuze, 74; W. Kolbe, *AM* 1912, 107).

An era *ab urbe condita* (from the founding of the city of Rome) did not, in reality, exist in the ancient world, and the use of reckoning the years in this way is modern. The Romans used this epoch only to measure time distance from it to some subsequent event: for example, Livy IV, 7 says that the consular tribunes came 310 years after the founding of the city (*cf.* III, 30, 7; VII, 18, 1). Similarly, an inscription states that Nerva restored liberty '848 years after the founding of the city' (Dessau, 274). This mode of relative dating was already used in the Roman Republic. For instance, an inscription of Puteoli (Dessau, 518) is dated '90 years *ab colonia deducta*' (that is, 105 BC) (*cf.* Dessau, 157; *genio municipii anno post Interamnam conditam 704*). Relative datings of this kind are incorrectly called 'eras'. Consequently, modern scholars speak of the 'era of Tanis', referring to an Egyptian inscription with the mention of '400 years of the city of Tanis' (K. Sethe, *AZ* 1930, 85; R. Stadelmann, *CE* 1965, 46). J. v. Beckerath, *Untersuchungen zur politischen Geschichte der zweiten Zwischenzeit in Aegypten* (1965), 153. H. Goedicke, *CE* 1966, 23. *Cf. Numb.* 13, 22: Hebron built seven years before Zoan (Tanis).

The principal reason for not using the system *ab urbe condita* was that the age of the city was disputed: *est enim inter scriptores de numero annorum controversia* (Cic. *Brut.* 18, 72). The date of the founding in Roman historiography—excluding the more extreme opinions (for example Cincius Alimentus in Dion. Hal. I, 74: 729/8 BC)—oscillates between 759 and 748 BC. For a long time the Polybian date of 751/0 served as a norm for Cicero, Livy and Diodorus (*cf.* Perl, 20); then Atticus in his *Liber annalis* moved the founding back to 753 BC (Cic. *Brut.* 18, 72). This date was taken up and popularized by Varro. The list of the magistrates of the Republic compiled under Augustus (*Fasti*

Capitolini) indicates the years *ab urbe condita*, which are, however, counted from 752 BC. Tradition established the festival
of Parilia on 21 April as the birthday of Rome. Thus a year *ab
urbe condita* which ran from 21 to 20 April corresponded to
parts of two consular years, and its identification with one of
them depended on the chosen system of conversion (*cf.* Leuze,
252).

INDICTION

The number of an indiction shows the position of the year within
a cycle of 15 years: AD 312–326, etc. The cycles themselves are
not numbered, so that the number of the indiction is usually
used only to relate to another dating system. This kind of time-
reckoning was introduced in AD 312 (*Chronicon Paschale*) and
became obligatory for the dating of documents from AD 537
(Justinian *Novel.* 47).

Indiction (='declaration', ἰνδικτίων, ἐπινέμησις) originally
referred to the announcement (*indictio*) of the compulsory
delivery of foodstuffs to the government (*annona*), an obligation
which under Diocletian became the cornerstone of the Roman
fiscal system. At first the term was used only with reference to
taxation (*cf.* U. Wilcken, *APF* 1911, 256). Thus, *e.g.*, in AD 368
a village had to pay 44,617 denarii, κατὰ τὸν τύπον τῆς ια ἰνδικ-
[τίοωνος] (Wilcken, *Chrest.* 281). The population knew the tax
year better than the official consular date. Accordingly, from the
second half of the fourth century on, the indiction appears in all
kinds of documents, for instance in a petition to offer to rent
3 *arourai* 'for sowing them in the 10th year of this prosperous
indiction' (Wilcken, ib., 380). The indictions, however, were not
numbered. For Julian equivalents of the years within an indiction,
from AD 312 on, see *RE* I, 666.

The origin of the indiction cycle and its meaning remain
unknown. In Egypt the fiscal period of 15 years was in use from
AD 297 (*cf.* Wilcken, *APF* XI, 313; Grumel, 192).

The year of indiction generally began on 1 September, but in
Egypt it varied according to the date of the tax announcement
in the summer. (For the table, see F. Hohmann, *Zur Chronologie*

der Papyrusurkunden (1911), 40.) Thus, June of the 14th indiction in Egypt fell in the 15th indiction of Constantinople (P. M. Meyer, *Juristische Papyri* (1920), no. 52 (of AD 551)). In the West, the inclusion of indictions in the Easter Table of Dionysius Exiguus (*cf.* p. 81) made this time reference popular. In the chaos of medieval datings this one was at least stable (*cf.* J. E. W. Wallis, *English Regnal Years and Tables* (1921), 9). Reckoning by indiction continued to be used by the Supreme Tribunal of the Holy Roman Empire until the dissolution of the latter in 1806, and is still carried on in some modern calendar tables, for instance in H. Lietzmann's *Zeitrechnung* (1934), who gives indictions from AD 298 until AD 2000.

The conversion rule for an indiction number is to add 3 to the year number of the Christian era and divide the sum by 15. The remainder gives the indiction number of the year. The Byzantine dates from the Creation are to be divided by 15 (O. Seeck, *RE* IX, 1330; Ginzel II, 148).

CHAPTER III

APPLIED CHRONOLOGY

THE KNOWLEDGE of ancient calendars and dating systems must in principle enable us to convert the dates of our sources into units of our reckoning. This is generally possible for the ancient datings expressed in terms of the Julian year. According to our sources, Caesar was murdered on the Ides of March in the year when Caesar was consul for the fifth time and Antony was his colleague. According to the consular list the year *C. Caesare V et M. Antonio consulibus* corresponded to 44 BC. The Ides of March corresponded to 15 March. Caesar, thus, was killed on 15 March 44 BC.

The same, or almost the same, certainty can be obtained for dates of the Babylonian cyclical calendar (see p. 24), and for Egyptian calendar dates—if the Julian year is known (*cf.* p. 40). For instance, a letter dated 2 Mesore, year 29 (of Ptolemy II), was written on 22 September 257 BC (*P. Cairo Zen.* 59096). For Greek history and Roman pre-Julian dates, except for some particular cases (for instance, the astronomically fixed dates), we must be satisfied with establishing the Julian year and the approximate season of the event in question.

For the Near East, the margin of error rapidly increases when we go back beyond *c.* 900 BC. Until the fourteenth century, in the most favourable cases, the margin will be about ten years and more; until the seventeenth century, about fifty years, and still earlier, about a hundred years. For the pre-literate period we have no historical dates, but must rely on the archaeological chronology (see p. 11).

Approximate as our knowledge may be, we must know how it is obtained. How do we get the equation between the ancient and our own datings? To answer this question we have first to understand the origin of our time reckoning.

PRINCIPLES OF REDUCTION

The Church required Easter to fall on the first Sunday after the spring full moon, that is, the first full moon after 21 March. This necessitated computation of the Easter cycles and tables. In AD 525, Dionysius Exiguus was asked by Pope John I to compile a new table. He used the table of the church of Alexandria which employed the era of Diocletian (see p. 72), but being unwilling to reckon from the reign 'of an impious persecutor', he chose 'to note the years' from the Incarnation. In his table, the year 532 *ab incarnatione* followed the year 247 of Diocletian (*PL* LXVII, 493). Accepted by the See of Rome, Dionysius' table was revised again and again, for instance by Bede in 725 (*PL* XC, 859), and served the Roman Catholic church up to the introduction of the Gregorian calendar in 1582. With Dionysius' Easter computation, the West also adopted his era. For instance, the era of Incarnation was already used by the author of the *Computatio Paschalis* compiled in AD 562.[63] Thus, our reckoning simply continues a Roman one. Therefore, all ancient datings which directly or indirectly can be related to the counting of the years of Diocletian can also be converted into Julian dates.

Secondly, the dating according to the Roman consuls was still used in the fifth century, and Dionysius himself wrote his work *consulatu Probi iunioris* (AD 525). The aforementioned *Computatio Paschalis* gives the equation AD 562 = year 21 *post consulatum Basilii*. As we have the complete *fasti* of the Roman consuls for 1,050 years from Brutus and Collatinus to the aforementioned Basilius, we can easily assign Julian years to each of them, provided that the ancient dates are trustworthy (*cf.* p. 69).

Third, we have the so-called 'Ptolemaic' canon, the list of kings preserved in Theon's commentary on Ptolemy's astronomical work. Composed by Alexandrian astronomers for their own calculations, this list, based on the Egyptian mobile year, begins with the accession of the Babylonian king Nabonassar on 27 February 747 BC. It gives astronomically exact dates of successive reigns (Babylonian, Persian, Ptolemies, the Roman and Byzantine emperors), and in some manuscripts the list is con-

tinued until the fall of Constantinople in 1453. Here again, modern
chronology is linked directly to an ancient system of reckoning.[6]

If, for example, we want to know which was the first year of
Diocletian's rule (which in itself does not have to be identical
with the beginning of the era of Diocletian), the *Chronicon
Paschale* tells us that he was proclaimed emperor on 17 September
under the consulate of Carinus II and Numerianus. From the
fasti consulares we get the corresponding Christian year, AD 284.
Petavius proceeded in this manner in 1627. Ideler, instead, made
use of an astronomical observation which is dated synchronisti-
cally: 81 years from Diocletian = 1,112 years from Nabonassar
(that is, from the beginning of the Canon of the Kings); the
equation gives AD 284 as the first year of Diocletian's rule. In
order to fix the first year of the emperor, Scaliger (*De emendatione
temporum*, V) in 1582 established that the Coptic church, in con-
tinuing to calculate the era of Diocletian, equated AD 1582 (from
29 August) with the 1299th year of Diocletian. In other words
all Roman dates, if they are complete and reliable, can be directly
expressed in Julian years. All the other datings of ancient chronology are linked to our reckoning by direct or indirect synchronisms with Roman dates. For instance, the Egyptian
chronology is based on the list of the Pharaohs, made by Manetho
under Ptolemy II (*FrGrH*, no. 609). His list contains the reigns
of Persian kings, beginning with Cambyses, who ruled in Egypt
and who also appear in the Royal Canon. In this way a correspondence with Roman chronology is obtained. Ancient Indian
chronology depends on the date of King Asoka, in whose edicts
five Hellenistic kings are mentioned (Antigonus Gonatas, etc.).
We can date these kings, thanks to Roman synchronisms.
Accordingly, the approximate date of Asoka can be established
(P. H. L. Eggermont, *Chronology of the Reign of Asoka* (1956)).

Where the link to Roman chronology is broken, we grope
vainly for certitude. Take, for example, Egyptian chronology.
The aforementioned king-list of Manetho has been preserved
only in Christian summaries (*FrGrH*, 609). As we have seen,
the mention of Persian rulers allows us to connect his list with
Roman reckoning. The references to later Pharaohs in Babylon

an texts and astronomical data in Egyptian documents confirm
the general reliability of Manetho's list for the New Kingdom
and later dynasties up to the sixteenth century BC (M. Alliot,
NES 1950, 211; R. A. Parker, *Revue d'Egyptologie* 1952, 101).
Yet the exact datings before *c.* 800 are rarely obtainable. The
accession of Ramesses II is dated by various egyptologists to 1304,
1292, or 1279 BC.[65]

Manetho's figures for the period of anarchy between the
Middle and the New Kingdom (*c.* 160 years) and for the first
intermediate period between the Old and the Middle Kingdoms
c. 900 years) are, however, unreliable. Thus, the link with
Roman chronology is twice broken. A papyrus letter states that
Sirius will rise on 16.VIII of the year 7. The king in question is,
in all probability, Sesostris III, or it may be Amenemmes III, his
successor (XII Dynasty). Secondly, the rise of Sirius is not observed
but predicted—that is, calculated—21 days in advance. We do
not, however, know how. The Julian date of the event is *c.* 1880.
Thus, we know that the XII Dynasty reigned from *c.* 2000 to
c. 1800. The royal canon preserved in a Turin papyrus (Gardiner,
47) gives a total figure of 995 years for the Old Kingdom until
the end of the VI Dynasty. Assuming that the figure is exact, we
still do not know the length of the interval between the VI and
the XII Dynasty. According to Manetho, the first Pharaoh,
Menes, ruled from 4242 (V. Struve, *Vestnik Drevnei Istorii* 1946,
fasc. 4, 9). The most recent estimates vary between 3100 and
2800. Yet, according to the same astronomical and historical
dates, Menes was also placed toward the end of the fifth millennium (*cf.* L. Borchardt, *Quellen und Forschungen zur Zeitbestimmung der ägyptischen Geschichte* II (1935), 117). We cannot disprove
this hypothesis. We can only say that archaeological considera-
tions suggest that it is best to accept the shorter chronology and
not to throw the XII Dynasty back to the fourth millennium
(Gardiner, 66).[66]

Assyro-Babylonian chronology is based on the Royal Canon
which begins with the Babylonian king Nabonassar. The king-
lists which go down to Nabonassar would in principle allow us to
convert all Assyro-Babylonian royal datings into Julian ones; but

these lists are often unreliable. The Assyrian scribes, for instance, suppressed some kings who were later considered usurpers (B. Landsberger, *JCS* 1954, 101). The compilers also made successive some dynasties which were contemporary with one another. The regnal years were already counted *c.* 2500 in the Sumerian city of Lagash (M. Lambert, *RH* 1960, 24; for Larsa, *cf.* F. B. Kraus, *ZA* 1959, 136). But this dating system came into common use only under the Kassite dynasty. Before this time, all years received official names which referred to some event marking the year. If, for example, we say that Rimsin of Larsa was defeated in the year 31 of Hammurabi, this means that the date-formula 'year in which Hammurabi destroyed Rimsin' received the 31st place in the Babylonian list of year names in the reign of Hammurabi. The Assyrians dated by annual eponyms. For instance, an original document of King Esarhaddon, found in his palace, is dated by the magistrate (*limmu*) of the year (=676 BC). But elsewhere in the second and first millennia the time-reckoning by regnal years prevailed.

The fixing in time of the famous Babylonian legislator, Hammurabi, on whose dating many others depend (*cf.* D. Edzard, *Die zweite Zwischenzeit Babyloniens* (1957), 15), illustrates the inherent difficulty of working with king-lists. Hammurabi was a king of the I Dynasty. A Babylonian king-list goes down from the I Dynasty to Kandalanu of the Royal Canon (647–626). Thus, we have here a link to Roman chronology. Though the list is damaged and includes the II Dynasty (of the Sealand on the Persian Gulf), which apparently never reigned over Babylon, it is possible, by using the dates of this list, to place Hammurabi in the second half of the twentieth century BC (*cf.* Ed. Meyer, *Die älteste Chronologie Babyloniens, Assyriens und Ägyptens* (1931), 1). Yet, recently discovered documents prove that Hammurabi was contemporary with Shamshi-Adad I of Assyria, who, according to the Assyrian list, reigned in the second half of the eighteenth century. Should we bring Hammurabi down or move Shamshi-Adad up? The rather fluid chronology of the Pharaohs and the Hittites and vague archaeological inferences led recent scholars to suggest 1792–1750 or 1728–1686 as the most probable dates of

Hammurabi. Other scholars prefer to place him in 1848 or even c. 1900. As a matter of fact, the Assyrian kings themselves disagree with each other and with the information supplied by the royal list when they state the interval between a given king and some predecessor.[67]

The Royal Canon is also basic for Greek chronology, together with a chronographic fragment from Eratosthenes (*FrGrH*, 241 F 1), in which are given the intervals between the main events of Greek history until the death of Alexander (dated in the Canon of Kings): 'From the fall of Troy to the return of the Heraclids 80 years, from here to the Ionian colonization (Ionian migration), 60 years, then until the guardianship of Lycurgus, 159 years, from here to the beginning of the Olympiads, 108 years; from the 1st Olympiad to the campaign of Xerxes, 297 years; from here to the beginning of the Peloponnesian Wars, 48 years, and until the end of these wars and of the Athenian hegemony, 27 years, and until the battle of Leuctra, 34 years; from this time to the death of Philip, 35 years, and, finally, until the death of Alexander, 12 years.'

In this way it is possible to say that the beginning of the Peloponnesian War was in 431 BC. Furthermore, Thucydides mentions the Olympic games (for instance) in the twelfth year of the war (V, 49). Because the distance of the Peloponnesian War from the first Olympiad is also established by Eratosthenes, the date of the Olympiad 1/1 is 776 BC; this is confirmed by Censorinus, who equates the consular year *Ulpii et Pontiniani* (AD 238) with the 266th Olympiad.

Let us now take another example. Diodorus (XI, 1, 2) places the expedition of Xerxes in the first year of the 75th Olympiad, when Calliades was archon in Athens and Sp. Cassius and P. Verginius consuls in Rome. The consular date seems to give a direct link to Roman chronology. But according to the Roman *fasti*, Sp. Cassius and Verginius were consuls in 486 BC. This disagrees with the Greek dating. In fact, the name of the Athenian archon Calliades is already given by Herodotus (VIII, 51), who also states that the battles were fought in the time of the Olympic games (VII, 206). Ol.75, 1 is 480/79 BC, the same year of the archon Calliades. Diodorus made a mistake in his Roman synchronism (*cf.* Perl, 106).

In this way, by means of reciprocal controls of synchronization and with the help of astronomy, the founders of modern chronology, J. Scaliger (1540–1609) and D. Petavius (1583–1652), calculated the fundamental dates, which, in turn, permitted the conversion of other dates. Petavius, in *Rationarium Temporum II*, presents the material which justifies the currently accepted equations between ancient datings and the Julian years.

The references to celestial phenomena, particularly the eclipses, allow us to control the systems of ancient chronology since their dates can be calculated astronomically, and thus, independently of the said system. The solar eclipse, which occurs during the period of the new moon, is observable only from that part of the earth on which the moon's shadow falls. The lunar eclipse, which can occur only at full moon, is visible everywhere. The eclipses recur in the same sequence within the period of 233 lunar revolutions, that is, every 18 years and 11 days (F. Boll, *RE* VI, 2338). Thus, the approximate date of the observation must be known in order to identify the phenomenon with an eclipse of the astronomers. Therefore, it is not possible to date with certainty the solar eclipse seen by Archilochus (frag. 74 D), generally thought to be that of 6 April 648 BC. The observations of Venus made under King Ammizaduga of the first Babylonian dynasty have been preserved. But since the same phenomena recur every 56 years on approximately the same dates in a lunar calendar, the observations can as well agree with the dates 1977 or 1581 BC, for the first year of Ammizaduga. (*Cf.* J. D. Weir, *Venus Tablets of Ammizaduga* (1971), 12; E. Huber, *BO* 1974, 86; R. Reiner and D. Pingree, *Venus Tablet of Ammizaduga* (1975).) Again, the Julian dates of Sirius (p. 41) would differ by several years according to the place of observation; *cf.* E. Hornung, *AZ* 1965, 38. Only historical evidence allows us to choose the right historical date.[68]

However, as soon as the cyclic period to which an observation belongs is known, astronomy can date the phenomenon with absolute precision and therefore establish with certainty a whole series of dates. Thus, for example, Assyrian chronology is pinned

down by the mention of the solar eclipse which occurred on
15 June 763 BC in the list of the eponyms of Assur. The disputed
dates of the scientist Heron of Alexandria (*c.* AD 62), of the
astrologer Vettius Valens (*c.* AD 152–162) and of the astronomer
Cleomedes (*c.* AD 370) were established by modern recalculation
of celestial phenomena mentioned by these writers (O. Neugebauer, 178; id. *HTR* 1954, 66; id. *AJPh* 1964, 418).[69] The
beginning of the Peloponnesian War in 431 is confirmed by
Thucydides' reference (II, 28, 1) to an eclipse which actually
occurred on 3 August 431 BC. Mithridates VI of Pontus died in
63 BC, as a Roman synchronism (Pompey's march to Petra)
shows. According to our sources, he reigned fifty-six years and
was thirteen years old at accession. This gives 133 and 120 BC
respectively as the dates of his birth and accession (Plin. XXV, 1,
6; Memnon, 32). According to Justinus (XXXVII, 2) brilliant
comets shone in the year he was begotten (134 BC), and in the
year he became king (120 BC). In fact, Chinese sources record the
appearance of comets in 134 and 120 BC (*cf.* Finegan, 242). The
Julian year of the battle at Thermopylae is fixed by the reference
to the Olympic and the archon year. Polyaenus (I, 32, 2) mentions
'the rising of a star' before Leonidas' battle. If he means the hero
of Thermopylae, and if this star is Sirius, the battle must have
been fought *c.* 1 August (J. Labarbe, *BCH* 1954, 1; id. *Revue
Belge de Philologie* 1959, 69). The seasonal occurrence of the
flooding of the Nile can help to establish the date of Pompey's
death (D. Bonneau, *REL* 1961, 105).

CHRONOGRAPHY

Hellanicus of Lesbos was the first who, in the time of the
Peloponnesian War, attempted to adjust various systems of
chronological references to a common standard, namely to the
years of the priestesses of Hera in Argos. Following his example,
later Greek savants prepared synchronistic tables. Since Timaeus
and Eratosthenes, these tables were generally based on the reckoning of the Olympiads. Castor of Rhodes (*c.* 60 BC) added Roman
and Oriental datings. Using the work of their predecessors, the
Christian chronographers put secular chronography into the

service of sacred history. A work of this kind, the 'Canon' in the second part of Eusebius' *Chronicle*, composed *c.* AD 300, was translated by Jerome and continued until 378. Jerome's compilation became the standard of chronological knowledge in the West. J. Scaliger, the founder of modern chronological science, aimed at reconstructing the work of Eusebius.

The Canon gives a continuous series of synchronisms. The years after Abraham (1 Abr.=2016 BC), with whom for Eusebius all reliable chronology began, are equated with the royal years, the Olympiads, etc., and events are mentioned under their respective dates. For instance, the birth of Christ is mentioned under the year 2015 of Abraham, which was also the 25th year of the reign of Augustus and fell into the 184th Olympiad, that is, incidentally, the year 2 BC according to our reckoning, which goes back to Dionysius Exiguus (see p. 81).[70]

The datings of Eusebius, often transmitted incorrectly in manuscripts, are of little use to us today, except in a few cases where no better information is available (*cf.* p. 11). However, a modern 'Eusebius', a work which would adequately summarize the present state of applied chronology, is still lacking.[71] We must realize that we cannot establish our own handy chronological tables except on the basis of tables, lists, and so on, prepared by the ancients themselves, who in turn were handicapped by the absence of the standard time-reckoning. Under 45 BC, a contemporary chronicler notes: *annus or[dinatione Caesaris] mutatus* ('*Fasti Ostienses*', ed. L. Vidman, *Rozpravy* of the Czechoslovak Academy LXVII, 6 (1957)). Yet the introduction of the Julian year alone could not standardize chronology, particularly since the Julian year itself began at different dates in each country. In England and its American colonies, the year began on 25 March until 1752. Two examples may illustrate the difficulties which confronted a chronologist even after the introduction of the Julian calendar. For instance, Porphyry was a specialist in chronological research; yet in his biography of Plotinus he had to use the regnal years of the Roman emperors. Thus, Porphyry's reader would have needed some handy tables of chronology to understand his datings. Yet the imperial years were not identical with the Julian years, and the reader would not know which form of the Imperial year was used by the author (*cf.* R. Waltz, *REA* 1949, 41; M. J. Boyde, *CPh* 1937, 241). Errors were unavoidable. Jerome, a chronologist himself, writing after AD 374 congratulates a certain Paul on his hundredth birthday (*Ep. ad Paulum*). Yet elsewhere (*De viris ill.* III, 53) he states that Paul knew personally Cyprian of Carthage who had died in AD 259. Mani used the Babylonian form of the Seleucid era (from 311 BC), and we have information coming from various sources about his life and death. Yet these sources disagree about his chronology, though he lived in the third century AD. This lack of certainty in the matter of chronology made it possible for the Sassanid traditions to reduce the period from Alexander to the Sassanids from 557 to 226 years. The Jews also allotted only 52 years to the Persian period of their history, though 206 years separate Cyrus from Alexander.[72]

Ancient historians often had to use different systems of dating concurrently since they were unable to unify the references they had found in their sources. See *e.g.* W. den Boer, *Mnemosyne* 1967, 30 on Herodotus; O. Mørkholm, *Antiochus IV of Syria* (1966), 196; J. Goldstein, *I Maccabees* (1976) 24.

PRACTICAL SUGGESTIONS

In ancient (and medieval) chronology we use the Julian calendar and not the Gregorian one which is used now. Both coincide *c.* AD 300; but then the Julian dates run behind the Gregorian calendar by three days every four hundred years. In the reverse direction, from *c.* 100 BC, the Julian year is in advance of the Gregorian calendar by three days every four hundred years, so that *e.g.* 29 December 102 BC (Gregorian) was already 1 January 101 BC Julian (*cf.* p. 10).

In using ancient datings given in era or regnal years, we must take into account two possible pitfalls. First, the beginning of the year was not standardized but left to local choice. For instance, the Actium era began on 23 September 31 BC at Philadelphia, but in 32 BC at Amisus (M. N. Tod, *ABSA* XXIII (1918–19), 212).

Similar were the variations for the Macedonian and Actium eras in Greece (F. Papazoglou, *BCH* 1963, 517).

The regnal years of the Achaemenids began in the spring for the Babylonians, in the autumn for the Egyptians, and were probably counted from the accession day by the Persian court (*cf.* Thuc. VIII, 58). Further, each city in the same realm for various reasons could count the regnal years differently from one another and from the court reckoning (H. Seyrig, *RN* 1964, 58).

Again, the numbering of regnal years does not need to agree with history. Charles II of England actually became king on 29 May 1660, but his regnal years were counted from the death of Charles I on 30 January 1649. Ancient rulers, too, could for various reasons antedate the beginning of their reigns (*cf.* E. J. Bickerman, *Berytus* 1944, 77). On the other hand, a disputed succession could confuse the scribes. Twelve years after the death of Philip Arrhidaeus, in 305 BC, a cuneiform document was dated: 'King Philip, year 19' (Isid. Lévy, *Journ. Asiat.* 1952, 269).

We use the standard Julian years and reckon them backward 'before Christ'. This reckoning postulates a zero year between the dates 'BC' and 'AD'. But such a year is lacking in our computation. This point is to be kept in mind when calculating the intervals between events before and after Christ. The simplest method is to use the astronomical convention: 1 BC=year 0; 2 BC=1, and so on. For example we ask how old Augustus was when he died in AD 14. He was born in 63 BC. Thus the equation is: $63 - 1 = 62$; $62 + 14 = 76$. In fact, Augustus died 35 days before reaching his 76th birthday (Suet. *Aug.* 100).

The lack of the zero era in Christian reckoning also explains the conversion rule for the era years. For instance, the first year of the Seleucid era (of Macedonian style) is 312/11 BC. This means that the zero year for this era is 313. Thus, to obtain the Julian year corresponding to a Seleucid year for the pre-Christian period, we have to subtract the number of the Seleucid year from 313. For instance, year 200 Sel.$=313 - 200 = 113$ BC and year 312 Sel. is $313 - 312 = 1$ BC. But year 313 Sel. is AD 1. Accordingly, for the post-Christian years of the Seleucid era, the number of the Julian year of the epoch (312) is to be subtracted from the number of the Seleucid year. Thus, 522 Sel.=522 – 312=AD 210 or rather October 210 – 30 September AD 211.

The lack of the zero year also explains the rules for the conversion of the number of an Olympiad. For the period BC, that is, up through Ol.194, the number of the Olympiad is reduced by one, multiplied by four, and the product is subtracted from 776. The result gives the Julian year BC in which the games were held, that is, the first year of the Olympiad in question. For example, what is the Julian year of the 180th Olympiad? The operation is as follows: 180 – 1=179; 179 × 4=716; 776 – 716 =60 BC, or, more precisely, 60/59. This is the first Julian year of the 180th Olympiad.

On the other hand, for the period AD, that is from the 195th Ol. on, the number of the given Olympiad is again to be reduced by one, the result multiplied by four, and 775 to be deducted from the product. For instance, Eusebius' *Chronicle* names the Olympic victors up to the 249th Ol. inclusively. Now, 249 – 1=248; 248 × 4 =992; 992 – 775=217. Julius Africanus gave a catalogue of the winners in Olympic games until his time, that is AD 217. Eusebius, without saying so, a century later reproduced Africanus' list (*cf.* Ed. Schwartz, *RE* VI, 1378). But using ancient datings expressed in terms of Olympic years, we should not forget the possible variations in synchronization: the source may have equated Ol. 180, 1, not with 60/59 BC, but with 61/60 BC, and so on (see p. 76). To put it bluntly: anyone trying to convert an ancient dating into one expressed in terms of our reckoning should remember the legal maxim: *caveat emptor.*

ABBREVIATIONS

JOURNALS AND COLLECTIONS

ABA	*Abhandlungen der Bayerischen Akademie*
ABSA	*Annual of the British School at Athens*
AFO	*Archiv für Orientforschung*
AGGG	*Abhandlungen der Göttinger Gelehrten Gesellschaft (Akademie)*
AJA	*American Journal of Archaeology*
AJPh	*American Journal of Philology*
AM	*Mitteilungen des Deutschen Archaeologischen Instituts, Athenische Abteilung*
APAW	*Abhandlungen der Preussischen Akademie der Wissenschaften*
APF	*Archiv für Papyrusforschung*
ARW	*Archiv für Religionswissenschaft*
ArchOr	*Archiv Orientálí*
ASAA	*Annuario della Scuola Archeologica d'Atene*
Ath	*Athenaeum*
AZ	*Zeitschrift für Aegyptische Sprache*
BASOR	*Bulletin of the American Schools of Oriental Research in Jerusalem and Baghdad*
BCH	*Bulletin de Correspondance Hellénique*
BIFAO	*Bulletin de l'Institut français d'archéologie orientale*
BO	*Bibliotheca Orientalis*
BSL	*Bulletin de la Société de Linguistique de Paris*
BSLL	*Bulletin de la Société des Lettres de Lund*
BSOAS	*Bulletin of the School of Oriental and African Studies*
CAH	*Cambridge Ancient History*
CAH²	*Cambridge Ancient History I–II, New Edition*
CE	*Chronique d'Égypte*
CIL	*Corpus Inscriptionum Latinarum*
CPh	*Classical Philology*
CR	*Comptes Rendus de l'Académie des Inscriptions*
DWA	*Denkschriften der Wiener Akademie*
FrGrH	*F. Jacoby, Fragmente der griechischen Historiker*
GDI	*Sammlung der griechischen Dialekt-Inschriften*
GGA	*Göttingische Gelehrte Anzeiger*
GGN	*Nachrichten der Göttingischen Gelehrten Gesellschaft*
Hesp.	*Hesperia*

HSCPh	Harvard Studies in Classical Philology
HTR	Harvard Theological Review
HUCA	Hebrew Union College Annual
IEJ	Israel Exploration Journal
IG	Inscriptiones Graecae
JAOS	Journal of the American Oriental Society
JBL	Journal of Biblical Literature
JCS	Journal of Cuneiform Studies
JEA	Journal of Egyptian Archaeology
JHS	Journal of Hellenic Studies
JNES	Journal of Near Eastern Studies
JOAI	Jahreshefte des Österreichischen Archaeologischen Instituts
JQR	Jewish Quarterly Review
JRS	Journal of Roman Studies
MOI	Mitteilungen des Orientalischen Instituts (Academy of Berlin)
OGIS	Orientis Graeci Inscriptiones Selectae ed. W. Dittenberger (1903–5)
OLZ	Orientalistische Literaturzeitung
PAAJR	Proceedings of the American Academy of Jewish Research
PAPhS	Proceedings of the American Philosophical Society
Phil	Philologus
PL	Patrologia Latina ed. Migne
RA	Revue archéologique
RAss	Revue d'Assyrologie
RE	Pauly-Wissowa, Real-Encyclopädie der classischen Altertums-wissenschaft
REA	Revue des études anciennes
REG	Revue des études grecques
REJ	Revue des études juives
REL	Revue des études latines
RH	Revue Historique
RHR	Revue de l'histoire des religions
RLA	Reallexikon der Assyriologie
RLAC	Reallexikon für Antike und Christentum
RN	Revue Numismatique
RhM	Rheinisches Museum
RPh	Revue de Philologie
SBA	Sitzungsberichte der Bayerischen Akademie
SCO	Studi classici e orientali
SEG	Supplementum Epigraphicum Graecum
SHAW	Sitzungsberichte der Heidelberger Akademie
SOAW	Sitzungsberichte der österreichischen Akademie (Wien)
SPAW	Sitzungsberichte der preussischen Akademie der Wissenschaften
Syll	Sylloge Inscriptionum Graecarum, 3rd ed (1915–24) ed. W. Dittenberger

TAPhA	*Transactions of the American Philological Association*
YCS	*Yale Classical Studies*
ZA	*Zeitschrift für Assyriologie*
ZDMG	*Zeitschrift der Deutschen Morgenländischen Gesellschaft*
ZNTW	*Zeitschrift für die neutestamentliche Wissenschaft*
ZPE	*Zeitschrift für Papyrologie und Epigraphik*

BOOKS

Busolt-Swoboda	G. Busolt and H. Swoboda, *Griechische Staatskunde* I–II (1920–26)
Degrassi	A. Degrassi, *Inscriptiones Latinae Liberae Reipublicae* (1957–63)
Dessau	H. Dessau, *Inscriptiones Latinae Selectae* (1892–1916)
Dinsmoor	W. B. Dinsmoor, *The Archons of Athens in the Hellenistic Age* (1931)
Finegan	J. Finegan, *Handbook of Biblical Chronology* (1964)
Gardiner	A. Gardiner, *Egypt of the Pharaohs* (1961)
Ginzel	F. K. Ginzel, *Handbuch der Chronologie* I–III (1906–14)
Grumel	V. Grumel, *La Chronologie* (1958)
Ideler	L. Ideler, *Handbuch der Chronologie* I–II (1825)
Ideler, *Lehrbuch*	L. Ideler, *Lehrbuch der Chronologie* (1831)
Jacoby	F. Jacoby, *Atthis* (1949)
Kubitschek	W. Kubitschek, *Grundriss der antiken Zeitrechnung* (1928)
Kugler	F. X. Kugler, *Sternkunde und Sterndienst in Babel* I–II and Suppl. I–III (1907–35)
Langdon	S. Langdon, *Semitic Menologies* (1935)
Leuze	O. Leuze, *Römische Jahrzählung* (1909)
Meritt	B. D. Meritt, *The Athenian Year* (1961)
Meyer	Ed. Meyer, *Forschungen zur Alten Geschichte* (1892–9)
Mommsen	Th. Mommsen, *Römische Chronologie* (1859)
Mommsen, *RStR*	Th. Mommsen, *Römisches Staatsrecht* (1887)
Neugebauer	O. Neugebauer, *The Exact Sciences in Antiquity* (1957)
Nilsson	M. P. Nilsson, *Primitive Time-Reckoning* (1920)
Nilsson, *Kalender*	M. P. Nilsson, *Die Enstehung und religiöse Bedeutung des griechischen Kalenders* (1918)
Perl	G. Perl, *Kritische Untersuchungen zu Diodors römischer Jahrzählung* (1957)
Pritchett	W. K. Pritchett, *Ancient Athenian Calendars on Stone* (1963)
Pritchett-Neugebauer	W. K. Pritchett and O. Neugebauer, *The Calendars of Athens* (1948)
Robert	J. and L. Robert, *Bulletin épigraphique* (*REG*)
Samuel	A. E. Samuel, *Greek and Roman Chronology* (1972)
Tod	M. N. Tod, *Selection of Greek Historical Inscriptions* (1946)

NOTES

1 There is no adequate, full-scale treatment of ancient chronology. L. Ideler, *Handbuch der Chronologie* I–II (1825–6) and his shorter *Lehrbuch der Chronologie* (1831), though outdated, offer even today the best over-all picture. F. K. Ginzel, *Handbuch der Chronologie* I–III (1906–14), useful as a collection of material, though often at second hand, is also antiquated. For Greece and Rome see A. E. Samuel, *Greek and Roman Chronology. Calendars and Years in Classical Antiquity* (1972). For comparative chronology see M. P. Nilsson, *Primitive Time-Reckoning* (*Skrifter of the Humanistika Vetenskapssamfunder i Lund*, 1920). For current bibliography *cf. L'Année Philologique* s.v. *Calendaria*, and for Greece see J. and L. Robert, Bulletin épigraphique in *REG*. For Egypt see J. Janssen, *Annual Egyptian Bibliography*, 1947 ff. Yearly bibliography on the Near Eastern chronology can be found in the journal *Orientalia*.

2 R. van Compernolle, *Études de chronologie et d'historiographie siciliotes. Institut historique belge de Rome. Études . . . d'histoire ancienne* V (1960); J. Boardman, *JHS* 1965, 5; Molly Miller, *The Sicilian Colony Dates* (1970). On the uncertainty of typological dating *cf. e.g.* J. Moreau, *Die Welt der Kelten* (1958), 132.

3 D. R. Brothwell, E. S. Higgs, G. Clark (ed.), *Science in Archaeology* (2nd ed. 1970); S. Fleming, *Dating in Archaeology* (1977). The radio-carbon dating is particularly important for prehistory, but for various reasons, *e.g.* the variations of the disintegration rate of C-14, the radio-carbon date may widely disagree with the true date. *Cf.* Trevor Watkins (ed.), *Radiocarbon Calibration and Prehistory* (1976) and *CAH* I, 1, s.v. *Radiocarbon*. For current information about dating techniques in archaeology, consult relevant articles in *Antiquity*. For recent estimates of prehistoric chronology *cf.* G. Clark, *World Prehistory* (2nd ed. 1969) and *CAH* I, 1 (1970).

4 On our own calendar see, *e.g.*, P. Couderc, *Le Calendrier* (1961). For Babylonia, our sources (in addition to information from ancient historians, which is incorporated in the works of Ideler and Ginzel, and documents) also include astronomical records. The following are basic works: F. X. Kugler, *Sternkunde und Sterndienst in Babel*, I–II (1907–24) and Suppl. I–III (1913–35); O. Neugebauer, *Astronomical Cuneiform Texts* (1955); A. Sachs, *Late Babylonian Astronomical Texts* (1955). *Cf.* O. Neugebauer, *The Exact Sciences in Antiquity* (1957), 97, and *JNES* 1945, 1. For Egypt *cf.* p. 40.

Among other ancient peoples, those of Western Asia generally followed the Babylonian system (p. 24); the calendars of the western lands (Gaul, Spain and Germany) are not known well. On the Celtic calendar, *cf.* P. M. Duval, *La vie privée en Gaule* (1952), 342. Id. *Mélanges Carcopino* (1966), 295. On Germans *cf.* Ginzel III, 55.

5 Here and often elsewhere, Geminus is quoted in the English translation of Sir Thomas L. Heath, *Greek Astronomy* (1932).

6 The Egyptian hours: K. Sethe, *GGN* 1920, 106; L. Borchardt, *Aegyptische Zeitmessung* (1920); Neugebauer, 82; J. Lauer, *BIFA* 1960, 171. For Babylonia *cf.* F. Thureau-Dangin, *RAss* 1930, 123; 1932, 133; 1933, 151; id. *Osiris* 1939, 112; B. L. van der Waerden, *JNES* 1949, 18; 1951, 25. For Greece and Rome *cf.* G. Bilfinger, *Die antiken Stundenangaben* (1888); id. *Der bürgerliche Tag* (1888). On clocks and sundials *cf.* A. Rehm, *RE* VIII, 2416; M. C. Schmidt, *Antike Wasseruhren* (1912), H. Diels, *Antike Technik* (1924), 157. Waterclocks in Egypt: S. Schoch, *Abhandl. Akad. Mainz* 1950, no. 10, 908. For Babylonia *cf.* S. Smith, *Iraq* 1969, 77. On sundials *cf.* S. Gibbs, *Greek and Roman Sundials* (1976). On portable and multiple sundials *cf.* E. Büchner, *Chiron* 1971, 457, R. J. Bull, *BASOR* 1975, 29. On the use of minutes *cf.* P. Tannery, *RA* 1895, 359. On the survival of variable hours *cf.* G. C. Lewis, *Historical Survey of the Astronomy of the Ancients* (1862), 242. On the introduction of sundials in Greece *cf.* D. R. Dicks, *JHS* 1966, 29.

7 *Cf. e.g.* F. Hiller von Gärtringen, *Inschriften von Priene* (1906) no. 112, line 60: ἔθηκεν δὲ τὸ ἄλειμμα ἀπὸ ἀνατολῆς ἡλίου δι᾽ ἡμέρας μέχρι πρώτης τῆς νυκτὸς ὥρας . . .

8 O. Schliessel, *Hermes* 1936, p. 104; O. Neugebauer, *SOAW* 240, 2 (1962), p. 27.

9 L. Ideler, *Über astronomische Beobachtungen der Alten* (1806), 20; O. Neugebauer and H. B. Van Hosen, *Greek Horoscopes, Memoirs of Amer. Philos. Soc.* 48 (1959), 95. The same kind of instrument was used in Athenian courts in order to give the same amount of time to the accuser and the defendant. *Cf.* Busolt-Swoboda II, 1161.

10 On Egyptian equal hours *cf.* O. Neugebauer, *Egyptian Astronomical Texts* I (1960), 119; Neugebauer, 81, 86; on Babylonian counting of hours *cf.* the papers of F. Thureau-Dangin quoted above, note 6.

11 R. Pfeiffer, *State Letters of Assyria* (*Amer. Orient. Series* VI, 1935), 298; H. Sauren, *Actes de la XVIIème Rencontre Assyrologique* (1970), 13. On direct observation of the moon *cf.* B. Z. Wacholder and D. B. Weinberg, *HUCA* 1971, 136.

12 C. Schoch, in S. Langdon and J. K. Fotheringham, *The Venus Tablets of Ammizaduga* (1928), 97. For Athens see Ginzel I, 93.

13 Kugler, Suppl. III (1935), 255.

14 R. Pfeiffer (note 11), no. 303.

15 *Cf.* Kugler II, 301; II, 232; Suppl. I, 136, 175, 186.

16 *Cf.* L. W. King, *Letters and Inscriptions of Hammurabi* III (1898), 12; A. L. Oppenheim, *Letters from Mesopotamia* (1967), 100.

17 N. Schneider, *Zeitbestimmung der Wirtschaftsurkunden der III Dynastie von Ur* (1936). *Cf.* F. Thureau-Dangin, *RAss* 1927, 181. The calendar was an instrument of State economy. The Sumerian administration began the fiscal year after the delivery of new barley to granaries and the settlement of

relevant accounts, *i.e.*, about two months after harvest. For other purposes the year began before or after harvest (*cf.* Kugler II, 301; Y. Rosengarten, *Le concept sumérien de consommation* (1960), 410). For Mari *cf.* M. Birot, *Archives royales de Mari* XII, 2, p. 20. Consequently, the same month could have several names in the same city; *e.g.* it might be called the month of sheep-shearing, when the account concerned sheep (*cf.* B. Landsberger, *JNES* 1949, 262, 273; Rosengarten, op. cit., 423). *Cf.* Nilsson, *Kalender*, 73.

18 R. A. Parker and W. H. Dubberstein, *Babylonian Chronology 626 BC–AD 75* (*Brown University Studies* XIX; 1956). As R. A. Parker kindly informs me, his diagram of intercalated years has to be corrected as follows: not 492–1 but 500–499 was intercalated. *Cf.* G. Cameron, *JNES* 1965, 181. *Cf.* also D. Sidersky, *Étude sur la chronologie assyro-babylonienne, Mémoires présentées à l'Acad. des Inscriptions* 13 (1920), 115; id. *RAss* 1933, 68 (the Julian dates of 1 Nisanu). On the 8-year cycle and, from 499 BC, the 19-year cycle in Babylonia *cf.* B. L. van der Waerden, *AFO* 1963, 97. But the latter cycle was followed without deviation only from 380 BC on (Neugebauer, 140). This cycle 'is quite accurate; only after 310 Julian years do the cyclically computed mean new months fall one day earlier than they should' (Neugebauer, 7). *Cf.* also note 20 and T. Heath, *Aristarchus of Samos* (1913), 293.

19 R. Labat, *Hémérologies et ménologies assyriennes* (1939), 25. *Cf.* id. *MIO* 1957, 229. The nature of the pre-Babylonian calendar of the Assyrians is uncertain. The problem of the Assyrian calendar is still insoluble (*cf.* M. B. Rowton, *CAH* I, 1, 229). On the Assyrian calendar in Cappadocia *cf.* N. B. Jankowska, *ArchOr* 1967, 524. On the Elamite calendar *cf.* R. Reiner, *AFO* 1973, 97.

20 E. Mahler, *Handbuch der jüdischen Chronologie* (1916) is out of date. On Biblical time-reckoning *cf.* R. de Vaux, *Ancient Israel* (1961), 178; Finegan. *Cf.* my review *BO* 1965, 184; J. van Goudever, *Fêtes et calendriers bibliques*[3] (1967); H. N. Smith, *The Jewish New Year Festival* (1947); A. Caquot, *RHR* 191, 1 (determination of the new moon). The names of four Hebrew months are recorded in Scripture (*cf.* A. Lemaire, *Vetus Testamentum* (1973), 243). On the Gezer calendar *cf.* S. Talmon, *JAOS* 1963, 177; John C. L. Gibson, *Textbook of Syrian Semitic Inscriptions* I (1971), 11.

On the modern Jewish calendar see Maimonides, *Sanctifications of the New Moon* (*Yale Judaica Series* XI, 1956); B. Zuckermann, Materialen zur alten jüdischen Zeitrechnung, *Jahresbericht der jüdisch-theologischen Seminars in* Breslau, 1882; D. Sidersky, Étude sur l'origine astronomique de la chronologie juive, *Mémoires pres. par divers savants à l'Acad. des Inscr.* XII, 2 (1916); id. *Études sur la chronologie assyro-babylonienne*, ib. XIII (1916), 140. It is a pity that none of later writers on Jewish chronology discusses, or even knows, the material collected and interpreted in Ed. Schwartz, Christliche und Jüdische Ostertafeln, *AGGG* N.F. VIII, 6 (1905), 121. In the present Jewish calendar the 19-year cycle is longer by about two hours than 19 solar years (*Jewish Encyclopaedia* III, 501). Accordingly, the Jewish New Year now disagrees by roughly one week with the sun (W. M. Feldman, *Rabbini*

Mathematics and Astronomy (1931), 207). See also S. Powels, *Der Kalender der Samaritaner* (1977), 25.

21 On the calendar used in the Elephantine documents *cf.* D. Sidersky, *Revue des études juives* 1926, 59; L. Borchardt, *Monatsschr. für Geschichte des Judentums* 1932, 299; R. A. Parker, *JNES* 1955, 71. *Cf.* also M. Lidzbarski, *Ephemeris für Semitische Epigraphie* II, 221: an Iranian uses the same calendar in Persian Egypt. On the same calendar used by the Persian administration at Persepolis see R. T. Hallock, *Persepolis Fortification Tablets* (1969), 74. Here the intercalation doubled the sixth month (*cf.* E. J. Bickerman, *ArchOr* 1967, 197). For equations of Babylonian and Egyptian months in late Egyptian texts: F. Hintze, *MOI* 3 (1955) 149; R. A. Parker, *A Vienna Demotic Papyrus* (1959), 30.

22 On the Seleucids *cf.* E. J. Bickerman, *Institutions des Séleucides* (1938) 144 and 205. The existence of the official calendar did not prevent cities from inserting names of particular months: *cf. e.g.* OGIS, 233 ('Pantheon' at Antioch in Persia); L. Robert, *RPh* 1936, 126 ('Antiocheion' in Stratonicea). For the Parthians, *cf.* W. W. Tarn, *CAH* IX, 650; G. Le Rider, 'Suse sous les Séleucids et les Parthes', *Mémoires de la mission archéologique en Iran* XXXVIII (1965), 35. *Cf.* E. J. Bickerman, *BO* 1966, 328.

23 *Cf.* J. Johnson, *Dura Studies*, Thesis, U. of Pennsylvania, 1932; Dura-Europos, *Preliminary Reports* VII–IX (1939), 309; C. B. Welles, *Eos* 1957, 469; Samuel, 143.

24 On the calendar of the people of the Dead Sea Scrolls *cf.* J. M. Baumgarten, *JBL* 1958, 249; S. Talmon, *Revue de Qumran* 1960, 474; J. A. Sanders, *The Psalm Scroll of the Cave* II (1965), 91; M. Limbeck, *Die Ordnung des Heils* (1971), 134. On the schematic calendar in the Book of Enoch *cf.* O. Neugebauer, *Orientalia* 1960, 60. The calendar quarrels between the Jews and the Karaites are very instructive for the understanding of the similar disagreements. *Cf.* Z. Ankori, *Karaites in Byzantium* (1959).

25 Biruni, *Chronology of the Ancient Nations*, tr. E. Sachau (1879), 68, states that the Jews began to use the precalculated calendar about two hundred years after Alexander (that is, *c.* year 200 of the Seleucid era, or *c.* 110 BC). This bit of information cannot be disproved or proved. It is possible that the calendar schemes were changed several times in Jerusalem, but it is also possible that Biruni reproduces an argument used in the polemics between the Jews and Karaites.

26 M. P. Nilsson, Die Entstehung und die religiöse Bedeutung des griechischen Kalenders, in *Lunds Univers. Årsskrift*, N.F. XIV (1918); 2nd ed. in *Scripta Minora* of the *K. Humanistika Vetenskapssamfundet i Lund*, 1960/61. On dates in pre-Homeric documents *cf.* J. Chadwick, *The Mycenean World* (1976), 97, 191; Samuel, 64. For Homer *cf.* E. Buchholtz, *Die homerischen Realien* I (1871), 33. Hesiod's calendar is entirely seasonal, that is, agricultural (*Theog.* 58), and the change of seasons is marked by rising and setting of stars. The mention of the month Lenaion (v. 504) is interpolated (*cf.* Samuel, 66; D. R.

Dicks, *Early Greek Astronomy* (1970), 25). On the subdivision of the month in Homeric hymns and Hesiod *cf.* T. W. Allen, W. R. Halliday, E. E. Sikes, *The Homeric Hymns*[2] (1936) ad *H. Merc.* 19; H. L. Lorimer, *BSA* 1951, 806.

27 M. P. Nilsson, *Geschichte der griechischen Religion* I[2] (1955), 644. *Cf.* F. Jacoby, *Atthis* (1949), 287. The arguments adduced for the very early use of the 8-year cycle (Ideler, *Lehrbuch*, 116; Nilsson, *RE* 17, 2387), namely, the celebration of the Olympic games alternately in 49 and 50 months, and of the Pythian games every eight years from 656 until 583 (*Sch. Hom. Il.* X, 252; *Sch. Pind. Ol.* III, 33) are of little value. *Cf.* J. L. Fotheringham, *JHS* 1919, 176. According to Censorinus, the octaeteris was devised by Cleostratus of Tenedos, who lived after Anaximander (Plin. *N.H.* II, 8, 31), that is, after *c.* 550. *Cf.* D. R. Dicks, *JHS* 1966, 26.

28 The counting of days within a decade could vary. For example, in Argos, the ninth day of a month was called ἠνάτα πράτα, the seventeenth ἑβδεμάτα μέσα, the twenty-sixth ἔκτα δευτάτα (A. Boethius, *Der Argivische Kalender* (1922), 64, and *cf.* Samuel, 91). In Athens, the first day was called νουμηνία, the days from the second to the tenth δευτέρα (τρίτη, etc.) ἱσταμένου, the days of the second decade πρώτη (etc.) ἐπι δέκα, the twentieth εἰκάς, and the last day of the month ἔνη καὶ νέα ('old' and 'new'). For the last decade, progressive numeration was used in documents from the time of Alexander the Great on: the twenty-first was δεκάτη ὑστέρα, the twenty-second δευτέρα μετ' ἐικάδας, and so on. On the other hand, until the end of the fourth century BC, retrogressive numeration (φθίνοντος) was common. *Cf.* e.g. Aristoph., *Nubes*, 1131 and 1134: πέμπτη, τετράς, τρίτη, μετὰ ταύτην δευτέρα, . . . εὐθὺς μετὰ ταύτην ἐσθ'ἔνη τε καὶ νέα. Thus, in a full month we have to subtract the number of the given Greek days from 31 to find the date of our notation. As to the hollow month, the position of the leap day is still debated. It was *dekate phthinontos*, that is, the '21' according to Meritt, 38; id. *Historia* 1962, 441; id. *Hesperia* 1964, 1, who refers to Schol. Arist., *Nubes*, 1131. *Cf.* Samuel, 60; B. D. Meritt, *AJPh* 1974, 264; W. K. Pritchett, *California Studies in Classical Philology* 1976, 181. Curious was the notation of days for the last decade in Rhodes, at least in the second century AD (*IG* XII, 1, 4): the last day of the month was always called *triakas*. The day before the last, the *pro(triakas)*, was omitted in the hollow month. Then days from 28 to 22 were counted backward, from 30th, so that our 22nd day was '29', our 28th day '23', but our 21st day was '21'.

29 On the term ἐμβόλιμος *cf.* W. Vollgraf, *Mnemosyne* 1916, 49; Meritt, *TAPhA* 1964, 200 ff.

30 W. K. Pritchett and O. Neugebauer, *The Calendars of Athens* (1948); B. D. Meritt, *The Athenian Year* (1961); W. K. Pritchett, *Ancient Athenian Calendars on Stone* (1963); id. *The Choiseul Marble* (1970); Meritt, *PAPhS* 115 (1971), 97 offers a new reconstruction of the Athenian calendar from 432 to 401, which is inevitably as uncertain as were the previous attempts.

31 *Cf.* B. Keil, *Hermes* 1894, 61; Meritt, 60; W. K. Pritchett, *AJPh* 1964, 40. On *IG* I, 304 b, *cf.* id. *BCH* 1964, 455; id. *Hesp.* 1965, 131.

32 *Cf.* Dem. 3, 4; 19, 57; 21, 86; 24, 26; 37, 6; 42, 5; 49, 6; 49, 22. See A. Mommsen, *Chronologische Untersuchungen* (1883), 143.

33 J. K. Fotheringham (*JHS* 1919, 172) was probably the first scholar to state that Geminus refers to the cycles propounded by astronomers which were never adopted by the cities. As a matter of fact, the Athenians did not even have a fixed leap month. *Cf.* W. K. Pritchett, *CPh* 1968, 53.

34 G. Daux, *BCH* 1963, 603. *Cf.* M. Jameson and S. Dow, ib. 1964, 154, 180; S. Dow, *Historia* 1960, 270; S. Dow and R. F. Healey, *Sacred Calendars of Eleusis* (1965); J. D. Mikalson, *The Sacred and Civilian Calendar of the Athenian Year* (1975).

35 The equations of the summer solstice of 27 June 432 BC and of 26 June 106 BC with 13 and 14 Skirophorion respectively given in the Milesian *parapegma* (see p. 58) probably concern the same 'ideal' astronomical calendar. B. L. van der Waerden, *JHS* 1960, 170 and 180.

36 A. E. Samuel, *Ptolemaic Chronology* (1962). *Cf.* also Samuel, 145. Julian dates of the Ptolemies: T. C. Skeat, *The Reigns of the Ptolemies* (1954); id. *JEA* 1960, 91; 1962, 100; A. E. Samuel, *Études de Papyrologie* IX (1964), 73; P. W. Pestman, *Chronologie égyptienne d'après les textes démotiques* (1967). For the reign of Ptolemy II *cf.* L. Koenen, *Eine agonistische Inschrift aus Ägypten* (1976). On the financial year see J. Bingen, *CE* 1975, 239.

37 R. A. Parker, *The Calendars of Ancient Egypt* (1950); Ed. Meyer, *Ägyptische Chronologie*, in *APAW*, 1904, and 1907; *AZ* 1907, 115; Ed. Meyer, *Chronologie égyptienne* (1912). K. Sethe, *GGN* 1919, 287-319; ib. 1920, 28-55 and 97-141; S. Schott, *Aegyptische Festdaten, Abhand. der Mainzer Akademie,* 1950. For the conversion of Egyptian dates, E. Lundsgaard, *Aegyptischer Kalender der Jahre 3000-200 v. Chr.* (Copenhagen, 1942). For the conversion of the Egyptian dates into Egyptian Julian dates (*cf.* p. 50) *cf.* B. L. van der Waerden, *Isis* 1956, 387; M. Chaine, *La chronologie des temps chrétiens de l'Égypte et de l'Ethiopie* (1923).

38 We do not even know to what level the waters of the Nile had to rise in the third millennium BC before the Egyptians considered the flood as having begun. Furthermore, the visibility of the rising of Sirius is uncertain. L. Borchardt and P. W. Neugebauer, *OLZ* 1924, 370.

39 On the Sassanian calendar *cf.* S. H. Taqizadeh, *Old Iranian Calendars* (1938); M. Boyce, *BSOAS* 1970, 513; id. in J. de Menasce, *Troisième livre du Denkart* (1972), 262; V. Lifshitz, in Russian translation of the present work (1975), 320; and Bickerman's chapter on Chronology in *Cambridge History of Iran* III (forthcoming). On the Armenian calendar *cf.* Ginzel I, 314. The Chorezmian calendar: V. Lifshitz, *Acta Antiqua* 1968, 435. The Cappadocian calendar is known only in its Julian form (*cf.* p. 50), and its functioning remains uncertain. *Cf.* Ginzel, *RE* X, 1917; K. Hannell, *BSLL* 1931/2, 22.

40 Our knowledge of the Roman calendar comes from two different sources:

from the living tradition and from ancient writers and documents. We still follow the Caesarian calendar, and the system of Roman dating (Nones and Kalends) was used until the sixteenth century (Ginzel III, 115). Among the basic sources are Macrobius, *Sat.* (I, 13) and Censorinus (*De die natali*, written in AD 238). In addition (excluding numerous lesser passages in different writers, etc.) we have stone calendars, among them one of the pre-Julian year [Fasti Antiates veteres: A. Degrassi, *Inscriptiones Latinae liberae reipublicae* (1957) no. 9]; id. *Inscriptiones latinae* XIII, 2 (1963); F. Maggi in *Atti Pontific. Accademia di archeologia*, Ser. III, vol. IX, 1 (1972). Among modern studies of the Roman calendar, Mommsen's *Römische Chronologie*² (1859) remains basic and unsurpassed. More recent surveys: A. K. Michels, *The Calendar of the Roman Republic* (1967) and Samuel, ch. V. *Cf.* also F. Della Corte, *Antico calendario dei Romani* (1969).

41 Ginzel II, 243; G. Wissowa, *Hermes* 1923, 392; L. van Johnson, *AJPh* 1959, 133; A. Magdelain, *REL* 1962, 201; A. K. Michels, *Hommages à Albert Grenier* (1962), 1174. On the linguistic aspect of dating, Ginzel II, 175; A. H. Salonius, *Zur römischen Datierung*, in *Annales Acad. Scient. Fenicae*, Ser. B, XV (1922). In the Republican period the inclusive calculation was not used for counting the years: J. Beaujeu, *REL* 1976, 329. Cumbersome as was the Roman counting of the days, it was sometimes used by Romans even in Greek cities: *cf.* L. Robert in *Laodicea du Lykos* (ed. J. des Gagniers) (1969), 325.

42 See M. P. Nilsson, in *Festskrift Per Persson* (1922) 13 = *Opuscula* II (1951), 979; H. J. Rose, *Primitive Culture in Italy* (1926), 88. For further conjectures about the pre-history of the Roman calendar *cf.* K. Hanell, *Das Altrömische eponym Amt* (1946), 99; J. Hubeaux, *Rome et Veies* (*Bibl. Fac. Phil. et Lettres*, Univ. Liège CXLV, 1958), 66; L. V. Johnson, *TAPhA* 1960, 101; id. *AJPh* 1963, 28; E. Gjerstadt, *Acta Archaeologica* 1961, 193; G. Radke, *RhM* 1963, 313; R. Werner, *Der Beginn der römischen Republik* (1963); Michels (*supra* note 40), 121; Samuel, 165. On the Etruscan calendar *cf.* K. Olszscha, *Glotta* 1954, 71; J. Heurgon, *JRS* 1966, 1. On other calendars in Italy *cf.* J. W. Whatmough, *HSCPh* 1932.

43 G. De Sanctis, *Storia dei Romani* III (1916), Index s.v. Calendario, and IV, I (1923), 368. *Cf.* also M. Holleaux, *Études d'épigraphie* IV (1952), 336; V (1957), 24; P. Meloni, *Latomus* 1954, 533. For some recent suggestions on Julian equivalents of the Roman pre-Julian calendar, *cf. e.g.* R. Derov, *Phoenix* 1973, 348, ib. 1976, 265; *Antiquité classique* 1976, 265 (covering the period 290–168 BC); M. Morgan, *Chiron* 1977, 89 (First Punic War); P. Marchetti, *Antiq. Class.* 1977, 473 (the years 203–196); id. *BCH* 1976, 411 (168 BC); M.-Th. Rapsaet-Charlier, *Historia* 1974, 278 (59–45 BC).

44 On the limits of *autumnus* see Ph. Fabia, *REA* 1931, 122. On three and four seasons in Greece, *cf.* G. M. A. Hanfmann, *The Season Sarcophagus in Dumbarton Oaks* (1951). On observing the movement of stars *cf.* K. Sethe, *GGN* 1919, 291; R. W. Sloley, *JEA* 1931, 166; Neugebauer, 84; id. in

Hypsikles, ed. V. de Falco, M. Krause, *AGGG* LXII (1965). On the Greek 'computers' *cf.* D. de Solla Price, Gears from the Greeks, *PAPhS* 64 (1974), 7.

45 The natural year: Nilsson, *Kalender* 21. The seasons: Ginzel II, 182, 308, and passim. Observation of the stars and meteorological forecasts: A. Rehm, *RE*, Suppl. VII, coll. 175–198. For the question of how much the sky was really observed, *cf.* H. Vogt, *SHAW*, Abh. 1 (1920), 54; R. Boeker, *RE*, Suppl. IX, 1610 ff. Further *cf.* Aristotle, *Hist. Animal.*, ed. A. L. Peck, II, p. 383 (Loeb Classics). On 'seasons' in Thucydides *cf.* O. Lushnat, *RE*, Suppl. XIV, 1134; D. P. Orsi, *Quaderni di storia* (1975), 117. Plato, too, seems to know only two seasons: *cf.* A. D. Nock, *Gnomon* 1934, 290. On the Roman natural year *cf.* J. E. Skydsgaard, *Varro the Scholar* (Analecta Romana Inst. Danici, Suppl. IV, 1968), 45. On the natural year in Egypt and Mesopotamia *cf.* A. M. Bakir, *The Cairo Calendar* (1974), R. Labat, *Le calendrier babylonien des travaux, des signes et des mois* (1965). For the dates of the most important phases of the stars for antiquity see Ginzel II, 517 and Table II below.

46 The zodiac: F. Cumont in *Dictionnaire des Antiquités* V, 1046; B. L. van der Waerden, *AFO* 1953, 216; Neugebauer, 140; H. F. Gundel, *RE* X, 462. A cuneiform text of about 1500–1000 BC mentions some zodiacal signs: E. F. Weidner, *Syria* 1956, 180. The division of the ecliptic into twelve equal signs by Babylonian astronomers is already attested in the early fifth century: B. C. A. Aabe and A. Sachs, *Centaurus* 1969, 1. On the symbolism of the zodiac *cf.* W. Hartner, *JNES* 1965, 1. Parapegmata: A. Rehm, *RE* XVIII 4, col. 1295; Pritchett and van der Waerden, *BCH* 1961, 31; A. Wilhelm, *Epitymbion H. Swoboda* (1927), 144.

47 *Cf.* Mommsen, 309; E. Diehl, *Inscriptiones Latinae Christianae* (1928), III, 311.

48 Latest survey and bibliography: E. Lohse, in *Theologisches Wörterbuch zum Neuen Testament* VII (1960), 1; F. H. Colson, *The Week* (1926); S. Eriksson, *Wochentagsgötter, Mond und Tierkreis* (1956). On the planetary week and its spread, see also Nilsson, *Geschichte der griechischen Religion* II (1950), 467; H. Gundel, *RE* XX, 2143; F. X. Doelger, *Antike und Christentum* VI (1941), 252; S. Gandz, *PAAJR* XVIII (1948–9), 213; H. Ingholt, 'Parthian Sculptures', *Memoirs of Connecticut Academy* XII (1954), 40; A. Degrassi, *Atti del III Congresso Internazionale di Epigrafia* (1959), 104. The Jewish week: H. and J. Lewy, *HUCA* XVII (1942/3), 1. On the *Nundinae cf.* W. Lintott, *Classical Quarterly* 1968, 189. On the market-days in the Roman empire *cf.* R. McMullen, *Phoenix* 1974, 333. On the Roman agricultural week, *cf.* J. Heurgon, *REL* 1947, 236.

49 For the *Marmor Parium* and similar texts, see *FrGrH*, nos. 239 and 252. Jacoby, 160; *cf.* D. W. Prakken, *Studies in Greek Genealogical Chronology* (1943).

50 Mommsen, *RStR*, 896; H. Mattingly, *JRS* 1930, 78; R. P. Longen, *JRS* 1931, 131; M. Hammond, *The Antonine Monarchy* (1959), 72. For Julian day-dates of accession, etc., of the emperors *cf.* L. Holzapfel, *Klio* 1912, 1913,

1918, 1921 (partly out of date). On the terms *etos* and *eniautos cf.* M. P. Nilsson, *Eranos* 1957, 115. *Cf.* the terms *chronos* and *tempus*, meaning 'a year': E. Lofstedt, *Late Latin* (1959), 117. For the naming of a year *cf. Archives royales de Mari* XIII (1964), no. 47: a year was first called 'King Zimri-Lim dedicated a throne to god Dagon.' But when the throne was not ready, another name for the year had to be found. On the accession dates of Roman emperors *cf.* Mommsen, *RStR*, II, 2, 796; F. de Martino, *Storia della costituzione romana* IV, 2 (1974), 171; J. Béranger, *Recherches sur l'aspect idéologique du Principat* (1953), 102.

51 See A. Gardiner, *JEA* 1945, 11; W. Helck, *Analecta Biblica* 1959, 113; Gardiner, 71; J. Czerny, *JEA* 1964, 58. For Babylonia see note 67. On regnal years of Hebrew kings: Finegan, 194; Jepsen, R. Hahnhardt, *Untersuchungen zur israelitisch-jüdischen Chronologie* (1964). Bar Kochba's years were counted from 1st Nisan: *cf.* B. Kanael, *IEJ* 1971, 411.

52 Some (often hypothetical) lists of eponyms of Greek cities outside Athens may be cited here. Alexandria (under the Ptolemies): W. Peremans and E. Van't Dick, *Prosopographia ptolemaica* III (1956); J. Ijsewijn, *De sacerdotibus Alexandri ... et Lagidarum eponymis* (*Verhandelingen von de K. Vlaamse Academie* XLII, 1961). Boeotia: P. Roesh, *Thespies et la confédération béotienne* (1961), 84; R. Etienne and D. Knoepf, *Hyettos de Béotie* (1976), 349 (for the period 250–171). Delphi: G. Daux, *Chronologie delphique* (1943); E. Manni, *Ath* 1950, 88. Delos: F. Durrbach, *Inscriptions de Délos* II (1929), 327. Miletus: A. Rehm, *Didyma* II, 380. Rhodes: F. Hiller v. Gärtringen, *RE*, Suppl. V, 835; Chr. Blinkenberg, *Lindos* II (1941); L. Morricone, *Annuario della scuola archeologica in Atene* (1952), 27, 351. Sparta: Samuel, 238. Thessaly: A. M. Babakos (Μπαπάκος) *Praxeis koines diatheseos ... kata to dikaion tes archaias Thessalias* (1962), 255. See also W. Schonfleder, *Stadt- und Bundesbeamten des griechischen Festlandes*, Diss. Leipzig (1917); R. Munsterberg, *Beamtennamen auf griechischen Münzen* (1917) = *Wiener Numismatische Zeitschrift* 1911 ff.

53 On the Athenian archon lists *cf.* Jacoby, 169. On the archons before 480 BC *cf.* T. J. Cadoux *JHS* 1948, 70; Samuel, 195; R. Meiggs and D. Lewis, *A Selection of Greek Historical Inscriptions* (1969), no. 6.

54 See T. R. S. Broughton, *The Magistrates of the Roman Republic* I–II and Supplement, 1951. A. Degrassi, *I Fasti Consolari dell'Impero Romano dal 30 a.C. al 613 d.C.* (1952). The consular *fasti* of the Republic have come down to us in three editions of the Augustan Age. (a) The *Fasti Capitolini* set up in the Forum between 36 and 30 BC. The text has been partly preserved; its gaps can be filled up with help of later sources, such as the Chronographer of the Year AD 354, the so-called *Fasti Hydatani*, compiled in AD 468 and the Paschal Chronicle compiled in Greek in AD 630. (b) Livy, and for the lost parts of his work, a list of consuls in Cassiodorus' *Chronicle*, published in AD 519. (c) The Roman eponyms for 486–302 BC in Diodorus XI–XX. *Cf.* Ed. Meyer, *Kleine Schriften* II (1924), 288. The consular lists of the afore-

mentioned chronographers are in *Chronica Minora* I–III, ed. Th. Mommsen (1892–8).

55 See in general Mommsen; id. *Römische Forschungen* II (1879), p. 151; O. Leuze, *Römische Jahrzählung* (1909); E. Pais, *Ricerche sulla storia del diritto pubblico di Roma* II (1916); K. J. Beloch, *Römische Geschichte* (1926); K. Hanell, *Das altrömische eponyme Amt* (1946); A. Degrassi, *Fasti et Elogia* (1947); id. *Fasti Capitolini* (1954); G. Perl, *Kritische Untersuchungen zu Diodors römischer Jahrzählung* (1957).

56 See L. Ideler, *Über astronomische Beobachtungen der Alten* (1806), 256. S. H. Taqizadeh, *BSOAS* X (1942), 129.

57 On the Arsacid calendar *cf.* p. 25 and note 22. On the Arsacid era in Babylonian documents *cf.* J. Oelsner, in *Altorientalische Forschungen*, III 1976, 25; in Hatra: J. Teixidor, *Syria* 1966, 93; 1973, 414. The Seleucid era continued to be used in Babylonia, particularly by astronomers and thus for the dating of important events. For instance, the Manicheans stated that Mani was born on 8th Nisan (14 April) of the Seleucid year 527 (AD 216). His first revelation is similarly dated to 1 April 228 and the second one to 19 April 240. *Cf.* L. Koenen, *ZPE* 1972, 249. The Seleucid era continued to be used in Christian Syria: *cf.* L. Bernhard, Die Chronologie der Syrer, *SBWA* 263, 3 (1969), 110.

58 E. Minns, *Scythians and Greeks* (1913), no. 646, note 17. *Cf.* G. Perl in *Studien zur Geschichte und Philosophie des Altertums* (ed. J. Harmatta) 1968, 299 (era of Bithynia, Pontus, and kingdom of Bosphorus.)

59 As a matter of fact, Diocletian's era antedates his accession. He was proclaimed emperor on 20 November 284. T. C. Skeat, *Papyri from Panopolis* (1964), 145. But the Julian year began in Egypt on 29 August. Thus, the second year of Diocletian started on 29 August 285, and in this way the years of his reign came to be counted in Egypt from 29 August AD 284.

60 See P. Herrmann, *DWA* LXXVII, 1959, 8. *Cf.* S. Accame, *Il dominio romano in Grecia* (1946), 11; M. N. Tod, *ABSA* XXIII (1918/19), 212; id. in *Studies presented to D. M. Robinson* II (1953), 383; H. Seyrig, *Syria* 1950, 6; J. Bingen, *CE* 1964, 14. On the era 'of Caesar' (that is, 'of Pharsalus') *cf.* Robert, 1972, 388. On the Actium era in Cyrene *cf.* L. Robert, *Hellenica* XI–XII (1960), 533; G. Perl, *Klio* 1970, 320. Two 'provincial' eras co-existed in Macedonia: that of the organization of the Roman province (148–7) and that from the 3rd year of Augustus which began 116 years later (*cf.* Robert, 1976, 359). Further recent bibliography about local eras: Samuel, 246.

61 Paphlagonia: see *e.g.* *OGIS* 532=Dessau, 8781. *Cf.* H. Dessau, *Zeitschr. für Numism.* 1906, 335; W. Ruge, *RE* XVIII, 2532. Athens: P. Graindor, *Athènes sous Hadrien* (1934). Manichees: W. B. Henning, *Asia Major* 1952, 198. *Cf.* the era from AD 10/11 in Thessaly: A. H. Kramolish, *Chiron* 1975, 337. G. Le Ridder, *RN* 1969, 280 suggests that the letters on the coins of Aradus (p. 74) refer to monetary magistrates.

62 Numbering of Olympiads: see Truesdell S. Brown, *Timaeus of Tauromenium*

(1958), 10; of the games, L. Robert, *RPh* 1930, 39. List of Olympic victors: L. Moretti, *Memorie dell'Accad. dei Lincei* VII ser. II (1957). Trustworthiness of this list: Th. Lenschau, *Phil.* 1936, 391; F. Jacoby, *Atthis* (1949), 58.

63 See P. Lehmann, *Phil.* 1912, 297. *Cf.* also Ed. Schwartz, *Christliche und Jüdische Ostertafeln*, *AGGG* N.F. VIII, 6 (1905); A. van der Vyer, *Revue d'histoire ecclésiastique* 1957, 197; G. Ogg, *Vigiliae Christianae* 1962, 2. On Dionysius *cf.* B. Krush, *APA* 1937, 57.

64 The royal canon: *Chronica Minora*, ed. Th. Mommsen, III, 359. *Cf.* Ginzel I, 139; Kubitschek, 61. Similar lists: *e.g.*, *FrGrH* Nos. 255 f., *Pap. Oxyrh.* 31, 2551, with a commentary by P. Sattler, *Studien aus dem Gebiete der alten Geschichte* (1962), 29; C. Corteman, *CE* 1956, 385.

65 An Egyptian papyrus records a moon observation in the 52nd year of Ramesses II. But as lunar dates are repetitive, the observation could refer to the year 1253, 1250 BC, etc. Thus, its place within the range of possible dates depends on synchronisms which can be found only in Mesopotamian chronology: *cf.* R. Parker, *JNES* 1957, 42. Accordingly, the recent estimations of the accession date of the Pharaoh are: Jon D. Schmidt, *Ramesses II* (1972): 1290 BC; W. C. Hayes, *CAH* I: 1173; and R. O. O. Faulkner, ib. II, 1, 225: 1304; M. L. Bierbier, *The Late New Kingdom in Egypt* (1975), 109: 1279.

66 On Manetho, see W. Helck, *Untersuchungen zu Manetho und den aegyptischen Königslisten* (1956). The recent reconstruction of the list of the Pharaohs: Gardiner, 429. The most recent surveys of chronological questions: Et. Drioton, J. Vandier, *L'Egypte* (1962); W. C. Hayes (*supra* n. 65) with addenda, ib. I, 2, 949; II, 1, 729, 760. On the XVIIIth dynasty *cf.* also J. G. Read, *JNES* 1970, 1; D. B. Redford, *BASOR* (1973) 211; 49. On the later period *cf.* K. A. Kitchen, *The Third Intermediate Period in Egypt, 1100–650 BC* (1973) and E. Wente, *JNES* 1976, 269.

67 M. B. Rowton, *CAH* I, 1 (1970), 193 (in fact, originally published in 1962); P. Garelli, *Le Proche-Orient asiatique* I–II (1969–74). See also chronological tables for third and second millennium in *CAH* I, 2; II, 1–2 and in Garelli (also for the first millennium BC). The chronology of the third millennium hinges on the still unknown length of the interval between the last dynasty of Akkad and the 3rd dynasty of Ur. *Cf.* Rowton, ib. 219 and W. W. Hallo, *RLA* III, 713. The essential work on the chronology of the ancient Near East (Egypt included) in the second millennium is H. Tadmor, in *The World History of the Jewish People*, First Series II (ed. B. Mazar, 1970), ch. V, with chronological tables from *c.* 1900 to *c.* 900 BC. On Assyrian and Babylonian lists of kings *cf.* F. Kraus, in *Mededelingen* of the Netherlands Academy, N.R. 28, no. 2 (1965) and A. K. Grayson, *Assyrian and Babylonian Chronicles* (1975). Further *cf.* J. J. Finkelstein, *JCS* 1966, 65 (royal genealogies); R. Hachmann, *Zeitschr. des Deutschen Palästina-Vereins* 1977, 97 (Assyrian royal dates). The Hittite chronology remains obscure: *cf.* A. Kammenhuber, *Orientalia* 1970, 278. For late Babylonian kings see J. A.

Brinkman, *Political History of the post-Kassite Babylonia 1158–722 BC* (1968) and id. *BO* 1970, 301. On neo-Babylonian rulers *cf.* R. Borger, *JCS* 1965, 74; J. Oates, *Iraq* 1965, 135.

68 Eclipses: for the period between 4200 and 900 BC: P. W. Neugebauer, *Spez. Kanon der Sonnenfinsternisse für Vorderasien und Aegypten (Astronomische Abhandlungen* VIII, 4 (1931), id. *Spez. Kanon der Mondfinsternisse für Vorderasien und Aegypten, 3450–1 v. Chr. (Astr. Abh.* IX, 2 (1934), Kiel); M. Kudlek, *Solar and Lunar Eclipses in the Ancient Near East* (1971). Lunar eclipses from 1400 to 100 BC: H. Dubbs, *JNES* 1947, 124. For the Greco-Roman age: F. K. Ginzel, *Spez. Kanon der Finsternisse* (1899). Eclipses recorded in ancient sources: Boll, *RE* VI, 2355. Solar eclipses in the Bible: F. R. Stephenson, *Palestine Exploration Quarterly* 1975, 107. Comets: Gundel, *RE* XI, 1183. Eclipses, comets and earthquakes in the Byzantine age (after AD 285): Grumel, 458 and 476. Instructions for converting astronomical dates, with tables: P. W. Neugebauer, *Astronomische Chronologie* I–II (1929), and *Tafeln zur astronomischen Chronologie* I–II (1912 ff.); R. Schramm, *Kalenderiographischer und chronologischer Tafeln* (1908); U. Baehr, *Tafeln zur Behandlung chronologischer Problemen* (1955) (*Veröffentlichungen des astronomischen Rechnen-Instituts zu Heidelberg* III, 1–3); B. Tuckermann, *Planetary, Lunar and Solar Positions* (for 601 BC–AD 1649): (*Memoirs of the American Philosophical Society* LVI, LIX, 1962, 1964); W. D. Stahlman, O. Gengerich, *Solar and Planetary Longitudes* (for 2500 BC–AD 2000) (1963); H. Goldstine, *New and Full Moons 1001 BC–AD 1650* (*Memoirs of the American Philosophical Society*, 90, 1973).

69 Likewise, the horoscope of the philosopher Proclus (Marinus, *V. Procli*, 35) establishes his birth-date: 8 Feb. 412. *Cf.* J. M. Dillon, *Classical Review* 1969, 274.

70 On ancient chronographers, *cf.* Ed. Schwartz, 'Die Königslisten des Eratosthenes und Kastor, *AGGG* XL (1894): *FrGrH*, 239–261. On Christian chronographers, *cf.* H. Gelzer, *Sextus Iulius Africanus* I–II, 1 (1880–5). Except for some fragments, the *Chronicle* of Eusebius has been preserved only in Armenian (German translation of J. Karst, 1911) and in Jerome's Latin compilation, which was re-edited by J. K. Fotheringham (1923) and R. Helm (1924–6, reprinted in 1956). The first part of Eusebius' *Chronicle*, dealing with the chronology of the various nations, was omitted by Jerome. The Eusebian origin of the Canon tables has been doubted; *cf.* Ed. Schwartz, *RE* VI, 1383; D. S. Wallace-Hadrell, *Eusebios* (1960), 155. *Cf.* A. Momigliano, in *The Conflict between Paganism and Christianity* (ed. A. Momigliano, 1963), 82; J. Sirinelli, *Les vues historiques d'Eusèbe de Césare* (1961), 31.

71 The *Fasti Graeci* and the *Fasti Romani* by H. Clinton (1841; 1850) are antiquated but not yet replaced. The same is true for the shorter work of Carl Peter, *Chronological Tables of Greek History* (1882). The tables of dates in *CAH* and similar works do not indicate the essential point: how the Julian date has been fixed. For Athens *cf.* p. 68 and Samuel, 195. Abundant material for local history can be found in the *Fasti* given in the new volumes

of *Inscriptiones Graecae*, *e.g.* for Epidaurus (IV, 1), for Arcadia (V, 2), and for Aetolia (IX, 1). *Cf.* also note 52. For the Ptolemies *cf.* note 36, for the Seleucids *cf.* R. A. Parker and W. H. Dubberstein, *Babylonian Chronology 626 BC–AD 75* (1956). For Julian day-dates of accession, etc., of the Roman emperors *cf.* L. Holzapfel, *Klio* 1912, 1013; 1918, 1921 (partly out of date); R. O. Fink (*et alii*), Feriale Duranum, *YCS* VII (1940); P. Buresh, *Les titulatures impériales dans les papyrus* (1964). Chronological lists of high Roman officials can often be of help in dating documents. *Cf.*, for instance, prefects of Egypt: O. W. Reinmuth, *Bulletin of the American Society of Papyrologists* 1967 and 1968, 11 (partly outdated); G. Bastianini, *ZPE*, 17 (1975), 263; Governors of Judaea (70–134) and Macedonia (57–IIIrd c.): H. G. Pflaum *IEJ* 1969, 227; G. Alfoeldi, *Fasti Hispanienses* (from Augustus to Diocletian) (1969); J. Winkler, *Die Reichsbeamten von Noricum* (1960); H. G. Pflaum, *Les carrières procuratoriennes sous le Haut-Empire romain* (1960–1); A. Chastagnol, *Fastes de la préfecture de Rome au Bas-Empire* (1962); W. Meyers, *L'administration de la province romaine de Belgique* (1964); A. Jagenteufel, *Die Statthalter . . . Dalmatia* (*Schriften der Balkankommission, Antiquar. Abt.* of the Austrian Academy XII, 1958); D. Magie, *Roman Rule in Asia Minor* (1950), 1579; H. K. Sherk, *The Legates of Galatia* (*Johns Hopkins University Studies in History* 69, no. 2, 1951); B. E. Thomasson, *Die Statthalter . . . Nord-afrikas* (*Acta Inst. Romani Regni Sueciae* IX, 1960). Governors of Coele-Syria: J. F. Gilliam, *AJPh* 1958, 225. Governors of Arabia: H. G. Pflaum, *Syria* 1957, 128. For the chronology of the period between the Severi and Diocletianus *cf.* the papers of X. Loroit (AD 235–49) and of M. Christole (AD 252–68) in *Aufsteig und Niedergang der römischen Welt* (ed. H. Temporini, Second Series II, 1958) and J. P. Rea, *Pap. Oxyrh.* XL (1972), 15 (for Egypt). For AD 294–313 *cf.* C. H. W. Sutherland and R. A. G. Carson, *The Roman Imperial Coinage* VI (1967). The dating in Egypt under Diocletian and the other tetrarchs: J. D. Thomas, *CE* 1971, 173.

72 G. F. Moore, *Judaism* I (1927), 6; R. N. Frye, *The Heritage of Persia* (1963), 171.

THE TABLES

TABLE I

The Astronomical Canon

The Canon, reproduced here after C. Wachsmuth, *Einleitung in das Studium der Alten Geschichte* (1895), 305, has been preserved in astronomical manuscripts which generally continue the list up to the time of the scribe, *e.g.* until AD 911. The Canon was established by astronomers of Alexandria as a chronological basis for their computations. It goes back to the Babylonian king Nabonassar since the continuous astronomical observations began under his reign. The astronomers of Alexandria, who used the Egyptian mobile year, reduced the dates of their sources to the same reckoning. For instance, Nabopolossar died on 8 Abu of his 21 regnal year, that is on 15 August 605. But the Canon ends his reign at the date of the last day of the Egyptian year 605/4, that is on 20 January 604. The names of Babylonian kings became corrupted in Greek translation and transmission. According to Babylonian documents they are as follows:

Nabonassar
Nabunadinzri
Ukinzir and Pulu (= Tiglathpileser III; *cf.* II *Kings* 15, 19)
Ululas = Shalmaneser IV
Mardukbaliddin
Arkeanos = Sargon II
'Kingless', that is the period of local pretenders, Mardukzakirshum and Mardukbaliddin, whose legitimacy was denied by the Babylonian author of the list
Belibni
Ashurnadinshum
Nergalushezib
Mushezib Marduk
'Kingless' (from the destruction of Babylon by Sennacherib to the restoration by Esarhaddon)
Esarhaddon
Shamashshumkin
Kandalanu =

Nabopolossar
Nebuchadrezzar
Amel-Marduk (Evil–Merodach)
Neriglissar
Nabonidus

Βασιλέων	ἔτων ἐπισυναγωγή						
Ναβονασσάρου	ιδ	ιδ	27 Feb.	747—22	Feb.	733
Ναδίου	β	ιϛ	23 Feb.	733—21	Feb.	731
Χινζῆρος καὶ Πώρου	ε	κα	22 Feb.	731—20	Feb.	726
Ἰλουλαίου	ε	κϛ	21 Feb.	726—19	Feb.	721
Μαρδοκεμπάδου	ιβ	λη	20 Feb.	721—16	Feb.	709
Ἀρκεανοῦ	ε	μγ	17 Feb.	709—14	Feb.	704
ἀβασίλευτα	β	με	15 Feb.	704—14	Feb.	702
Βιλίβου	γ	μη	15 Feb.	702—13	Feb.	699
Ἀπαραναδίου	ϛ	νδ	14 Feb.	699—12	Feb.	693
Ῥηγεβήλου	α	νε	13 Feb.	693—11	Feb.	692
Μεσησιμορδάκου	δ	νθ	12 Feb.	692—10	Feb.	688
ἀβασίλευτα	η	ξζ	11 Feb.	688— 8	Feb.	680
Ἀσαραδίνου	ιγ	π	9 Feb.	680— 5	Feb.	667
Σαοσδουχίνου	κ	ρ	6 Feb.	667—31	Jan.	647
Κινηλαδάνου	κβ	ρκβ	1 Feb.	647—26	Jan.	625
Ναβοπολασσάρου	κα	ρμγ	27 Jan.	625—20	Jan.	604
Ναβοκολασσάρου	μγ	ρπϛ	21 Jan.	604—10	Jan.	561
Ἰλλοαρουδάμου	β	ρπη	11 Jan.	561— 9	Jan.	559
Νηριγασολασσάρου	δ	ρϞβ	10 Jan.	559— 8	Jan.	555
Ναβοναδίου	ιζ	σθ	9 Jan.	555— 4	Jan.	538

Περσῶν βασιλεῖς

Κύρου	θ	σιη	5 Jan.	538— 2	Jan.	529
Καμβύσου	η	σκϛ	3 Jan.	529—31	Dec.	522
Δαρείου πρώτου	λϛ	σξβ	1 Jan.	521—22	Dec.	486
Ξέρξου	κα	σπγ	23 Dec.	486—16	Dec.	465
Ἀρταξέρξου πρώτου	μα	τκδ	17 Dec.	465— 8˙	Dec.	424
Δαρείου δευτέρου	ιθ	τμγ	7 Dec.	424— 1	Dec.	405
Ἀρταξέρξου δευτέρου	μϛ	τπδ	2 Dec.	405—20	Nov.	359
Ὤχου	κα	υι	21 Nov.	359—15	Nov.	338
Ἀρωγοῦ	β	υιβ	16 Nov.	338—14	Nov.	336
Δαρείου τρίτου	δ	υιϛ	15 Nov.	336—13	Nov.	332
Ἀλεξάνδρου Μακεδόνος	η	υκδ	14 Nov.	332—11	Nov.	324

βασιλεῖς Μακεδόνων

Φιλίππου τοῦ μετ' Ἀλέξανδρον τὸν κτίστην	ζ	υλα	ζ	12	Nov. 324— 9	Nov.	317
Ἀλεξάνδρου ἑτέρου	ιβ	υμγ	ιθ	10	Nov. 317— 6	Nov.	305
Ἰτολεμαίου Λάγου	κ	υξγ	λθ	7	Nov. 305— 1	Nov.	285
Φιλαδέλφου	λη	φα	οζ	2	Nov. 285—23	Oct.	247
Εὐεργέτου	κε	φκς	ρβ	24	Oct. 247—17	Oct.	222
Φιλοπάτορος	ιζ	φμγ	ριθ	18	Oct. 222—12	Oct.	205
Ἐπιφάνους	κδ	φξζ	ρμγ	13	Oct. 205— 6	Oct.	180
Φιλομήτορος	λε	χβ	ροη	7	Oct. 180—28	Sept.	146
Εὐεργέτου δευτέρου	χθ	χλα	σζ	29	Sept. 146—20	Sept.	117
Σωτῆρος	λς	χξζ	σμγ	21	Sept. 117—11	Sept.	81
Διονύσου νέου	κθ	χϟς	σοβ	12	Sept. 81— 4	Sept.	52
Κλεοπάτρας	κβ	ψιη	σϟδ	5	Sept. 52—30	Aug.	30

Examples of Babylonian Royal Lists

XVIII Vorlauf. *Bericht über die Ausgrabungen von Uruk-Warka*, ed. H. J. ₋enzen, 53 and 55.)

A

Nebuchadrezzar	
Amel-Marduk (Evil-Merodach)	2 years
Neriglissar	2 years 8 months
₋abashi-Marduk	3 months
Nabonidus	5 years

B

Alexander	7 (?) years
Philip	6 years
Antigonus	6 years
Seleucus	31 years
Antiochus (I)	22 years
Antiochus (II)	15 years
Seleucus (II)	20 years

TABLE II

Rising and Setting of Stars

Heliacal phenomena: near sunrise. Acronical and cosmical phenomena: near sunset. The dates indicate the Julian day and the fraction of the day (Greenwich meantime) counted from Midday. For instance, May 17.20 means 17 May 4 hours 48 minutes P.M. The difference between Greenwich time and the hour in Rome and Athens is 50 minutes and 1 hour 35 minutes respectively. (Adapted from Ginzel, pp. 520 ff.)

					Year					
LATITUDE	− 500		− 300		− 100		+ 100		+ 300	

η Tauri (Pleiades)
Heliacal Risings

LATITUDE	− 500		− 300		− 100		+ 100		+ 300	
34°	May	17.20	May	18.20	May	19.20	May	20.17	May	21.1
38	„	20.71	„	21.65	„	22.57	„	23.46	„	24.3
42	„	25.97	„	26.81	„	27.60	„	28.36	„	29.1
46	June	3.88	June	4.50	June	5.07	June	5.59	June	6.0

Heliacal Settings

34	April	5.33	April	6.60	April	7.88	April	9.15	April	10.3
38	„	5.29	„	6.55	„	7.80	„	9.06	„	10.2
42	„	5.16	„	6.39	„	7.63	„	8.85	„	10.0
46	„	4.89	„	6.12	„	7.33	„	8.52	„	9.7

Acronical Risings

34	Sept.	29.38	Sept.	30.83	Oct.	2.28	Oct.	3.80	Oct.	5.3
38	„	25.85	„	27.36	Sept.	28.86	Sept.	30.42	„	2.0
42	„	21.08	„	22.62	„	24.16	„	25.78	Sept.	27.4
46	„	14.11	„	15.70	„	17.36	„	19.07	„	20.8

Cosmical Settings

34	Nov.	3.46	Nov.	4.83	Nov.	6.21	Nov.	7.60	Nov.	9.0
38	„	3.96	„	5.34	„	6.74	„	8.16	„	9.5
42	„	4.53	„	5.94	„	7.36	„	8.80	„	10.2
46	„	5.21	„	6.64	„	8.09	„	9.57	„	11.0

LATITUDE	− 500		− 300		− 100		+ 100		+ 300	

α Orionis (Betelgeuse)
Heliacal Risings

	− 500		− 300		− 100		+ 100		+ 300	
34°	June	25.27	June	25.71	June	26.15	June	26.60	June	27.06
38	,,	29.04	,,	29.35	,,	29.66	,,	29.99	,,	30.34
42	July	3.44	July	3.59	July	3.75	July	3.92	July	4.13
46	,,	8.67	,,	8.61	,,	8.57	,,	8.57	,,	8.60

Heliacal Settings

34	May	3.11	May	4.00	May	4.85	May	5.69	May	6.49
38	,,	1.42	,,	2.26	,,	3.08	,,	3.88	,,	4.62
42	April	29.57	April	30.37	,,	1.14	,,	1.89	,,	2.59
46	,,	27.53	,,	28.27	April	29.00	April	29.69	April	30.31

Acronical Risings

34	Nov.	27.84	Nov.	28.76	Nov.	29.67	Nov.	30.58	Dec.	1.46
38	,,	29.55	,,	30.41	Dec.	1.27	Dec.	2.14	,,	2.99
42	Dec.	1.46	Dec.	2.28	,,	3.08	,,	3.89	,,	4.69
46	,,	3.67	,,	4.42	,,	5.16	,,	5.90	,,	6.62

Cosmical Settings

34	Nov.	22.12	Nov.	23.19	Nov.	24.23	Nov.	25.26	Nov.	26.27
38	,,	21.04	,,	22.09	,,	23.13	,,	24.16	,,	25.17
42	,,	19.93	,,	20.97	,,	21.99	,,	23.01	,,	24.01
46	,,	18.76	,,	19.80	,,	20.80	,,	21.81	,,	22.79

LATITUDE	− 500		− 300		− 100		+ 100		+ 300	

α Canis major (Sirius)
Heliacal Risings

	− 500		− 300		− 100		+ 100		+ 300	
34°	July	23.61	July	23.69	July	23.77	July	23.87	July	23.99
38	,,	28.13	,,	28.11	,,	28.10	,,	28.13	,,	28.17
42	Aug.	2.01	Aug.	1.89	Aug.	1.79	Aug.	1.73	Aug.	1.70
46	,,	7.25	,,	7.04	,,	6.84	,,	6.68	,,	6.54

Heliacal Settings

34	May	6.91	May	7.24	May	7.54	May	7.82	May	8.06
38	,,	3.31	,,	3.60	,,	3.86	,,	4.09	,,	4.28
42	April	29.49	April	29.74	April	29.94	April	30.10	April	30.23
46	,,	25.38	,,	25.57	,,	25.72	,,	25.82	,,	25.88

Acronical Risings

34	Dec.	29.54	Dec.	29.89	Dec.	30.25	Dec.	30.63	Dec.	31.00
38	Jan.	2.11	Jan.	2.40	Jan.	2.69	Jan.	3.03	Jan.	3.34
42	,,	5.99	,,	6.19	,,	6.42	,,	6.68	,,	6.93
46	,,	10.21	,,	10.33	,,	10.47	,,	10.63	,,	10.81

Cosmical Settings

34	Nov.	25.83	Nov.	26.37	Nov.	26.88	Nov.	27.38	Nov.	27.83
38	,,	22.92	,,	23.43	,,	23.91	,,	24.36	,,	24.79
42	,,	19.84	,,	20.33	,,	20.77	,,	21.18	,,	21.58
46	,,	16.58	,,	17.03	,,	17.43	,,	17.80	,,	18.14

LATITUDE	− 500		− 300		− 100		+ 100		+ 300	
				α Bootis (Arcturus)						
				Heliacal Risings						
34°	Sept.	21.73	Sept.	23.29	Sept.	24.79	Sept.	26.24	Sept.	27.67
38	,,	18.85	,,	20.49	,,	22.07	,,	23.60	,,	25.07
42	,,	15.69	,,	17.48	,,	19.18	,,	20.80	,,	22.30
46	,,	12.15	,,	14.11	,,	15.98	,,	17.76	,,	19.44
				Heliacal Settings						
34	Oct.	25.96	Oct.	25.97	Oct.	26.00	Oct.	26.08	Oct.	26.10
38	Nov.	2.27	Nov.	1.92	Nov.	1.61	Nov.	1.36	Nov.	1.17
42	,,	11.08	,,	10.23	,,	9.46	,,	8.80	,,	8.23
46	,,	21.80	,,	20.27	,,	18.92	,,	17.72	,,	16.63
				Acronical Risings						
34	Feb.	29.56	March	2.14	March	3.67	March	5.15	March	6.50
38	,,	26.23	Feb.	27.94	Feb.	29.58	,,	2.14	,,	3.61
42	,,	22.51	,,	24.39	,,	26.17	Feb.	27.87	Feb.	29.47
46	,,	18.17	,,	20.30	,,	22.30	,,	24.18	,,	25.93
				Cosmical Settings						
34	May	25.59	May	25.23	May	24.90	May	24.60	May	24.31
38	June	4.18	June	3.43	June	2.73	June	2.07	June	1.47
42	,,	15.11	,,	13.90	,,	12.76	,,	11.71	,,	10.73
46	,,	27.40	,,	25.65	,,	24.02	,,	22.52	,,	21.13

LATITUDE	− 500		− 300		− 100		+ 100		+ 300	
				α Lyrae						
				Heliacal Risings						
34°	Nov.	16.04	Nov.	16.23	Nov.	16.34	Nov.	16.46	Nov.	16.51
38	,,	10.16	,,	10.35	,,	10.47	,,	10.58	,,	10.62
42	,,	3.51	,,	3.71	,,	3.83	,,	3.93	,,	3.98
46	Oct.	26.32	Oct.	26.60	Oct.	26.76	Oct.	26.89	Oct.	26.9
				Heliacal Settings						
34	Jan.	16.48	Jan.	16.20	Jan.	15.96	Jan	15.75	Jan.	15.56
38	,,	22.98	,,	22.61	,,	22.27	,,	21.98	,,	21.71
42	,,	30.36	,,	29.88	,,	29.44	,,	29.06	,,	28.7
46	Feb.	8.43	Feb.	7.76	Feb.	7.14	Feb.	6.62	Feb.	6.1
				Acronical Risings						
34	April	27.00	April	27.01	April	26.98	April	26.90	April	26.79
38	,,	20.47	,,	20.48	,,	20.46	,,	20.39	,,	20.28
42	,,	13.09	,,	13.13	,,	13.12	,,	13.06	,,	12.9
46	,,	4.07	,,	4.22	,,	4.28	,,	4.25	,,	4.16
				Cosmical Settings						
34	Aug.	9.45	Aug.	9.02	Aug.	8.59	Aug.	8.24	Aug.	7.90
38	,,	16.42	,,	15.91	,,	15.40	,,	14.98	,,	14.58
42	,,	24.24	,,	23.62	,,	23.04	,,	22.55	,,	22.16
46	Sept.	2.66	Sept.	1.88	Sept.	1.19	,,	31.57	,,	31.0

TABLE III

Synchronistic Table

Olympic years, years ab *urbe condita* (according to Varro) and Egyptian mobile years. (After Table V in Ginzel.)

Year BC	Varr. a.u.c.	Olymp.	I Thoth	Year BC	Varr. a.u.c.	Olymp.	I Thoth	Year BC	Varr. a.u.c.	Olymp.	I Thoth
			Feb.				Feb.				Feb.
776		1,1									
775		2		735	19	11,2	23	694	60	21,3	13
774		3		734	20	3	23	693	61	4	13
773		4		733	21	4	23	692	62	22,1	12
772		2,1		732	22	12,1	22	691	63	2	12
771		2		731	23	2	22	690	64	3	12
770		3		730	24	3	22	689	65	4	12
769		4		729	25	4	22	688	66	23,1	11
768		3,1		728	26	13,1	21	687	67	2	11
767		2		727	27	2	21	686	68	3	11
766		3		726	28	3	21	685	69	4	11
765		4		725	29	4	21	684	70	24,1	10
764		4,1		724	30	14,1	20	683	71	2	10
763		2		723	31	2	20	682	72	3	10
762		3		722	32	3	20	681	73	4	10
761		4		721	33	4	20	680	74	25,1	9
760		5,1		720	34	15,1	19	679	75	2	9
759		2		719	35	2	19	678	76	3	9
758		3		718	36	3	19	677	77	4	9
757		4		717	37	4	19	676	78	26,1	8
756		6,1		716	38	16,1	18	675	79	2	8
755		2		715	39	2	18	674	80	3	8
754		3		714	40	3	18	673	81	4	8
753	1	4		713	41	4	18	672	82	27,1	7
752	2	7,1		712	42	17,1	17	671	83	2	7
751	3	2		711	43	2	17	670	84	3	7
750	4	3		710	44	3	17	669	85	4	7
749	5	4		709	45	4	17	668	86	28,1	6
748	6	8,1		708	46	18,1	16	667	87	2	6
			Feb.	707	47	2	16	666	88	3	6
747	7	2	26	706	48	3	16	665	89	4	6
746	8	3	26	705	49	4	16	664	90	29,1	5
745	9	4	26	704	50	19,1	15	663	91	2	5
744	10	9,1	25	703	51	2	15	662	92	3	5
743	11	2	25	702	52	3	15	661	93	4	5
742	12	3	25	701	53	4	15	660	94	30,1	4
741	13	4	25	700	54	20,1	14	659	95	2	4
740	14	10,1	24	699	55	2	14	658	96	3	4
739	15	2	24	698	56	3	14	657	97	4	4
738	16	3	24	697	57	4	14	656	98	31,1	3
737	17	4	24	696	58	21,1	13	655	99	2	3
736	18	11,1	23	695	59	2	13	654	100	3	3

Year BC	Varr. a.u.c.	Olymp.	1 Thoth	Year BC	Varr. a.u.c.	Olymp.	1 Thoth	Year BC	Varr. a.u.c.	Olymp.	1 Thoth
			Feb.				Jan.				Jan.
653	101	31,4	3	603	151	2	21	551	203	57,2	8
652	102	32,1	2	602	152	44,3	21	550	204	3	8
651	103	2	2	601	153	4	21	549	205	4	8
650	104	3	2	600	154	45,1	20	548	206	58,1	7
649	105	4	2	599	155	2	20	547	207	2	7
648	106	33,1	1	598	156	3	20	546	208	3	7
647	107	2	1	597	157	4	20	545	209	4	7
646	108	3	1	596	158	46,1	19	544	210	59,1	6
645	109	4	1	595	159	2	19	543	211	2	6
				594	160	3	19	542	212	3	6
			Jan.	593	161	4	19	541	213	4	6
644	110	34,1	31	592	162	47,1	18	540	214	60,1	5
643	111	2	31	591	163	2	18	539	215	2	5
642	112	3	31	590	164	3	18	538	216	3	5
641	113	4	31	589	165	4	18	537	217	4	5
640	114	35,1	30	588	166	48,1	17	536	218	61,1	4
639	115	2	30	587	167	2	17	535	219	2	4
638	116	3	30	586	168	3	17	534	220	3	4
637	117	4	30	585	169	4	17	533	221	4	4
636	118	36,1	29	584	170	49,1	16	532	222	62,1	3
635	119	2	29	583	171	2	16	531	223	2	3
634	120	3	29	582	172	3	16	530	224	3	3
633	121	4	29	581	173	4	16	529	225	4	3
632	122	37,1	28	580	174	50,1	15	528	226	63,1	2
631	123	2	28	579	175	2	15	527	227	2	2
630	124	3	28	578	176	3	15	526	228	3	2
629	125	4	28	577	177	4	15	525	229	4	2
628	126	38,1	27	576	178	51,1	14	524	230	64,1	1
627	127	2	27	575	179	2	14	523	231	2	1
626	128	3	27	574	180	3	14	522	232	3	1
625	129	4	27	573	181	4	14				Dec.
624	130	39,1	26	572	182	52,1	13	521	233	4	31
623	131	2	26	571	183	2	13	520	234	65,1	31
622	132	3	26	570	184	3	13	519	235	2	31
621	133	4	26	569	185	4	13	518	236	3	31
620	134	40,1	25	568	186	53,1	12	517	237	4	30
619	135	2	25	567	187	2	12	516	238	66,1	30
618	136	3	25	566	188	3	12	515	239	2	30
617	137	4	25	565	189	4	12	514	240	3	30
616	138	41,1	24	564	190	54,1	11	513	241	4	29
615	139	2	24	563	191	2	11	512	242	67,1	29
614	140	3	24	562	192	3	11	511	243	2	29
613	141	4	24	561	193	4	11	510	244	3	29
612	142	42,1	23	560	194	55,1	10	509	245	4	28
611	143	2	23	559	195	2	10	508	246	68,1	28
610	144	3	23	558	196	3	10	507	247	2	28
609	145	4	23	557	197	4	10	506	248	3	28
608	146	43,1	22	556	198	56,1	9	505	249	4	27
607	147	2	22	555	199	2	9	504	250	69,1	27
606	148	3	22	554	200	3	9	503	251	2	27
605	149	4	22	553	201	4	9	502	252	3	27
604	150	44,1	21	552	202	57,1	8	501	253	4	26

Year BC	Varr. a.u.c.	Olymp.	I Thoth	Year BC	Varr. a.u.c.	Olymp.	I Thoth	Year BC	Varr. a.u.c.	Olymp.	I Thoth
			Dec.				Dec.				Dec.
500	254	70,1	26	450	304	82,3	14	400	354	95,1	1
499	255	2	26	449	305	4	13	399	355	2	1
498	256	3	26	448	306	83,1	13	398	356	3	1
497	257	4	25	447	307	2	13				Nov.
496	258	71,1	25	446	308	3	13	397	357	4	30
495	259	2	25	445	309	4	12	396	358	96,1	30
494	260	3	25	444	310	84,1	12	395	359	2	30
493	261	4	24	443	311	2	12	394	360	3	30
492	262	72,1	24	442	312	3	12	393	361	4	29
491	263	2	24	441	313	4	11	392	362	97,1	29
490	264	3	24	440	314	85,1	11	391	363	2	29
489	265	4	23	439	315	2	11	390	364	3	29
488	266	73,1	23	438	316	3	11	389	365	4	28
487	267	2	23	437	317	4	10	388	366	98,1	28
486	268	3	23	436	318	86,1	10	387	367	2	28
485	269	4	22	435	319	2	10	386	368	3	28
484	270	74,1	22	434	320	3	10	385	369	4	27
483	271	2	22	433	321	4	9	384	370	99,1	27
482	272	3	22	432	322	87,1	9	383	371	2	27
481	273	4	21	431	323	2	9	382	372	3	27
480	274	75,1	21	430	324	3	9	381	373	4	26
479	275	2	21	429	325	4	8	380	374	100,1	26
478	276	3	21	428	326	88,1	8	379	375	2	26
477	277	4	20	427	327	2	8	378	376	3	26
476	278	76,1	20	426	328	3	8	377	377	4	25
475	279	2	20	425	329	4	7	376	378	101,1	25
474	280	3	20	424	330	89,1	7	375	379	2	25
473	281	4	19	423	331	2	7	374	380	3	25
472	282	77,1	19	422	332	3	7	373	381	4	24
471	283	2	19	421	333	4	6	372	382	102,1	24
470	284	3	19	420	334	90,1	6	371	383	2	24
469	285	4	18	419	335	2	6	370	384	3	24
468	286	78,1	18	418	336	3	6	369	385	4	23
467	287	2	18	417	337	4	5	368	386	103,1	23
466	288	3	18	416	338	91,1	5	367	387	2	23
465	289	4	17	415	339	2	5	366	388	3	23
464	290	79,1	17	414	340	3	5	365	389	4	22
463	291	2	17	413	341	4	4	364	390	104,1	22
462	292	3	17	412	342	92,1	4	363	391	2	22
461	293	4	16	411	343	2	4	362	392	3	22
460	294	80,1	16	410	344	3	4	361	393	4	21
459	295	2	16	409	345	4	3	360	394	105,1	21
458	296	3	16	408	346	93,1	3	359	395	2	21
457	297	4	15	407	347	2	3	358	396	3	21
456	298	81,1	15	406	348	3	3	357	397	4	20
455	299	2	15	405	349	4	2	356	398	106,1	20
454	300	3	15	404	350	94,1	2	355	399	2	20
453	301	4	14	403	351	2	2	354	400	3	20
452	302	82,1	14	402	352	3	2	353	401	4	19
451	303	2	14	401	353	4	1	352	402	107,1	19
								351	403	2	19

Table — Group 1

Year BC	Varr. a.u.c.	Olymp.	I Thoth
			Nov.
350	404	107,3	19
349	405	4	18
348	406	108,1	18
347	407	2	18
346	408	3	18
345	409	4	17
344	410	109,1	17
343	411	2	17
342	412	3	17
341	413	4	16
340	414	110,1	16
339	415	2	16
338	416	3	16
337	417	4	15
336	418	111,1	15
335	419	2	15
334	420	3	15
333	421	4	14
332	422	112,1	14
331	423	2	14
330	424	3	14
329	425	4	13
328	426	113,1	13
327	427	2	13
326	428	3	13
325	429	4	12
324	430	114,1	12
323	431	2	12
322	432	3	12
321	433	4	11
320	434	115,1	11
319	435	2	11
318	436	3	11
317	437	4	10
316	438	116,1	10
315	439	2	10
314	440	3	10
313	441	4	9
312	442	117,1	9
311	443	2	9
310	444	3	9
309	445	4	8
308	446	118,1	8
307	447	2	8
306	448	3	8
305	449	4	7
304	450	119,1	7
303	451	2	7
302	452	3	7
301	453	4	6

Table — Group 2

Year BC	Varr. a.u.c.	Olymp.	I Thoth
			Nov.
300	454	120,1	6
299	455	2	6
298	456	3	6
297	457	4	5
296	458	121,1	5
295	459	2	5
294	460	3	5
293	461	4	4
292	462	122,1	4
291	463	2	4
290	464	3	4
289	465	4	3
288	466	123,1	3
287	467	2	3
286	468	3	3
285	469	4	2
284	470	124,1	2
283	471	2	2
282	472	3	2
281	473	4	1
280	474	125,1	1
279	475	2	1
278	476	3	1
			Oct.
277	477	4	31
276	478	126,1	31
275	479	2	31
274	480	3	31
273	481	4	30
272	482	127,1	30
271	483	2	30
270	484	3	30
269	485	4	29
268	486	128,1	29
267	487	2	29
266	488	3	29
265	489	4	28
264	490	129,1	28
263	491	2	28
262	492	3	28
261	493	4	27
260	494	130,1	27
259	495	2	27
258	496	3	27
257	497	4	26
256	498	131,1	26
255	499	2	26
254	500	3	26
253	501	4	25
252	502	132,1	25
251	503	2	25

Table — Group 3

Year BC	Varr. a.u.c.	Olymp.	I Thoth
			Oct.
250	504	132,3	25
249	505	4	24
248	506	133,1	24
247	507	2	24
246	508	3	24
245	509	4	23
244	510	134,1	23
243	511	2	23
242	512	3	23
241	513	4	22
240	514	135,1	22
239	515	2	22
238	516	3	22
237	517	4	21
236	518	136,1	21
235	519	2	21
234	520	3	21
233	521	4	20
232	522	137,1	20
231	523	2	20
230	524	3	20
229	525	4	19
228	526	138,1	19
227	527	2	19
226	528	3	19
225	529	4	18
224	530	139,1	18
223	531	2	18
222	532	3	18
221	533	4	17
220	534	140,1	17
219	535	2	17
218	536	3	17
217	537	4	16
216	538	141,1	16
215	539	2	16
214	540	3	16
213	541	4	15
212	542	142,1	15
211	543	2	15
210	544	3	15
209	545	4	14
208	546	143,1	14
207	547	2	14
206	548	3	14
205	549	4	13
204	550	144,1	13
203	551	2	13
202	552	3	13
201	553	4	12

Year BC	Varr. a.u.c.	Olymp.	I Thoth
			Oct.
200	554	145,1	12
199	555	2	12
198	556	3	12
197	557	4	11
196	558	146,1	11
195	559	2	11
194	560	3	11
193	561	4	10
192	562	147,1	10
191	563	2	10
190	564	3	10
189	565	4	9
188	566	148,1	9
187	567	2	9
186	568	3	9
185	569	4	8
184	570	149,1	8
183	571	2	8
182	572	3	8
181	573	4	7
180	574	150,1	7
179	575	2	7
178	576	3	7
177	577	4	6
176	578	151,1	6
175	579	2	6
174	580	3	6
173	581	4	5
172	582	152,1	5
171	583	2	5
170	584	3	5
169	585	4	4
168	586	153,1	4
167	587	2	4
166	588	3	4
165	589	4	3
164	590	154,1	3
163	591	2	3
162	592	3	3
161	593	4	2
160	594	155,1	2
159	595	2	2
158	596	3	2
157	597	4	1
156	598	156,1	1
155	599	2	1
154	600	3	1
			Sept.
153	601	4	30
152	602	157,1	30
151	603	2	30

Year BC	Varr. a.u.c.	Olymp.	I Thoth
			Sept.
150	604	157,3	30
149	605	4	29
148	606	158,1	29
147	607	2	29
146	608	3	29
145	609	4	28
144	610	159,1	28
143	611	2	28
142	612	3	28
141	613	4	27
140	614	160,1	27
139	615	2	27
138	616	3	27
137	617	4	26
136	618	161,1	26
135	619	2	26
134	620	3	26
133	621	4	25
132	622	162,1	25
131	623	2	25
130	624	3	25
129	625	4	24
128	626	163,1	24
127	627	2	24
126	628	3	24
125	629	4	23
124	630	164,1	23
123	631	2	23
122	632	3	23
121	633	4	22
120	634	165,1	22
119	635	2	22
118	636	3	22
117	637	4	21
116	638	166,1	21
115	639	2	21
114	640	3	21
113	641	4	20
112	642	167,1	20
111	643	2	20
110	644	3	20
109	645	4	19
108	646	168,1	19
107	647	2	19
106	648	3	19
105	649	4	18
104	650	169,1	18
103	651	2	18
102	652	3	18
101	653	4	17

Year BC	Varr. a.u.c.	Olymp.	I Thoth
			Sept.
100	654	170,1	17
99	655	2	17
98	656	3	17
97	657	4	16
96	658	171,1	16
95	659	2	16
94	660	3	16
93	661	4	15
92	662	172,1	15
91	663	2	15
90	664	3	15
89	665	4	14
88	666	173,1	14
87	667	2	14
86	668	3	14
85	669	4	13
84	670	174,1	13
83	671	2	13
82	672	3	13
81	673	4	12
80	674	175,1	12
79	675	2	12
78	676	3	12
77	677	4	11
76	678	176,1	11
75	679	2	11
74	680	3	11
73	681	4	10
72	682	177,1	10
71	683	2	10
70	684	3	10
69	685	4	9
68	686	178,1	9
67	687	2	9
66	688	3	9
65	689	4	8
64	690	179,1	8
63	691	2	8
62	692	3	8
61	693	4	7
60	694	180,1	7
59	695	2	7
58	696	3	7
57	697	4	6
56	698	181,1	6
55	699	2	6
54	700	3	6
53	701	4	5
52	702	182,1	5
51	703	2	5

Year BC	Varr. a.u.c.	Olymp.	I Thoth	Year AD	Varr. a.u.c.	Olymp.	I Thoth	Year AD	Varr. a.u.c.	Olymp.	I Thoth
			Sept.				Aug.				Aug.
50	704	182,3	5	1	754	195,1	23	51	804	207,3	11
49	705	4	4	2	755	2	23	52	805	4	10
48	706	183,1	4	3	756	3	23	53	806	208,1	10
47	707	2	4	4	757	4	22	54	807	2	10
46	708	3	4	5	758	196,1	22	55	808	3	10
45	709	4	3	6	759	2	22	56	809	4	9
44	710	184,1	3	7	760	3	22	57	810	209,1	9
43	711	2	3	8	761	4	21	58	811	2	9
42	712	3	3	9	762	197,1	21	59	812	3	9
41	713	4	2	10	763	2	21	60	813	4	8
40	714	185,1	2	11	764	3	21	61	814	210,1	8
39	715	2	2	12	765	4	20	62	815	2	8
38	716	3	2	13	766	198,1	20	63	816	3	8
37	717	4	1	14	767	2	20	64	817	4	7
36	718	186,1	1	15	768	3	20	65	818	211,1	7
35	719	2	1	16	769	4	19	66	819	2	7
34	720	3	1	17	770	199,1	19	67	820	3	7
			Aug.	18	771	2	19	68	821	4	6
33	721	4	31	19	772	3	19	69	822	212,1	6
32	722	187,1	31	20	773	4	18	70	823	2	6
31	723	2	31	21	774	200,1	18	71	824	3	6
30	724	3	31	22	775	2	18	72	825	4	5
29	725	4	30	23	776	3	18	73	826	213,1	5
28	726	188,1	30	24	777	4	17	74	827	2	5
27	727	2	30	25	778	201,1	17	75	828	3	5
26	728	3	30	26	779	2	17	76	829	4	4
25	729	4	29	27	780	3	17	77	830	214,1	4
24	730	189,1	29	28	781	4	16	78	831	2	4
23	731	2	29	29	782	202,1	16	79	832	3	4
22	732	3	29	30	783	2	16	80	833	4	3
21	733	4	28	31	784	3	16	81	834	215,1	3
20	734	190,1	28	32	785	4	15	82	835	2	3
19	735	2	28	33	786	203,1	15	83	836	3	3
18	736	3	28	34	787	2	15	84	837	4	2
17	737	4	27	35	788	3	15	85	838	216,1	2
16	738	191,1	27	36	789	4	14	86	839	2	2
15	739	2	27	37	790	204,1	14	87	840	3	2
14	740	3	27	38	791	2	14	88	841	4	1
13	741	4	26	39	792	3	14	89	842	217,1	1
12	742	192,1	26	40	793	4	13	90	843	2	1
11	743	2	26	41	794	205,1	13	91	844	3	1
10	744	3	26	42	795	2	13				July
9	745	4	25	43	796	3	13	92	845	4	31
8	746	193,1	25	44	797	4	12	93	846	218,1	31
7	747	2	25	45	798	206,1	12	94	847	2	31
6	748	3	25	46	799	2	12	95	848	3	31
5	749	4	24	47	800	3	12	96	849	4	30
4	750	194,1	24	48	801	4	11	97	850	219,1	30
3	751	2	24	49	802	207,1	11	98	851	2	30
2	752	3	24	50	803	2	11	99	852	3	30
1	753	4	23					100	853	4	29

Year AD	Varr. a.u.c.	Olymp.	I Thoth
			July
101	854	220,1	29
102	855	2	29
103	856	3	29
104	857	4	28
105	858	221,1	28
106	859	2	28
107	860	3	28
108	861	4	27
109	862	222,1	27
110	863	2	27
111	864	3	27
112	865	4	26
113	866	223,1	26
114	867	2	26
115	868	3	26
116	869	4	25
117	870	224,1	25
118	871	2	25
119	872	3	25
120	873	4	24
121	874	225,1	24
122	875	2	24
123	876	3	24
124	877	4	23
125	878	226,1	23
126	879	2	23
127	880	3	23
128	881	4	22
129	882	227,1	22
130	883	2	22
131	884	3	22
132	885	4	21
133	886	228,1	21
134	887	2	21
135	888	3	21
136	889	4	20
137	890	229,1	20
138	891	2	20
139	892	3	20
140	893	4	19
141	894	230,1	19
142	895	2	19
143	896	3	19
144	897	4	18
145	898	231,1	18
146	899	2	18
147	900	3	18
148	901	4	17
149	902	232,1	17
150	903	2	17

Year AD	Varr. a.u.c.	Olymp.	I Thoth
			July
151	904	232,3	17
152	905	4	16
153	906	233,1	16
154	907	2	16
155	908	3	16
156	909	4	15
157	910	234,1	15
158	911	2	15
159	912	3	15
160	913	4	14
161	914	235,1	14
162	915	2	14
163	916	3	14
164	917	4	13
165	918	236,1	13
166	919	2	13
167	920	3	13
168	921	4	12
169	922	237,1	12
170	923	2	12
171	924	3	12
172	925	4	11
173	926	238,1	11
174	927	2	11
175	928	3	11
176	929	4	10
177	930	239,1	10
178	931	2	10
179	932	3	10
180	933	4	9
181	934	240,1	9
182	935	2	9
183	936	3	9
184	937	4	8
185	938	241,1	8
186	939	2	8
187	940	3	8
188	941	4	7
189	942	242,1	7
190	943	2	7
191	944	3	7
192	945	4	6
193	946	243,1	6
194	947	2	6
195	948	3	6
196	949	4	5
197	950	244,1	5
198	951	2	5
199	952	3	5
200	953	4	4

Year AD	Varr. a.u.c.	Olymp.	I Thoth
			July
201	954	245,1	4
202	955	2	4
203	956	3	4
204	957	4	3
205	958	246,1	3
206	959	2	3
207	960	3	3
208	961	4	2
209	962	247,1	2
210	963	2	2
211	964	3	2
212	965	4	1
213	966	248,1	1
214	967	2	1
215	968	3	1
			June
216	969	4	30
217	970	249,1	30
218	971	2	30
219	972	3	30
220	973	4	29
221	974	250,1	29
222	975	2	29
223	976	3	29
224	977	4	28
225	978	251,1	28
226	979	2	28
227	980	3	28
228	981	4	27
229	982	252,1	27
230	983	2	27
231	984	3	27
232	985	4	26
233	986	253,1	26
234	987	2	26
235	988	3	26
236	989	4	25
237	990	254,1	25
238	991	2	25
239	992	3	25
240	993	4	24
241	994	255,1	24
242	995	2	24
243	996	3	24
244	997	4	23
245	998	256,1	23
246	999	2	23
247	1000	3	23
248	1001	4	22
249	1002	257,1	22
250	1003	2	22

Year AD	Varr. a.u.c.	Olymp.	I Thoth	Year AD	Varr. a.u.c.	Olymp.	I Thoth	Year AD	Varr. a.u.c.	Olymp.	I Thoth
			June	267	1020	3	18	284	1037	4	13
251	1004	257,3	22	268	1021	4	17	285	1038	266,1	13
252	1005	4	21	269	1022	262,1	17	286	1039	2	13
253	1006	258,1	21	270	1023	2	17	287	1040	3	13
254	1007	2	21	271	1024	3	17	288	1041	4	12
255	1008	3	21	272	1025	4	16	289	1042	267,1	12
256	1009	4	20	273	1026	263,1	16	290	1043	2	12
257	1010	259,1	20	274	1027	2	16	291	1044	3	12
258	1011	2	20	275	1028	3	16	292	1045	4	11
259	1012	3	20	276	1029	4	15	293	1046	268,1	11
260	1013	4	19	277	1030	264,1	15	294	1047	2	11
261	1014	260,1	19	278	1031	2	15	295	1048	3	11
262	1015	2	19	279	1032	3	15	296	1049	4	10
263	1016	3	19	280	1033	4	14	297	1050	269,1	10
264	1017	4	18	281	1034	265,1	14	298	1051	2	10
265	1018	261,1	18	282	1035	2	14	299	1052	3	10
266	1019	2	18	283	1036	3	14	300	1053	4	9

*In leap years 25 Feb. = bis VI (bissextilis); 26 Feb. = V; 27 Feb. = IV; 28 Feb. = III
a.d. Kal. Mar.; 29 Feb. = pridie Kal. Mar.*

In the pre-Julian Roman calendar *Martius, Maius, Quintilis,* and *October* had
each 31 days, February had 28 days, and the seven other months 29 days each.
For the counting of days before the Ides see the Julian calendar. For the days
between the Ides and the next Calends, subtract the Roman number of the
day from the number of the days in the month and add 2. For instance,
IX a.d. Kal. Nov. will be 31 (the number of days in October) − 9 = 22 + 2 = 24
October.

TABLE IV

The Roman Julian Calendar

Day	January	February	March	April	May	June	July	August	September	October	November	December
1	Kal.	Kal.	Kal.	Kal.	Kal.	Kal.	Kal.	Kal.	Kal.	Kal.	Kal.	Kal.
2	IV	IV	VI	IV	VI	IV	VI	IV	IV	VI	IV	IV
3	III	III	V	III	V	III	V	III	III	V	III	III
4	pr.	pr.	IV	pr.	IV	pr.	IV	pr.	pr.	IV	pr.	pr.
5	Non.	Non.	III	Non.	III	Non.	III	Non.	Non.	III	Non.	Non.
6	VIII	VIII	pr.	VIII	pr.	VIII	pr.	VIII	VIII	pr.	VIII	VIII
7	VII	VII	Non.	VII	Non.	VII	Non.	VII	VII	Non.	VII	VII
8	VI	VI	VIII	VI	VIII	VI	VIII	VI	VI	VIII	VI	VI
9	V	V	VII	V	VII	V	VII	V	V	VII	V	V
10	IV	IV	VI	IV	VI	IV	VI	IV	IV	VI	IV	IV
11	III	III	V	III	V	III	V	III	III	V	III	III
12	pr.	pr.	IV	pr.	IV	pr.	IV	pr.	pr.	IV	pr.	pr.
13	Id.	Id.	III	Id.	III	Id.	III	Id.	Id.	III	Id.	Id.
14	XIX	XVI	pr.	XVIII	pr.	XVIII	pr.	XIX	XVIII	pr.	XVIII	XIX
15	XVIII	XV	Id.	XVII	Id.	XVII	Id.	XVIII	XVII	Id.	XVII	XVIII
16	XVII	XIV	XVII	XVI	XVII	XVI	XVII	XVII	XVI	XVII	XVI	XVII
17	XVI	XIII	XVI	XV	XVI	XV	XVI	XVI	XV	XVI	XV	XVI
18	XV	XII	XV	XIV	XV	XIV	XV	XV	XIV	XV	XIV	XV
19	XIV	XI	XIV	XIII	XIV	XIII	XIV	XIV	XIII	XIV	XIII	XIV
20	XIII	X	XIII	XII	XIII	XII	XIII	XIII	XII	XIII	XII	XIII
21	XII	IX	XII	XI	XII	XI	XII	XII	XI	XII	XI	XII
22	XI	VIII	XI	X	XI	X	XI	XI	X	XI	X	XI
23	X	VII	X	IX	X	IX	X	X	IX	X	IX	X
24	IX	VI	IX	VIII	IX	VIII	IX	IX	VIII	IX	VIII	IX
25	VIII	V	VIII	VII	VIII	VII	VIII	VIII	VII	VIII	VII	VIII
26	VII	IV	VII	VI	VII	VI	VII	VII	VI	VII	VI	VII
27	VI	III	VI	V	VI	V	VI	VI	V	VI	V	VI
28	V	pr.	V	IV	V	IV	V	V	IV	V	IV	V
29	IV		IV	III	IV	III	IV	IV	III	IV	III	IV
30	III		III	pr. Kal. May	III	pr. Kal. July	III	III	pr. Kal. Oct.	III	pr. Kal. Dec.	III
31	pr. Kal. Feb.		pr. Kal. April		pr. Kal. June		pr. Kal. Aug.	pr. Kal. Sept.		pr. Kal. Nov.		pr. Kal. Jan.

TABLE V

Lists of Rulers

KINGS OF SPARTA

The earliest datable kings are Polydoris and Theopompus (first half of the seventh century). A reliable list of kings begins with Anaxandridas and Ariston, contemporaries of Croesus of Lydia.

AGIADS

Anaxandridas	*c.* 560–520	Agesipolis II	371–37?
Cleomenes I	*c.* 520–490	Cleomenes II	370–309
Leonidas I	490–480	Areus I	309–26?
Pleistarchus	480–459	Acrotatus	265–26?
Pleistoanax	459–409	Areus II	262–25?
Pausanias	409–395	Leonidas II	254–23?
Agesipolis I	395–380	Cleomenes III	235–22?
Cleombrotus I	380–371	Agesipolis III	219–21?

EURYPONTIDS

Ariston	*c.* 550–515	Eudamidas II	*c.* 275–24?
Demaratus	*c.* 515–491	Agis IV	*c.* 244–24?
Leotychidas II	491–469	Eudamidas III	241–*c.* 22?
Archidamus II	469–427	Archidamus V	228–22?
Agis II	427–400	Eucleidas	227–22?
Agesilaus II	399–360	Lycurgus	219–*c.* 21?
Archidamus III	360–338	Pelops	*c.* 212–*c.* 20?
Agis III	338–331	(under guardianship of Machanidas
Eudamidas I	331–*c.* 305	and, from *c.* 206 on, of Nabis)
Archidamus IV	*c.* 305–275	Nabis	before 195–19?

KINGS OF MACEDON

Amyntas I	second half of sixth century BC
Alexander I	*c.* 495–*c.* 450/40
Perdiccas II	*c.* 450/40–413
Archelaus	413–399
Orestes	399–396
Aeropus	396–393
Amyntas II	393–2
Pausanias	393–2
Amyntas III	393–370
Alexander II	370–369/8
Ptolemaeus	369/8–365
Perdiccas III	365–359
Philip II	359–336
Alexander the Great	336–323

KINGS OF BABYLON

According to the Babylonian computation. *Cf.* R. A. Parker and W. H. Dubberstein, *Babylonian Chronology* (1956) and D. J. Wiseman, *Chronicles of the Chaldean Kings* (1956).

Nabopolossar	23 Nov. 626–15 August 605 BC
Nebuchadnezzar II	605–562 (died in the first days of October)
Amel-Marduk	562–560 (died between 7 and 13 August)
Nergal-shar-Usur	560–556
Labash Marduk	556– May
Nabunaid	May 556–29 October 539

KINGS OF PERSIA

According to the Babylonian computation. *Cf.* R. A. Parker and W. H. Dubberstein, *Babylonian Chronology* (1956).

Cyrus (in Iran)	559–530
Cyrus (in Babylonia)	539–530
Cambyses	530–522
Bardya (Smerdis, Gaumata)	522– killed by Darius 29 September 522
(Nebuchadnezzar III)	
Darius I	522–521
(Nebuchadnezzar IV)	521
Darius I	521–486
Xerxes	486–465
Artaxerxes I	464–423
Darius II	423–404

Artaxerxes II	404–359
Artaxerxes III	359–338
Arses	338–336
Darius III	336–331

Both Nebuchadnezzars were Babylonian pretenders not recognized in Persia.

KINGS OF EGYPT (XXVI–XXX DYNASTIES)

Cf. A. Gardiner, *Egypt of the Pharaohs* (1961) 451: E. Drioton and J. Vandier, *l'Egypte*[4] (1962) 680. All dates except the first and the last are more or less conjectural.

XXVI DYNASTY:

Psammetichus I	664–610
Necho II	610–595
Psammetichus II	595–589
Apries	589–570
Amasis	570–526
Psammetichus III	526–525

XXVII DYNASTY: Persian Kings (*cf.* Table above)

XXVIII DYNASTY:

Amyrtaeus	404–399

XXIX DYNASTY

Nepherites I	399–393
Psammuthis	393
Achoris	393–381
Nepherites II	381–380

XXX DYNASTY

Nectanebo I	380–363
Tachos	363–360
Nectanebo II	360–343

THE PTOLEMIES

According to T. C. Skeat, *The Reigns of the Ptolemies* (1954) and A. E. Samuel *Ptolemaic Chronology* (1962). *Cf.* also P. W. Pestman, *Chronologie égyptienne d'après les textes démotiques* (1967).

Ptolemy I Soter[1]	305–282
Ptolemy II Philadelphus	282–29 Jan. 246
Ptolemy III Euergetes I	246–222
Ptolemy IV Philopator	222–205
Ptolemy V Epiphanes	204–180
Ptolemy VI Philometor	180–145

Joint rule of Ptolemy VI, Ptolemy VIII and Cleopatra II, 5 Oct 170 (expulsion of Philometor 164–3)

Ptolemy VII Neos Philopator	145–4 associated on the throne
Ptolemy VIII Euergetes (Physcon)	145–116
Cleopatra III and Ptolemy IX Soter II (Lathyros)	116–107
Cleopatra III and Ptolemy X Alexander	107–101
Ptolemy X Alexander I and Cleopatra Berenice	101–88
Ptolemy IX Soter II	88–81
Cleopatra Berenice and Ptolemy XI Alexander II	80
Ptolemy XII (Auletes)	80–58
Berenice IV	58–55
Ptolemy XII (Auletes)	55–51
Cleopatra VII and Ptolemy XIII	51–47
Cleopatra VII and Ptolemy XIV	47–44
Cleopatra VII and Ptolemy XV (Caesarion)	44–30 Aug. 31

[1] Ptolemy I counted his years from the death of Alexander the Great (323).

ALEXANDER THE GREAT, HIS SUCCESSORS AND THE SELEUCIDS

According to the Babylonian computation. *Cf.* R. A. Parker and W. H. Dubberstein, *Babylonian Chronology* (1956) and A. R. Bellinger, *The End of the Seleucids* (1949). On Babylonian chronology in 331–305 BC *cf.* J. Oelsner, in *Altorientalische Forschungen* I (1974), 129 and in *ZA* 1974, 261.

Alexander	336–10 June 323
Philip Arrhidaeus	323–316
Alexander IV	316–312
Seleucus I Nicator	311–281
Antiochus I Soter	281–2 June 261
Antiochus II Theos	261–(Summer) 246
Seleucus II Callinicus	246–225
Seleucus III Soter	225–223
Antiochus III (the Great)	223–187 (early summer)
Seleucus IV Philopator	187–175 (3 Sept.)
Antiochus IV Epiphanes	175–164 (?)
Antiochus V Eupator	163–162
Demetrius I Soter	162–150
Alexander Balas	150–145
Demetrius II Nicator	145–140
Antiochus VI Epiphanes	145–142
Antiochus VII (Sidetes)	138–129

Demetrius II Nicator	129–125
Cleopatra Thea	126
Cleopatra Thea and Antiochus VIII	
(Grypus)	125–121
Seleucus V	125
Antiochus VIII (Grypus)	121–96
Antiochus IX (Cyzicenus)	115–95
Seleucus VI Epiphanes Nicanor	96–5
Demetrius III Philopator	95–88
Antiochus X Eusebes	95–83
Antiochus XI Philadelphus	94
Philip I Philadelphus	94–83
Antiochus XII Dionysus	87–84
(simultaneously Tigranes of Armenia)	(83–69)
Antiochus XIII (Asiaticus)	69–64
Philip II	65–64

THE ANTIGONIDS OF MACEDONIA

Antigonus I	306–301
Demetrius I (Poliorcetes)	306–283
Antigonus II (Gonatas)[1]	283–239
Demetrius II	239–229
Antigonus III (Doson)	229–221
Philip V	221–179
Perseus	179–168

[1] According to E. Manni, *Fasti ellenistici e romani* 75, Antigonus II died in 241/0. His actual rule in Macedonia began in 276. Likewise, Demetrius I reigned in Macedonia only from 294 to 287.

THE ATTALIDS OF PERGAMUM

Philetaerus	283–263
Eumenes I	263–241
Attalus I Soter	241–197
Eumenes II Soter	197–160
Attalus II	160–139
Attalus III	139–133
(Eumenes III = Aristonicus)[1]	133–129

[1] *Cf.* E. S. G. Robinson, *Numism. Chron.* 1954, p. 1.

THE PARTHIAN KINGS

According to G. Le Rider, *Suse sous les Séleucides et les Parthes* (1965), 460, On the kings from 121 to 68 BC *cf.* K. Dobbins, *Numism. Chronicle* 1975, 19. The dynasty era began in 248/7 (*cf. supra* p. 72).

Arsaces I	c. 238–215
Arsaces II	c. 190 (died)
Phriapitius	c. 190–176

Phraates I	c. 176–171
Mithridates I	c. 170–139
Phraates II	c. 139–129
Artabanus I	c. 128–124
Mithridates II	c. 124–88
Gotarzes I	c. 90–c. 80
Orodes I	c. 80–78
Sinatruces	c. 77–70
Phraates III	c. 70–58
Orodes II	c. 58–39
Mithridates III	c. 57–55
Pacorus I, died in	38
Phraates IV	c. 40–3 BC
Tiridates	c. 30–25 ·
Phraates V	3 BC–AD3
Orodes III	c. 4–7
Vonones I	c. 7–12
Artabanus II	10–c. 38
Vardanes I	c. AD 39–45
Gotarzes II	c. 43–50
Vologeses I	c. 50–76
Vologeses II	77–78
Pacorus II	77–86
Artabanus III	79–80
Vologeses II	89–90
Oroses	89–90
Pacorus II	92–95
Oroses	108–127
Vologeses III	111–146
Pacorus II	113–114
Mithridates IV	c. 130–c. 147
Vologeses IV	148–190
Vologeses V	190–206
Vologeses VI	207–221
Artabanus IV	c. 213–c. 227
Artavasdes	c. 226–7

(The identity of some kings who issued coins, *e.g.* Arsaces Theopator Euergetes, remains uncertain; not all pretenders and temporary rulers are mentioned in this list. With some exceptions, the dates are tentative.)

THE SASSANIDS

According to R. N. Frye, *The Heritage of Persia* (1963), 294.

Ardashir	AD 240
Shapur	240–c. 272
Hormizd Ardashir	272–273
Varahran I	273–276
Varahran II	276–293
Varahran III	293
Nerseh	299–302
Hormizd II	302–309
Shapur II	309–379
Ardashir II	379–383
Shapur III	383–388
Varahran IV	388–399
Yazdagird I	399–421
Varahran V	421–439
Yazdagird II	439–457
Hormizd III	457–459

The dynasty continued until the Arab conquest (651)

KINGS OF THE CIMMERIAN BOSPORUS

According to R. Werner, *Historia* 1955, 430.

Spartocus I	438/7–433/2
Seleucus (with Satyrus I)	433/2–393/2
Satyrus I (alone)	433/2–389/8
Leucon I (with Gorgippos)	389/8–349/8
Spartocus II (with Parisades I)	349/8–344/3
Parisades	344/3–311/0
Satyrus II (with Prytanis)	311/10–310/9
Prytanis	310/09
Eumelus	310/9–304/3
Spartocus III	304/3–284/3
Parisades II	284/3–c. 245
Spartocus IV	c. 245–240
Leucon II	240–220
Hygiaenon	220–200
Spartocus V	200–180
Parisades III	180–150
Parisades IV	150–125
Parisades V	125–109
Mithridates VI of Pontus	107–63
Pharnaces	63–47

Asander	*c.* 47–17 BC
Dynamis	17–16
Scribonius	15 (?)
Polemo	14–8
Dynamis	8 BC–AD 7/8
Unknown ruler for two years	
Aspurgus	AD 10/11–37/8
Gepaepyris (widow of Aspurgus)	37/8–39
Mithridates (for a time jointly with Gepaepyris)	39–44/5
Cotys (perhaps deposed in 62)	44/5–67
Rescuporis	68/9–90
Sauromates I	93/4–123/4
Cotys II	123/4–132/3
Rhoemetalcus	131/2–153/4
T. Iulius Eupator	153/4–173 (?)
Sauromates II	173/4–210/11
Rescuporis	210/11–226/7
Cotys III	227/8–233/4
Sauromates III	229/30–231/2
Rescuporis II	233/4
Pharsanzes	
Ininthimaeus	236
Sauromates IV	
C. Iulius Teiranes	275/6–278/9
Chedosbius	*c.* 280
Phophorses	286/7–308/9
Radamsadius	308/9–318 (?)
Rescuporis	318/9–335 (or later)

KINGS OF THRACE

The kings of the Odrysae	
Teres	*c.* 450
Sitalces	*c.* 440–424
Amdocus (Medocus)	*c.* 408
Hebryzelmis	*c.* 385
Cotys I	*c.* 383–360/59
(Division of the kingdom between three princes)	
Macedonian conquest	342/1

(For local princes of the Hellenistic period and Macedonian and client kings under the Roman rule *cf.* Wolf-D. Barloweven (ed.), *Abriss der Geschichte antiker Randkulturen* (1961), 239.)

KINGS OF PONTUS: THE MITHRIDATIDS

Mithridates dynast of Cius	337/6–302/1
Mithridates I	302/1–266/5 BC
Ariobarzanes	266/5–c. 255
Mithridates II	c. 225–c. 220
Mithridates III	c. 220–c. 185
Pharnaces I	c. 185–c. 170
Mithridates IV Philopator Philadelphus	c. 170–c. 150
Mithridates V Euergetes	c. 150–121/0
Mithridates VI Eupator	121/0–63
Pharnaces II (ruler of the Cimmerian Bosporus)	63–47
Darius	39–37?

KINGS OF CAPPADOCIA

The first ruler to assert independence was Ariarathes III, 255/1–220. The list then runs:

Ariarathes IV Eusebes	220–c. 162
Ariarathes V Eusebes Philopator	c. 163–c. 130
Ariarathes VI Epiphanes Philopator	c. 120–c. 111
Ariarathes VII Philometor	c. 111–c. 100
Ariarathes Eusebes Philopator[1]	c. 100–c. 88
Ariarathes VIII	c. 96

End of dynasty. Then the Cappadocians elected a noble, Ariobarzanes, as king.

Ariobarzanes I Philoromaios	c. 95–c. 62
Ariobarzanes II Philopator	62–c. 54
Ariobarzanes III Eusebes Philoromaios	c. 54–42
Ariarathes IX	42–36
Archelaus	36–AD 17

[1] This king was a son of Mithridates VI of Pontus. From c. 100 until 63 Cappadocia was mostly in the hands of Mithridates.

KINGS OF BITHYNIA

	BC
Zipoetes (king from 298/7)	c. 315–c. 280
Nicomedes I	c. 280, died before 242
Ziaelas	c. 250, died before 227
Prusias I	c. 230–c. 182
Prusias II	c. 182–149
Nicomedes II Epiphanes	149–c. 127
Nicomedes III Euergetes	c. 127–c. 94
Nicomedes IV Philopator	c. 94–74

KINGS OF COMMAGENE

Ptolemaeus, dependent *epistates* of Commagene from *c.* 170 BC, asserted his independence from Syria *c.* 163/2.

Ptolemaeus	*c.* 163/2–*c.* 130
Samus II Theosebes Dikaios	*c.* 130–*c.* 100
Mithridates I Callinicus	*c.* 100–*c.* 70
Antiochos I Theos Dikaios Epiphanes Philoromaios Philhellen	*c.* 70–*c.* 35
Mithridates II	*c.* 31
(Antiochus II, did not reign)	died 29
Mithridates III	*c.* 20
Antiochus III	died AD 17
(After his death, Commagene was annexed by Rome)	
Antiochus IV	AD 38–72

KINGS OF ARMENIA

(*Cf.* K. Toumanov, *Studies in Christian Caucasian History* (1963), 293. H. Seyrig, *Revue Numismatique* 1955, 111)

Orontes	*c.* 320
Samus	*c.* 260
Arsames	*c.* 260–*c.* 230
Xerxes	*c.* 230–*c.* 212
Orontes	*c.* 212–*c.* 200

THE DYNASTY OF ARTAXIAS

Artaxias, son of Zariadris	*c.* 189–*c.* 164
Tigranes I	?
Artavasdes	died *c.* 95
Tigranes II (the Great)	*c.* 95–55
Artavasdes II	55–34
Artaxes	34–20 BC
Tigranes III	20–*c.* 8 BC
Tigranes IV	*c.* 8 BC–AD 1
Short reign of a pretender Artavasdes II	
Ariobarzanes	*c.* AD 2–4
Artavasdes III	*c.* 4–*c.* 6

Short reigns of Tigranes V and Erato (widow of Tigranes IV); then an interregnum. Between AD 11 and 16 the Armenian throne is occupied by Vonones, unrecognized by either Rome or Parthia.

Artaxias	18–*c.* 34
Arsaces	*c.* 34–36
Mithridates (exiled by Gaius, but restored by Claudius)	36–51

Short usurpation of Radamistus	c. 52–c. 54
Tiridates	51–60
Tigranes VI of Cappadocia	60–62
Tiridates (restored)	63–75
Axidares	c. 110
Parthamasiris	113–114
Sanatruces	c. 115
Vologases	116–c. 140
Pacorus	c. 160–163
Sohaemus	c. 163–c. 175
Tiridates II	c. 215
Tiridates III	c. 287–c. 330

INDO-GREEK KINGS

According to A. K. Narain, *The Indo-Greeks* (1957). All dates are approximate and many hypothetical. The existence of Demetrius II remains doubtful; he may be identified with Demetrius I (*cf.* V. M. Masson, *Vestn. Drevn. Ist.* no. 76 (1961), 39).

Diodotus I	256–248 BC
Diodotus II	248–235
Euthydemus I	235–200
Demetrius I	200–185
Euthydemus II	200–190
Antimachus I	190–180
Pantaleon	185–175
Demetrius II	180–165
Agathocles	180–165
Eucratides I	171–155
Menander	155–130
Plato	155–
Heliocles I	155–140
Eucratides II	140–
Antimachus II	130–125
Strato I	130–95
Archebius	130–120
Philoxenus	125–115
Zoilus	–125
Heliocles II	120–115
Lysias	120–110
Antialcidas	115–100
Apollodotus	115–95
Zoilus, Dionysius, Apollophanes	95–80
Nicias	95–85
Diomedes	95–85

Telephus	95–80
Hippostratus	85–70
Amyntas	85–75
Theophilus	before 75
Hermaeus	75–55

THE DYNASTY OF MASSINISSA IN NUMIDIA

Massinissa	c. 215–149
Micipsa, Gulussa, Mastanabal	149–c. 145
Micipsa alone	c. 145–118
Adherbal, Hiempsal, Jugurtha	118–116
Jugurtha alone	112–105
Gauda	105–?
Hiempsal II	c. 88–c. 50
Juba I	c. 50–46
Juba II (after 25 BC ruler of Mauritania)	c. 30–c. AD 22
Ptolemy	c. AD 22–AD 40

RULERS OF THE JEWS

THE HASMONEANS

Jonathan	152–142
Simon	142–134
John Hyrcanus	134–104
Aristobulus	104–103
Alexander Jannaeus	103–76
Salome Alexandra	76–67
Aristobulus II	67–63
Hyrcanus II	63–40
Antigonus	40–37

THE HERODIANS

Herod I	37–4
Archelaus (in Judaea)	4–AD 6
Herod Antipas (in Galilea)	4–AD 39
Philip (northeastern districts)	4–AD 34
Herod Agrippa I (succeeded Philip in AD 37, Antipas c. 40 and Archelaus in 41)	died AD 44
Agrippa II (in northern Palestine)	AD 53–100 (?)

TABLE VI

The Athenian Archons from 528 to 292 BC

(After Diodorus and Dion. Halic. *Din.* 9. For the archons 528–522, 496–481 and 293–282 see Samuel, 204 and 212. The sequence of archons in 521–498 remains uncertain.)

BC		BC		BC	
528	Philoneos	463	Tlepolemos	422	Alkaios
527	Onetorides	462	Konon	421	Aristion
526	Hippias	461	Euthippos	420	Astyphilos
525	Kleisthenes	460	Phrasikleides	419	Archias
524	Miltiades	459	Philokles	418	Antiphon
523	Kalliades?	458	Habron	417	Euphemos
522	Peisistratos?	457	Mnesitheides	416	Arimnestos
497	Archias	456	Kallias	415	Charias
496	Hipparchos	455	Sosistratos	414	Teisandros
495	Philippos	454	Ariston	413	Kleokritos
494	Pythokritos	453	Lysikrates	412	Kallias
493	Themistokles	452	Chairephanes	411	Mnesilochos and
492	Diognetos	451	Antidotos		Theopompos
491	Hybrilides	450	Euthynos	410	Glaukippos
490	Phainippos	449	Pedieus	409	Diokles
489	Aristeides	448	Philiskos	408	Euktemon
488	Anchises	447	Timarchides	407	Antigenes
487	Telesines	446	Kallimachos	406	Kallias
486	?	445	Lysimachides	405	Alexias
485	Philokrates	444	Praxiteles	404	Pythodoros
484	Leostratos	443	Lysanias	403	Eukleides
483	Nikodemos	442	Diphilos	402	Mikon
482	?	441	Timokles	401	Xenainetos
481	Hypsichides	440	Morychides	400	Laches
480	Kalliades	439	Glaukinos	399	Aristokrates
479	Xanthippos	438	Theodoros	398	Euthykles
478	Timosthenes	437	Euthymenes	397	Suniades
477	Adeimantos	436	Lysimachos	396	Phormion
476	Phaidon	435	Antiochides	395	Diophantos
475	Dromokleides	434	Krates	394	Eubulides
474	Akestorides	433	Apseudes	393	Demostratos
473	Menon	432	Pythodoros	392	Philokles
472	Chares	431	Euthydemos	391	Nikoteles
471	Praxiergos	430	Apollodoros	390	Demostratos
470	Demotion	429	Epameinon	389	Antipatros
469	Apsephion	428	Diotimos	388	Pyrgion
468	Theagenides	427	Eukles Molonos	387	Theodotos
467	Lysistratos	426	Euthynos	386	Mystichides
466	Lysanias	425	Stratokles	385	Dexitheos
465	Lysitheos	424	Isarchos	384	Diotrephes
464	Archedemides	423	Ameinias	383	Phanostratos

BC		BC		BC	
382	Euandros	352	Aristodemos	322	Philokles
381	Demophilos	351	Theellos	321	Archippos
380	Pytheas	350	Apollodoros	320	Neaichmos
379	Nikon	349	Kallimachos	319	Apollodoros
378	Nausinikos	348	Theophilos	318	Archippos
377	Kalleas	347	Themistokles	317	Demogenes
376	Charisandros	346	Archias	316	Demokleides
375	Hippodamas	345	Eubulos	315	Praxibulos
374	Sokratides	344	Lykiskos	314	Nikodoros
373	Asteios	343	Pythodotos	313	Theophrastos
372	Alkisthenes	342	Sosigenes	312	Polemon
371	Phrasikleides	341	Nikomachos	311	Simonides
370	Dysniketos	340	Theophrastos	310	Hieromnemon
369	Lysistratos	339	Lysimachides	309	Demetrios
368	Nausigenes	338	Chairondas	308	Charinos
367	Polyzelos	337	Phrynichos	307	Anaxikrates
366	Kephisodoros	336	Pythodelos	306	Koroibos
365	Chion	335	Euainetos	305	Euxenippos
364	Timokrates	334	Ktesikles	304	Pherekles
363	Charikleides	333	Nikokrates	303	Leostratos
362	Molon	332	Niketes	302	Nikokles
361	Nikophemos	331	Aristophanes	301	Klearchos
360	Kallimedes	330	Aristophon	300	Hegemachos
359	Eucharistos	329	Kephisophon	299	Euktemon
358	Kephisodotos	328	Euthykritos	298	Mnesidemos
357	Agathokles	327	Hegemon	297	Antiphates
356	Elpines	326	Chremes	296	Nikias
355	Kallistratos	325	Antikles	295	Nikostratos
354	Diotimos	324	Hegesias	294	Olympiodoros
353	Thudemos	323	Kephisodoros	293	Olympiodoros II
				292	Philippos

TABLE VII

Roman Consuls, 509 BC–AD 337

See A. Degrassi, *Fasti Capitolini* (1954) and *I Fasti consolari dell' impero romano* (1952). For the Republic *cf.* T. R. S. Broughton, *The Magistrates of the Roman Republic*, 2 vols and Suppl. (1951–60). After AD 14 only the *consules ordinarii*, and not the *suffecti*, are cited.

BC	ab urbe condita	
509	245	L. Iunius M.f. Brutus. L. Tarquinius Collatinus
		suffecti:
		P. Valerius Volusi f. Publicola
		Sp. Lucretius T.?f. Tricipitinus
		M. Horatius M.f. Pulvillus
508	246	P. Valerius Volusi f. Publicola II. T. Lucretius T.f. Tricipitinus
507	247	P. Valerius Volusi f. Publicola III. M. Horatius M.f. Pulvillus II
506	248	Sp. Larcius Rufus. T. Herminius Aquilinus
505	249	M. Valerius Volusi f. (Volusus?). P. Postumius Q.f. Tubertus
504	250	P. Valerius Volusi f. Publicola IV. T. Lucretius T.f. Tricipitinus II
503	251	Agrippa Menenius C.f. Lanatus. P. Postumius Q.f. Tubertus II
502	252	Opiter Verginius Opit. f. Tricostus. Sp. Cassius Vecellinus
501	253	Postumius Cominius Auruncus. T. Larcius Flavus (or Rufus)
500	254	Ser. Sulpicius P.f. Camarinus Cornutus. M'. Tullius Longus
499	255	T. Aebutius T.f. Helva. C. (or P.) Veturius Geminus Cicurinus
498	256	Q. Cloelius Siculus. T. Larcius Flavus (or Rufus) II
497	257	A. Sempronius Atratinus. M. Minucius Augurinus
496	258	A. Postumius P.f. Albus (Regillensis). T. Verginius A.f. Tricostus Caeliomontanus
495	259	Ap. Claudius M.f. Sabinus Inregillensis. P. Servilius P.f. Priscus Structus
494	260	A. Verginius A.f. Tricostus Caeliomontanus. T. Veturius Geminus Cicurinus
493	261	Postumus Cominius Auruncus II. Sp. Cassius Vecellinus II
492	262	T. Geganius Macerinus. P. Minucius Augurinus
491	263	M. Minucius Augurinus II. A. Sempronius Atratinus II
490	264	Q. Sulpicius Camerinus Cornutus. Sp. Larcius Flavus (or Rufus) II
489	265	C. Iulius Iullus. P. Pinarius Mamertinus Rufus
488	266	Sp. Nautius Sp.?f. Rutilus. Sex. Furius Medullinus? Fusus?
487	267	T. Sicinius Sabinus? C. Aquillius Tuscus?
486	268	Sp. Cassius Vicellinus III. Proculus Verginius Tricostus Rutilus

BC	a.u.c.	
485	269	Ser. Cornelius Maluginensis. Q. Fabius K.f. Vibulanus
484	270	L. Aemilius Mam.f. Mamercus. K. Fabius K.f. Vibulanus
483	271	M. Fabius K.f. Vibulanus. L. Valerius M.f. Potitus
482	272	Q. Fabius K.f. Vibulanus II. C. Iulius C.f. Iullus
481	273	K. Fabius K.f. Vibulanus II. Sp. Furius Fusus
480	274	M. Fabius K.f. Vibulanus II. Cn. Manlius P.f. Cincinnatus
479	275	K. Fabius K.f. Vibulanus III. T. Verginius Opet.f. Tricostus Rutilus
478	276	L. Aemilius Man.f. Mamercus II. C. Servilius Structus Ahala. *suff.*: Opet. Verginius Esquilinus
477	277	C. (or M.) Horatius M.f. Pulvillus. T. Menenius Agrippae f. Lanatus
476	278	A. Verginius Tricostus Rutilus. Sp. Servilius (P.f.?) Structus
475	279	P. Valerius P.f. Publicola. C. Nautius Sp.f. Rutilus
474	280	L. Furius Medullinus. A. Manlius Cn.f. Vulso
473	281	L. Aemilius Mam.f. Mamercus III. Vopiscus Iulius C.f. Iullus
472	282	L. Pinarius Mamercinus Rufus. P. Furius Medullinus Fusus
471	283	Ap. Claudius Ap.f. Crassinus Inregillensis Sabinus. T. Quinctius L.f. Capitolinus Barbatus
470	284	L. Valerius M.f. Potitus II. Ti. Aemilius L.f. Mamercus
469	285	T. Numicius Priscus. A. Verginius Caeliomontanus
468	286	T. Quinctius L.f. Capitolinus Barbatus II. Q. Servilius Structus Priscus
467	287	Ti. Aemilius L.f. Mamercus II. Q. Fabius M.f. Vibulanus
466	288	Q. Servilius Priscus II. Sp. Postumius A.f. Albus Regillensis
465	289	Q. Fabius M.f. Vibulanus II. T. Quinctius L.f. Capitolinus Barbatus III
464	290	A. Postumius A.f. Albus Regillensis. Sp. Furius Medullinus Fusus
463	291	P. Servilius Sp.f. Priscus. L. Aebutius T.f. Helva
462	292	L. Lucretius T.f. Tricipitinus. T. Veturius T.f. Geminus Cicurinus
461	293	P. Volumnius M.f. Amintinus Gallus. Ser. Sulpicius Camerinus Cornutus
460	294	P. Valerius P.f. Poblicola. C. Claudius Ap.f. Inregillensis Sabinus *suff.*: L. Quinctius L.f. Cincinnatus
459	295	Q. Fabius M.f. Vibulanus III. L. Cornelius Ser.f. Maluginensis Uritus
458	296	C. Nautius Sp.f. Rutilus II.—Carvetus ? *suff.*: L. Minucius. P.f. Esquilinus Augurinus
457	297	C. (or M.) Horatius M.f. Pulvillus II. Q. Minucius P.f. Esquilinus
456	298	M. Valerius M'.f. Maximus Lactuca. Sp. Verginius A.f. Tricostus Caeliomontanus
455	299	T. Romilius T.f. Rocus Vaticanus. C. Veturius P.f. Cicurinus
454	300	Sp. Tarpeius M.f. Montanus Capitolinus. A. Aternius Varus Fontinalis
453	301	Sex. Quinctilius Sex.f. P. Curiatus Fistus Trigeminus

BC	a.u.c.	
452	302	T. Menenius Agripp.f. Lanatus. P. Sestius Q.f. Capito Vaticanu
451	303	Ap. Claudius Ap.f. Crassus Inregillensis Sabinus II. T. Genuciu L.f. Augurinus
450	304	Decemviri
449	305	L. Valerius P.f. Potitus. M. Horatius Barbatus
448	306	Lars (or Sp.) Herminius Coritinesanus. T. Verginius Tricostu Caeliomontanus
447	307	M. Geganius M.f. Macerinus. C. Iulius (Iullus?)
446	308	T. Quinctius L.f. Capitolinus Barbatus IV. Agrippa Furius Fusu
445	309	M. Genucius Augurinus. C. (or Agripp.) Curtius Philo
444	310	Trib. Mil. Cons. Pot.
		Suff.: L. Papirius Mugillanus. L. Sempronius A.f. Atratinus
443	311	M. Geganius M.f. Macerinus II. T. Quinctius L.f. Capitolinu Barbatus V
442	312	M. Fabius Q.f. Vibulanus. Post. Aebutius Helva Cornicen
441	313	C. Furius Pacilus Fusus. M'. (or M.) Papirius Crassus
440	314	Proculus Geganius Macerinus. T. Menenius Agripp. Lanatus
439	315	Agrippa Menenius T.f. Lanatus. T. Quinctius L.f. Capitolinu Barbatus VI
438	316	Trib. Mil. Cons. Pot.
437	317	M. Geganius M.f. Macerinus III. L. Sergius L.f. Fidenas
		Suff.: M. Valerius M.f. Lactuca Maximus
436	318	L. Papirius Crassus. M. Cornelius Maluginensis
435	319	C. Iulius (Iullus?) II. L. (or Proc.) Verginius Tricostus
434	320	C. Iulius Iullus III. L. (or Proc.) Verginius Tricostus II or M Manlius Capitolinus. Q. Sulpicius Ser.?f. Camerinus Praetextatu
433–432	321–322	Trib. Mil. Cons. Pot.
431	323	T. Quinctius L.f. Poenus Cincinnatus. C. (or Cn.) Iulius Ment
430	324	L. (or C.) Papirius Crassus L. Iulius Vop.f. Iullus
429	325	Hostus Lucretius Tricipitinus. L. Sergius C.f. Fidenas II
428	326	A. Cornelius M.f. Cossus. T. Quinctius L.f. Poenus Cincinnatus Listed by Diodorus between the colleges of 428 and 427: L. Quin ctius (L.f. Cincinnatus). A. Sempronius (L.f. Atratinus)
427	327	C. Servilius Structus Ahala. L. Papirius L.f. Mugillanus
426–424	328–330	Trib. Mil. Cons. Pot.
423	331	C. Sempronius Atratinus. Q. Fabius Q.f. Vibulanus
422	332	Trib. Mil. Cons. Pot.
421	333	Cn. (or N.) Fabius Vibulanus. T. Quinctius T.f. Capitolinu Barbatus
420–414	334–340	Trib. Mil. Cons. Pot.
413	341	A. (or M.?) Cornelius Cossus. L. Furius L.f. Medullinus
412	342	Q. Fabius Ambustus Vibulanus. C. Furius Pacilus

11	343	L. Papirius L.f. Mugillanus. Sp. (or C.) Nautius Sp.f. Rutilus
10	344	M'. Aemilius Mam.f. Mamercinus. C. Valerius L.f. Potitus Volusus
09	345	Cn. Cornelius A.f. Cossus. L. Furius L.f. Medullinus II
08–	346–	Trib. Mil. Cons. Pot
394	360	
93	361	L. Valerius L.f. Potitus. P.? (or Ser.) Cornelius Maluginensis *Suff.:* L. Lucretius Tricipitinus Flavus. Ser. Sulpicius Q.f. Camerinus
92	362	L. Valerius L.f. Potitus II. M. Manlius T.f. Capitolinus
91–	363–	Trib. Mil. Cons. Pot.
376	378	
70–	384–	Trib. Mil. Cons. Pot.
367	387	
66	388	L. Aemilius L.f. Mamercinus. L. Sextius f. Sextinus Lateranus
65	389	L. Genucius M.f. Aventinensis. Q. Servilius Q.f. Ahala
64	390	C. Sulpicius M.f. Peticus. C. Licinius C.f. Stolo or Calvus
63	391	Cn. Genucius M.f. Aventinensis. L. Aemilius L.f. Mamercinus II
62	392	Q. Servilius Q.f. Ahala II. L. Genucius M.f. Aventinensis II
61	393	C. Licinius C.f. Calvus or Stolo. C. Sulpicius M.f. Peticus II
60	394	M. Fabius N.f. Ambustus. C. Poetelius C.f. Libo Visolus
59	395	M. Popillius M.f. Laenas. Cn. Manlius L.f. Capitolinus Imperiosus
58	396	C. Fabius N.f. Ambustus. C. Plautius P.f. Proculus
57	397	C. Marcius L.f. Rutilus. Cn. Manlius L.f. Capitolinus Imperiosus II
56	398	M. Fabius N.f. Ambustus II. M. Popillius M.f. Laenas II
55	399	C. Sulpicius M.f. Peticus III. M. Valerius L.f. Poplicola
54	400	M. Fabius N.f. Ambustus III. T. Quinctius Poenus Capitolinus Crispinus
53	401	C. Sulpicius M.f. Peticus IV. M. Valerius L.f. Poplicola II
52	402	P. Valerius P.f. Poplicola. C. Marcius L.f. Rutilus II
51	403	C. Sulpicius M.f. Peticus V. T. Quinctius Poenus Capitolinus Crispinus II
50	404	M. Popillius M.f. Laenas III. L. Cornelius P.f. Scipio
49	405	L. Furius M.f. Camillus. Ap. Claudius P.f. Crassus Inregillensis Listed under this year by Diodorus: M. Aemilius, T. Quinctius
48	406	M. Valerius M.f. Corvus. M. Popillius M.f. Laenas IV
47	407	C. Plautius Venno (or Venox). T. Manlius L.f. Imperiosus Torquatus
46	408	M. Valerius M.f. Corvus II. C. Poetelius C.f. Libo Visolus II
45	409	M. Fabius Dorsuo. Ser. Sulpicius Camerinus Rufus
44	410	C. Marcius L.f. Rutilus III. T. Manlius L.f. Imperiosus Torquatus II
43	411	M. Valerius M.f. Corvus III. A. Cornelius P.f. Cossus Arvina
42	412	Q. Servilius Q.f. Ahala III. C. Marcius L.f. Rutilus IV

BC	a.u.c.	
341	413	C. Plautius Venno (Venox) II. L. Aemilius L.f. Mamercinus Privernas
340	414	T. Manlius L.f. Imperiosus Torquatus III. P. Decius Q.f. Mus
339	415	Ti. Aemilius Mamercinus. Q. Publilius Q.f. Philo
338	416	L. Furius Sp.f. Camillus. C. Maenius P.f.
337	417	C. Sulpicius Ser.f. Longus. P. Aelius Paetus
336	418	L. Papirius L.f. Crassus. K. Duillius
335	419	M. Atilius Regulus Calenus. M. Valerius M.f. Corvus IV
334	420	Sp. Postumius Albinus (Caudinus). T. Veturius Calvinus
333	421	Dictator year
332	422	Cn. Domitius Cn.F. Calvinus. A. Cornelius P.f. Cossus Arvina
331	423	C. Valerius L.f. Potitus. M. Claudius C.f. Marcellus
330	424	L. Papirius L.f. Crassus II. L. Plautius L.f. Venno (Venox)
329	425	L. Aemilius L.f. Mamercinus Privernas II. C. Plautius P.f. Decianus
328	426	C. Plautius Decianus II or P. Plautius Proculus
		P. Cornelius Scapula or P. Cornelius Scipio Barbatus
327	427	L. Cornelius Lentulus. Q. Publilius Q.f. Philo II
326	428	C. Poetelius C.f. Libo Visolus III. L. Papirius Sp.f. Cursor
325	429	L. Furius Sp.f. Camillus II. D. Iunius Brutus Scaeva
324	430	Dictator year
323	431	C. Sulpicius Ser.f. Longus II. Q. Aulius Q.f. Cerretanus
322	432	Q. Fabius M.f. Maximus Rullianus. L. Fulvius L.f. Curvus
321	433	T. Veturius Calvinus II. Sp. Postumius Albinus (Caudinus) II
320	434	L. Papirius Sp.f. Cursor II. Q. Publilius Q.f. Philo III
319	435	L. Papirius Sp.f. Cursor III. Q. Aulius Q.f. Cerretanus II
318	436	L. Plautius L.f. Venno (Venox). M. Folius C.f. Flaccinator
317	437	Q. Aemilius Q.f. Barbula. C. Iunius C.f. Bubulcus Brutus
316	438	Sp. Nautius Sp.f. Rutilus. M. Popillius M.f. Laenas
315	439	L. Papirius Sp.f. Cursor IV. Q. Publilius Q.f. Philo IV
314	440	M. Poetelius M.f. Libo. C. Sulpicius Ser.f. Longus III
313	441	L. Papirius Sp.f. Cursor V. C. Iunius C.f. Bubulcus Brutus II
312	442	M. Valerius M.f. Maximus (Corrinus). P. Decius P.f. Mus
311	443	C. Iunius C.f. Bubulcus Brutus III. Q. Aemilius Q.f. Barbula II
310	444	Q. Fabius M.f. Maximus Rullianus II. C. Marcius C.f. Rutilus (Censorinus)
309	445	Dictator year
308	446	P. Decius P.f. Mus II. Q. Fabius M.f. Maximus Rullianus III
307	447	Ap. Claudius C.f. Caecus. L. Volumnius C.f. Flamma Violens
306	448	Q. Marcius Q.f. Tremulus. P. Cornelius A.f. Arvina
305	449	L. Postumius L.f. Megellus. Ti. Minucius M.f. Augurinus
		Suff.: M. Fulvius L.f. Curvus Paetinus
304	450	P. Sempronius P.f. Sophus. P. Sulpicius Ser.f. Saverrio
303	451	Ser. Cornelius Cn.f. Lentulus. L. Genucius Aventinensis
302	452	M. Livius Denter. M. Aemilius L.f. Paullus

144

BC	a.u.c.	
301	453	Dictator year
300	454	M. Valerius M.f. Corvus V. Q. Appuleius Pansa
299	455	M. Fulvius Cn.f. Paetinus. T. Manlius T.f. Torquatus
		Suff.: M. Valerius M.f. Corvus VI
298	456	L. Cornelius Cn.f. Scipio Barbatus. Cn. Fulvius Cn.f. Maximus Centumalus
297	457	Q. Fabius M.f. Maximus Rullianus IV. P. Decius P.f. Mus III
296	458	Ap. Claudius C.f. Caecus II. L. Volumnius C.f. Flamma Violens II
295	459	Q. Fabius M.f. Maximus Rullianus V. P. Decius P.f. Mus IV
294	460	L. Postumius L.f. Megellus II. M. Atilius M.f. Regulus
293	461	L. Papirius L.f. Cursor. Sp. Carvilius C.f. Maximus
292	462	Q. Fabius Q.f. Maximus Gurges. D. Iunius D.f. Brutus Scaeva
291	463	L. Postumius L.f. Megellus III. C. Iunius C.f. Bubulcus Brutus
290	464	M'. Curius M'.f. Dentatus. P. Cornelius Cn.f. Rufinus
289	465	M. Valerius M.f. Maximus Corvinus II. Q. Caedicius Q.f. Noctua
288	466	Q. Marcius Q.f. Tremulus II. P. Cornelius A.f. Arvina II
287	467	M. Claudius M.f. Marcellus. C. Nautius Rutilus
286	468	M. Valerius Maximus (Potitus?). C. Aelius Paetus
285	469	C. Claudius M.f. Canina. M. Aemilius Lepidus
284	470	C. Servilius Tucca. L. Caecilius Metellus Denter
283	471	P. Cornelius Dolabella. Cn. Domitius Cn.f. Calvinus Maximus
282	472	C. Fabricius C.f. Luscinus. Q. Aemilius Cn.f. Papus
281	473	L. Aemilius Q.f. Barbula. Q. Marcius Q.f. Philippus
280	474	P. Valerius Laevinus. Ti. Coruncanius Ti.f.
279	475	P. Sulpicius P.f. Saverrio. P. Decius P.f. Mus
278	476	C. Fabricius C.f. Luscinus II. Q. Aemilius Cn.f. Papus II
277	477	P. Cornelius Cn.f. Rufinus II. C. Iunius C.f. Bubulcus Brutus I
276	478	Q. Fabius Q.f. Maximus Gurges II. C. Genucius L.f. Clepsina
275	479	M'. Curius M'.f. Dentatus II. L. Cornelius Ti.f. Lentulus Caudinus
274	480	M'. Curius M'.f. Dentatus III. Ser. Cornelius P.f. Merenda
273	481	C. Fabius M.f. Licinus. C. Claudius M.f. Canina II
272	482	L. Papirius L.f. Cursor II. Sp. Carvilius C.f. Maximus II
271	483	K. Quinctius L.f. Claudus. L. Genucius L.f. Clepsina
270	484	C. Genucius L.f. Clepsina II. Cn. Cornelius P.f. Blasio
269	485	Q. Ogulnius L.f. Gallus. C. Fabius C.f. Pictor
268	486	P. Sempronius P.f. Sophus. Ap. Claudius Ap.f. Russus
267	487	M. Atilius M.f. Regulus. L. Iulius L.f. Libo
266	488	D. Iunius D.f. Pera. N. Fabius C.f. Pictor
265	489	Q. Fabius Q.f. Maximus Gurges. L. Mamilius Q.f. Vitulus
264	490	Ap. Claudius C.f. Caudex. M. Fulvius Q.f. Flaccus
263	491	M'. Valerius M.f. Maximus (Messalla). M'. Otacilius C.f. Crassus
262	492	L. Postumius L.f. Megellus. Q. Mamilius Q.f. Vitulus
261	493	L. Valerius M.f. Flaccus. T. Otacilius C.f. Crassus.
260	494	Cn. Cornelius L.f. Scipio Asina. C. Duilius M.f.

BC	a.u.c.	
259	495	L. Cornelius L.f. Scipio. C. Aquillius M.f. Florus
258	496	A. Atilius A.f. Caiatinus. C. Sulpicius Q.f. Paterculus
257	497	C. Atilius M.f. Regulus. Cn. Cornelius P.f. Blasio II
256	498	L. Manlius A.f. Vulso Longus. Q. Caedicius Q.f.
		Suff.: M. Atilius M.f. Regulus II
255	499	Ser. Fulvius M.f. Paetinus Nobilior. M. Aemilius M.f. Paullu
254	500	Cn. Cornelius L.f. Scipio Asina II. A. Atilius A.f. Caiatinus
253	501	Cn. Servilius Cn.f. Caepio. C. Sempronius Ti.f. Blaesus
252	502	C. Aurelius L.f. Cotta. P. Servilius Q.f. Geminus
251	503	L. Caecilius L.f. Metellus. C. Furius C.f. Pacilus
250	504	C. Atilius M.f. Regulus II. L. Manlius A.f. Vulso II
249	505	P. Claudius Ap.f. Pulcher. L. Iunius C.f. Pullus
248	506	C. Aurelius L.f. Cotta II. P. Servilius Q.f. Geminus II
247	507	L. Caecilius L.f. Metellus II. N. Fabius M.f. Buteo
246	508	M'. Otacilius C.f. Crassus II. M. Fabius C.f. Licinus
245	509	M. Fabius M.f. Buteo. C. Atilius A.f. Bulbus
244	510	A. Manlius T.f. Torquatus Atticus. C. Sempronius Ti.f. Blaesus I
243	511	C. Fundanius C.f. Fundulus. C. Sulpicius C.f. Galus
242	512	C. Lutatius C.f. Catulus. A. Postumius A.f. Albinus
241	513	A. Manlius T.f. Torquatus Atticus II. Q. Lutatius C.f. Cerco
240	514	C. Claudius Ap.f. Centho. M. Sempronius C.f. Tuditanus
239	515	C. Mamilius Q.f. Turrinus. Q. Valerius Q.f. Falto
238	516	Ti. Sempronius Ti.f. Gracchus. P. Valerius Q.f. Falto
237	517	L. Cornelius L.f. Lentulus Caudinus. Q. Fulvius M.f. Flaccus
236	518	P. Cornelius L.f. Lentulus Caudinus. C. Licinius P.f. Varus
235	519	T. Manlius T.f. Torquatus. C. Atilius A.f. Bulbus II
234	520	L. Postumius A.f. Albinus. Sp. Carvilius Sp.f. Maximus (Ruga)
233	521	Q. Fabius Q.f. Maximus Verrucosus. M'. Pomponius M'.f. Matho
232	522	M. Aemilius M.f. Lepidus. M. Publicius L.f. Malleolus
231	523	M. Pomponius M'.f. Matho. C. Papirius C.f. Maso
230	524	M. Aemilius L.f. Barbula. M. Iunius D.f. Pera
229	525	L. Postumius A.f. Albinus II. Cn. Fulvius Cn.f. Centumalus
228	526	Sp. Carvilius Sp.f. Maximus II. Q. Fabius Q.f. Maximus Verrucosus II
227	527	P. Valerius L.f. Flaccus. M. Atilius M.f. Regulus
226	528	M. Valerius M'.f. (Maximus) Messalla. L. Apustius L.f. Fullo
225	529	L. Aemilius Q.f. Papus. C. Atilius M.f. Regulus
224	530	T. Manlius T.f. Torquatus II. Q. Fulvius M.f. Flaccus II
223	531	C. Flaminius C.f. P. Furius Sp.f. Philus
222	532	Cn. Cornelius L.f. Scipio Calvus. M. Claudius M.f. Marcellus
221	533	P. Cornelius Cn.f. Scipio Asina. M. Minucius C.f. Rufus
		Suff.: M. Aemilius M.f. Lepidus II
220	534	M. Valerius P.f. Laevinus. Q. Mucius P.f. Scaevola
		Suff (?): L. Veturius L.f. Philo. C. Lutatius C.f. Catulus

BC	a.u.c.	
219	535	L. Aemilius M.f. Paullus. M. Livius M.f. Salinator
218	536	P. Cornelius L.f. Scipio. Ti. Sempronius C.f. Longus
217	537	Cn. Servilius P.f. Geminus. C. Flaminius C.f. II
		Suff.: M. Atilius M.f. Regulus II
216	538	L. Aemilius M.f. Paullus II. C. Terentius C.f. Varro
215	539	Ti. Sempronius Ti.f. Gracchus. L. Postumius A.f. Albinus III
		Suff.: M. Claudius M.f. Marcellus II abd. Q. Fabius Q.f. Maximus Verrucosus III
214	540	Q. Fabius Q.f. Maximus Verrucosus IV. M. Claudius M.f. Marcellus III
213	541	Q. Fabius Q.f. Maximus. Ti. Sempronius Ti.f. Gracchus II
212	542	Ap. Claudius P.f. Pulcher. Q. Fulvius M.f. Flaccus III
211	543	P. Sulpicius Ser.f. Galba Maximus. Cn. Fulvius Cn.f. Centumalus Maximus
210	544	M. Valerius P.f. Laevinus II. M. Claudius M.f. Marcellus IV
209	545	Q. Fabius Q.f. Maximus Verrucosus V. Q. Fulvius M.f. Flaccus IV
208	546	M. Claudius M.f. Marcellus V. T. Quinctius L.f. Crispinus
207	547	C. Claudius Ti.f. Nero. M. Livius M.f. Salinator II
206	548	Q. Caecilius L.f. Metellus. L. Veturius L.f. Philo
205	549	P. Cornelius P.f. Scipio (Africanus). P. Licinius P.f. Crassus Dives
204	550	M. Cornelius M.f. Cethegus. P. Sempronius C.f. Tuditanus
203	551	Cn. Servilius Cn.f. Caepio. C. Servilius C.f. Geminus
202	552	Ti. Claudius P.f. Nero. M. Servilius C.f. Pulex Geminus
201	553	Cn. Cornelius L.f. Lentulus. P. Aelius Q.f. Paetus
200	554	P. Sulpicius Ser.f. Galba Maximus II. C. Aurelius C.f. Cotta
199	555	L. Cornelius L.f. Lentulus. P. Villius Ti.f. Tappulus
198	556	T. Quinctius T.f. Flamininus. Sex. Aelius Q.f. Paetus Catus
197	557	C. Cornelius L.f. Cethegus. Q. Minucius C.f. Rufus
196	558	L. Furius Sp.f. Purpureo. M. Claudius M.f. Marcellus
195	559	M. Porcius M.f. Cato. L. Valerius P.f. Flaccus
194	560	P. Cornelius P.f. Scipio Africanus II. Ti. Sempronius Ti.f. Longus
193	561	L. Cornelius L.f. Merula. A. Minucius Q.f. Thermus
192	562	L. Quinctius T.f. Flamininus. Cn. Domitius L.f. Ahenobarbus
191	563	M'. Acilius C.f. Glabrio. P. Cornelius Cn.f. Scipio Nasica
190	564	L. Cornelius P.f. Scipio (Asiaticus). C. Laelius C.f.
189	565	Cn. Manlius Cn.f. Vulso. M. Fulvius M.f. Nobilior
188	566	C. Livius M.f. Salinator. M. Valerius M.f. Messalla
187	567	M. Aemilius M.f. Lepidus. C. Flaminius C.f.
186	568	Sp. Postumius L.f. Albinus. Q. Marcius L.f. Philippus
185	569	Ap. Claudius Ap.f. Pulcher. M. Sempronius M.f. Tuditanus
184	570	P. Claudius Ap.f. Pulcher. L. Porcius L.f. Licinus
183	571	Q. Fabius Q.f. Labeo. M. Claudius M.f. Marcellus
182	572	L. Aemilius L.f. Paullus. Cn. Baebius Q.f. Tamphilus
181	573	P. Cornelius L.f. Cethegus. M. Baebius Q.f. Tamphilus

147

BC	a.u.c.	
180	574	A. Postumius A.f. Albinus (Luscus). C. Calpurnius C.f. Piso
		Suff.: Q. Fulvius Cn.f. Flaccus.
179	575	L. Manlius L.f. Acidinus Fulvianus. Q. Fulvius Q.f. Flaccus
178	576	M. Iunius M.f. Brutus. A. Manlius Cn.f. Vulso
177	577	C. Claudius Ap.f. Pulcher. Ti. Sempronius P.f. Gracchus
176	578	Cn. Cornelius Cn.f. Scipio Hispallus. Q. Petillius
		Suff.: C. Valerius M.f. Laevinus
175.	579	P. Mucius Q.f. Scaevola. M. Aemilius M.f. Lepidus II
174	580	Sp. Postumius A.f. Albinus Paullulus. Q. Mucius Q.f. Scaevola
173	581	L. Postumius A.f. Albinus. M. Popillius P.f. Laenas
172	582	C. Popillius P.f. Laenas. P. Aelius P.f. Ligus
171	583	P. Licinius C.f. Crassus. C. Cassius C.f. Longinus
170	584	A. Hostilius L.f. Mancinus. A. Atilius C.f. Serranus
169	585	Q. Marcius L.f. Philippus II. Cn. Servilius Cn.f. Caepio
168	586	L. Aemilius L.f. Paullus II. C. Licinius C.f. Crassus
167	587	Q. Aelius P.f. Paetus. M. Iunius M.f. Pennus
166	588	C. Sulpicius C.f. Galus. M. Claudius M.f. Marcellus
165	589	T. Manlius A.f. Torquatus. Cn. Octavius Cn.f.
164	590	A. Manlius A.f. Torquatus. Q. Cassius L.f. Longinus
163	591	Ti. Sempronius P.f. Gracchus II. M'. Iuventius T.f. Thalna
162	592	P. Cornelius P.f. Scipio Nasica (Corculum). C. Marcius C.f. Figulus
		Suff.: P. Cornelius L.f. Lentulus. Cn. Domitius Cn.f. Ahenobarbus
161	593	M. Valerius M.f. Messalla. C. Fannius C.f. Strabo
160	594	L. Anicius L.f. Gallus. M. Cornelius C.f. Cethegus
159	595	Cn. Cornelius Cn.f. Dolabella. M. Fulvius M.f. Nobilior
158	596	M. Aemilius M'.f. Lepidus. C. Popillius P.f. Laenas II
157	597	Sex. Iulius Sex.f. Caesar. L. Aurelius L.f. Orestes
156	598	L. Cornelius Cn.f. Lentulus Lupus. C. Marcius C.f. Figulus II
155	599	P. Cornelius P.f. Scipio Nasica II. M. Claudius M.f. Marcellus II
154	600	Q. Opimius Q.f. L. Postumius Sp.f. Albinus
		Suff.: M'. Acilius M'.f. Glabrio
153	601	Q. Fulvius M.f. Nobilior. T. Annius T.f. Luscus
152	602	M. Claudius M.f. Marcellus III. L. Valerius L.f. Flaccus
151	603	L. Licinius M.f. Lucullus. A. Postumius A.f. Albinus
150	604	T. Quinctius T.f. Flamininus. M'. Acilius L.f. Balbus
149	605	L. Marcius C.f. Censorinus. M'. Manilius P.f.
148	606	Sp. Postumius Sp.f. Albinus Magnus. L. Calpurnius C.f. Piso Caesoninus
147	607	P. Cornelius P.f. Scipio Africanus Aemilianus. C. Livius M. Aemiliani f. Drusus
146	608	Cn. Cornelius Cn.f. Lentulus. L. Mummius L.f.
145	609	Q. Fabius Q.f. Maximus Aemilianus. L. Hostilius L.f. Mancinus
144	610	Ser. Sulpicius Ser.f. Galba. L. Aurelius L.?f. Cotta

148

BC	a.u.c.	
143	611	Ap. Claudius C.f. Pulcher. Q. Caecilius Q.f. Metellus Macedonicus
142	612	L. Caecilius Q.f. Metellus Calvus. Q. Fabius Q.f. Maximus Servilianus
141	613	Cn. Servilius Cn.f. Caepio. Q. Pompeius A.f.
140	614	C. Laelius C.f. Q. Servilius Cn.f. Caepio
139	615	Cn. Calpurnius Piso. M. Popillius M.f. Laenas
138	616	P. Cornelius P.f. Scipio Nasica Serapio. D. Iunius M.f. Brutus (Callaicus)
137	617	M. Aemilius M.f. Lepidus Porcina. C. Hostilius A.f. Mancinus
136	618	L.? Furius Philus. Sex. Atilius M.f. Serranus
135	619	Ser. Fulvius Q.f. Flaccus. Q. Calpurnius C.f. Piso
134	620	P. Cornelius P.f. Scipio Africanus Aemilianus II. C. Fulvius Q.f. Flaccus
133	621	P. Mucius P.f. Scaevola. Calpurnius L.f. Piso Frugi
132	622	P. Popillius C.f. Laenas. P. Rupilius P.f.
131	623	P. Licinius P.f. Crassus Mucianus. L. Valerius L.f. Flaccus
130	624	L. Cornelius Lentulus. M. Perperna M.f.
		Suff.: Ap. Claudius Pulcher.
129	625	C. Sempronius C.f. Tuditanus. M'. Aquillius M'.f.
128	626	Cn. Octavius Cn.f. T. Annius Rufus
127	627	L. Cassius Longinus Ravilla. L. Cornelius L.f. Cinna
126	628	M. Aemilius Lepidus. L. Aurelius L.f. Orestes
125	629	M. Plautius Hypsaeus. M. Fulvius M.f. Flaccus
124	630	C. Cassius Longinus. C. Sextius C.f. Calvinus
123	631	Q. Caecilius Q.f. Metellus (Baliaricus). T. Quinctius T.f. Flamininus
122	632	Cn. Domitius Cn.f. Ahenobarbus. C. Fannius M.f.
121	633	L. Opimius Q.f. Q. Fabius Q. Aemiliani f. Maximus
120	634	P. Manilius P.?f. C. Papirius Carbo
119	635	L. Caecilius L.f. Metellus (Delmaticus). L. Aurelius Cotta
118	636	M. Porcius M.f. Cato. Q. Marcius Q.f. Rex
117	637	L. Caecilius Q.f. Metellus Diadematus. Q. Mucius Q.f. Scaevola
116	638	C. Licinius P.f. Geta. Q. Fabius Q. Serviliani f. (Augur) Maximus Eburnus
115	639	M. Aemilius M.f. Scaurus. M. Caecilius Q.f. Metellus
114	640	M'. Acilius M'.f. Balbus. C. Porcius M.f. Cato
113	641	C. Caecilius Q.f. Metellus Caprarius. Cn. Papirius C.f. Carbo
112	642	M. Livius C.f. Drusus. L. Calpurnius L.f. Piso Caesoninus
111	643	P. Cornelius P.f. Scipio Nasica Serapio. L. Calpurnius Bestia
110	644	M. Minucius Q.f. Rufus. Sp. Postumius Albinus
109	645	Q. Caecilius L.f. Metellus (Numidicus). M. Iunius D.f. Silanus
108	646	Ser. Sulpicius Ser.f. Galba. Q.? Hortensius
		Suff.: M. Aemilius Scaurus
107	647	L. Cassius L.f. Longinus. C. Marius C.f.
106	648	C. Atilius Serranus. Q. Servilius Cn.f. Caepio

BC	a.u.c.	
105	649	P. Rutilius P.f. Rufus. Cn. Mallius Cn.f. Maximus
104	650	C. Marius C.f. II. C. Flavius C.f. Fimbria
103	651	C. Marius C.f. III. L. Aurelius L.f. Orestes
102	652	C. Marius C.f. IV. Q. Lutatius Q.f. Catulus
101	653	C. Marius C.f. V. M'. Aquillius M'.f.
100	654	C. Marius C.f. VI. L. Valerius L.f. Flaccus
99	655	M. Antonius M.f. A. Postumius Albinus
98	656	Q. Caecilius Q.f. Metellus Nepos. T. Didius T.f.
97	657	Cn. Cornelius Cn.f. Lentulus. P. Licinius M.f. Crassus
96	658	Cn. Domitius Cn.f. Ahenobarbus. C. Cassius L.f. Longinus
95	659	L. Licinius L.f. Crassus. Q. Mucius P.f. Scaevola
94	660	C. Coelius C.f. Caldus. L. Domitius Cn.f. Ahenobarbus
93	661	C. Valerius C.f. Flaccus. M. Herennius M.f.
92	662	C. Claudius Ap.f. Pulcher. M. Perperna M.f.
91	663	L. Marcius Q.f. Philippus. Sex. Iulius C.f. Caesar
90	664	L. Iulius L.f. Caesar. P. Rutilius L.f. Lupus
89	665	Cn. Pompeius Sex.f. Strabo. L. Porcius M.f. Cato
88	666	L. Cornelius L.f. Sulla (Felix). Q. Pompeius Q.f. Rufus
87	667	Cn. Octavius Cn.f. L. Cornelius L.f. Cinna
		Suff.: L. Cornelius Merula
86	668	L. Cornelius L.f. Cinna II. C. Marius C.f. VII
		Suff.: L. Valerius C.?f. Flaccus
85	669	L. Cornelius L.f. Cinna III. Cn. Papirius Cn.f. Carbo
84	670	Cn. Papirius Cn.f. Carbo II. L. Cornelius L.f. Cinna IV
83	671	L. Cornelius L.f. Scipio Asiaticus. C. Norbanus
82	672	C. Marius C.f. Cn. Papirius Cn.f. Carbo III
81	673	M. Tullius M.f. Decula. Cn. Cornelius Cn.f. Dolabella
80	674	L. Cornelius L.f. Sulla Felix II. Q. Caecilius Q.f. Metellus Pius
79	675	P. Servilius C.f. Vatia (Isauricus). Ap. Claudius Ap.f. Pulcher
78	676	M. Aemilius Q.f. Lepidus. Q. Lutatius Q.f. Catulus
77	677	D. Iunius D.f. Brutus. Mam. Aemilius Mam.f. Lepidus Livianus
76	678	Cn. Octavius M.f. C. Scribonius C.f. Curio
75	679	L. Octavius Cn.f. C. Aurelius M.f. Cotta
74	680	L. Licinius L.f. Lucullus. M. Aurelius M.f. Cotta
73	681	M. Terentius M.f. Varro Lucullus. C. Cassius L.f. Longinus (Varus?)
72	682	L. Gellius L.f. Poplicola. Cn. Cornelius Cn.f. Lentulus Clodianus
71	683	P. Cornelius P.f. Lentulus Sura. Cn. Aufidius Cn.f. Orestes
70	684	Cn. Pompeius Cn.f. Magnus. M. Licinius P.f. Crassus
69	685	Q. Hortensius L.f. Hortalus. Q. Caecilius C.f. Metellus (Creticus)
68	686	L. Caecilius C.f. Metellus. Q. Marcius Q.f. Rex
		Suff.: Servilius Vatia
67	687	C. Calpurnius Piso. M'. Acilius M'.f. Glabrio
66	688	M'. Aemilius Lepidus. L. Volcacius Tullus
65	689	L. Aurelius M.f. Cotta. L. Manlius L.f. Torquatus

BC	a.u.c.	
64	690	L. Iulius L.f. Caesar. C. Marcius C.f. Figulus
63	691	M. Tullius M.f. Cicero. C. Antonius M.f. Hybrida
62	692	D. Iunius M.f. Silanus. L. Licinius L.f. Murena
61	693	M. Pupius M.f. Piso Frugi Calpurnianus. M. Valerius M.f. Messalla Niger
60	694	Q. Caecilius Q.f. Metellus Celer. L. Afranius A.f.
59	695	C. Iulius C.f. Caesar. M. Calpurnius C.f. Bibulus
58	696	L. Calpurnius L.f. Piso Caesoninus. A. Gabinius A.f.
57	697	P. Cornelius P.f. Lentulus Spinther. Q. Caecilius Q.f. Metellus Nepos
56	698	Cn. Cornelius P.f. Lentulus Marcellinus. L. Marcius L.f. Philippus
55	699	Cn. Pompeius Cn.f. Magnus II. M. Licinius P.f. Crassus II
54	700	L. Domitius Cn.f. Ahenobarbus. Ap. Claudius Ap.f. Pulcher
53	701	Cn. Domitius M.f. Calvinus. M. Valerius Messalla Rufus
52	702	Cn. Pompeius Cn.f. Magnus III. Q. Caecilius Q.f. Metellus Pius Scipio
51	703	Ser. Sulpicius Q.f. Rufus. M. Claudius M.f. Marcellus
50	704	L. Aemilius M.f. Paullus Lepidus. C. Claudius C.f. Marcellus
49	705	C. Claudius M.f. Marcellus. L. Cornelius P.f. Lentulus Crus
48	706	C. Iulius C.f. Caesar II. P. Servilius P.f. Vatia Isauricus
47	707	Q. Fufius Q.f. Calenus. P. Vatinius P.f.
46	708	C. Iulius C.f. Caesar III. M. Aemilius M.f. Lepidus
45	709	C. Iulius C.f. Caesar IV (without *collega*) *Suff.:* Q. Fabius Q.f. Maximus. C. Trebonius C.f. C. Caninius C.f. Rebilus
44	710	C. Julius C.f. Caesar V. M. Antonius M.f. *Suff.:* P. Cornelius P.f. Dolabella
43	711	C. Vibius C.f. Pansa Caetronianus. A. Hirtius A.f. *Suff.:* C. Julius C.f. Caesar (Octavianus). Q. Pedius (Q.f.?) P. Ventidius P.f. C. Carrinas C.f.
42	712	M. Aemilius M.f. Lepidus II. L. Munatius L.f. Plancus
41	713	L. Antonius M.f. P. Servilius P.f. Vatia Isauricus II
40	714	Cn. Domitius M.f. Calvinus II. C. Asinius Cn.f. Pollio *Suff.:* L. Cornelius L.f. Balbus. P. Canidius P.f. Crassus
39	715	L. Marcius L.f. Censorinus. C. Calvisius C.f. Sabinus *Suff.* C. Cocceius (Balbus). P. Alfenus P.f. Varus
38	716	Ap. Claudius C.f. Pulcher. C. Norbanus C.f. Flaccus *Suff.:* L. Cornelius. L. Marcius L.f. Philippus
37	717	M. Vipsanius L.f. Agrippa. L. Caninius L.f. Gallus *Suff.:* T. Statilius T.f. Taurus
36	718	L. Gellius L.f. Poplicola. M. Cocceius Nerva *Suff.:* L. Nonius (L.f. Asprenas). Marcius
35	719	L. Cornificius L.f. Sex. Pompeius Sex.f. *Suff.:* P. Cornelius (P.f. Scipio). T. Peducaeus

BC	a.u.c.	
34	720	M. Antonius M.f. II. L. Scribonius L.f. Libo
		Suff.: L. Sempronius L.f. Atratinus. Paullus Aemilius L.f. Lepidus
		C. Memmius C.f. M. Herennius
33	721	Imp. Caesar Divi f. II. L. Volcacius L.f. Tullus
		Suff.: L. Autronius P.f. Paetus. L. Flavius
		C. Fonteius C.f. Capito. M. Acilius (M'. f.?) Glabrio
		L. Vinicius M.f. Q. Laronius
32	722	Cn. Domitius L.f. Ahenobarbus. C. Sosius C.f.
		Suff.: L. Cornelius. M. Valerius Messalla
31	723	Imp. Caesar Divi f. III. M. Valerius M.f. Messalla Corvinus
		Suff.: M. Titius L.f. Cn. Pompeius Q.f.
30	724	Imp. Caesar Divi f. IV. M. Licinius M.f. Crassus
		Suff.: C. Antistius C.f. Vetus. M. Tullius M.f. Cicero. L. Saenius
		L.f.
29	725	Imp. Caesar Divi f. V. Sex. Appuleius Sex.f.
		Suff.: Potitus Valerius M.f. Messalla
28	726	Imp. Caesar Divi f. VI. M. Vipsanius L.f. Agrippa II
27	727	Imp. Caesar Divi f. VII. M. Vipsanius L.f. Agrippa III
26	728	Imp. Caesar Divi f. Augustus VIII. T. Statilius T.f. Taurus II
25	729	Imp. Caesar Divi f. Augustus IX. M. Junius M.f. Silanus
24	730	Imp. Caesar Divi f. Augustus X. C. Norbanus C.f. Flaccus
23	731	Imp. Caesar Divi f. Augustus XI. A. Terentius A.f. Varro Murena
		Suff.: L. Sestius P.f. Quirinalis. Cn. Calpurnius Cn.f. Piso
22	732	M. Claudius M.f. Marcellus Aeserninus. L. Arruntius L.f.
21	733	M. Lollius M.f. Q. Aemilius M'.f. Lepidus
20	734	M. Appuleius Sex.f. P. Silius P.f. Nerva
19	735	C. Sentius C.f. Saturninus. Q. Lucretius Q.f. Vespillo
		Suff.: M. Vinicius P.f.
18	736	P. Cornelius P.f. Lentulus Marcellinus. Cn. Cornelius L.f.
		Lentulus
17	737	C. Furnius C.f. C. Junius C.f. Silanus
16	738	L. Domitius Cn.f. Ahenobarbus. P. Cornelius P.f. Scipio
		Suff.: L. Tarius Rufus
15	739	M. Livius L.f. Drusus Libo. L. Calpurnius L.f. Piso Frugi
		(Pontifex)
14	740	M. Licinius M.f. Crassus. Cn. Cornelius Cn.f. Lentulus (Augur)
13	741	Ti. Claudius Ti.f. Nero. P. Quinctilius Sex.f. Varus
12	742	M. Valerius M.f. Messalla Barbatus Appianus. P. Sulpicius P.f.
		Quirinius
		Suff.: C. Valgius C.f. Rufus
		C. Caninius C.f. Rebilus. L. Volusius Q.f. Saturninus
11	743	Q. Aelius Q.f. Tubero. Paullus Fabius Q.f. Maximus
10	744	Africanus Fabius Q.f. Maximus. Iullus Antonius M.f.
9	745	Nero Claudius Ti.f. Drusus. T. Quinctius T.f. Crispinus
		(Sulpicianus)

BC	a.u.c.	
8	746	C. Marcius L.f. Censorinus. C. Asinius C.f. Gallus
7	747	Ti. Claudius Ti.f. Nero II. Cn. Calpurnius Cn.f. Piso
6	748	D. Laelius D.f. Balbus. C. Antistius C.f. Vetus
5	749	Imp. Caesar Divi f. Augustus XII. L. Cornelius P.f. Sulla
		Suff.: L. Vinicius L.f.
		Q. Haterius. C. Sulpicius C.f. Galba
4	750	C. Calvisius C.f. Sabinus. L. Passienus Rufus
		Suff.: C. Caelius. Galus Sulpicius
3	751	L. Cornelius L.f. Lentulus. M. Valerius M.f. Messalla Messallinus
2	752	Imp. Caesar Divi f. Augustus XIII. M. Plautius M.f. Silvanus
		Suff.: L. Caninius L.f. Gallus
		C. Fufius Geminus. Q. Fabricius
1	753	Cossus Cornelius Cn.f. Lentulus. L. Calpurnius Cn.f. Piso (Augur)
		Suff.: A. Plautius. A. Caecina (Severus)

AD	a.u.c.	
1	754	C. Caesar Aug.f. L. Aemilius Paulli f. Paullus
		Suff.: M. Herennius M.f. Picens
2	755	P. Vinicius M.f. P. Alfenus P.f. Varus
		Suff.: P. Cornelius Cn.f. (Lentulus) Scipio. T. Quinctius T.f. Crispinus Valerianus
3	756	L. Aelius L.f. Lamia. M. Servilius M.f.
		Suff.: P. Silius P.f. L. Volusius L.f. Saturninus
4	757	Sex. Aelius Q.f. Catus. C. Sentius C.f. Saturninus
		Suff. Cn. Sentius C.f. Saturninus. C. Clodius C.f. Licinus
5	758	L. Valerius Potiti f. Messalla Volesus. Cn. Cornelius L.f. Cinna Magnus
		Suff.: C. Vibius C.f. Postumus. C. Ateius L.f. Capito
6	759	M. Aemilius Paulli f. Lepidus. L. Arruntius L.f.
		Suff.: L. Nonius L.f. Asprenas
7	760	Q. Caecilius Q.f. Metellus Creticus Silanus. A. Licinius A.f. Nerva Silianus
		Suff.: Lucilius Longus
8	761	M. Furius P.f. Camillus. Sex. Nonius L.f. Quinctilianus
		Suff.: L. Apronius C.f. A. Vibius C.f. Habitus
9	762	C. Poppaeus Q.f. Sabinus. Q. Sulpicius Q.f. Camerinus
		Suff.: M. Papius M.f. Mutilus. Q. Poppaeus Q.f. Secundus
10	763	P. Cornelius P.f. Dolabella. C. Junius C.f. Silanus
		Suff.: Ser. Cornelius Cn.f. Lentulus Maluginensis. Q. Iunius Blaesus
11	764	M'. Aemilius Q.f. Lepidus. T. Statilius T.f. Taurus
		Suff.: L. Cassius L.f. Longinus
12	765	Germanicus Ti.f. Caesar. C. Fonteius C.f. Capito
		Suff.: C. Visellius C.f. Varro
13	766	C. Silius P.f. A. Caecina Largus. L. Munatius L.f. Plancus

14	767	Sex. Pompeius Sex.f. Sex. Appuleius Sex.f.

Hereafter neither the *consules suffecti* nor filiation are given

15	768	Drusus Caesar. C. Nortanus Flaccus
16	769	Sisenna Statilius Taurus. L. Scribonius Libo
17	770	L. Pomponius Flaccus. C. Caelius Rufus (or Nepos)
18	771	Ti. Caesar Augustus III. Germanicus Caesar II
19	772	M. Iunius Silanus Torquatus. L. Norbanus Balbus.
20	773	M. Valerius Messalla Messallinus. M. Aurelius Cotta Maximus Messallinus
21	774	Ti. Caesar IV. Drusus Caesar II.
22	775	D. Haterius Agrippa. C. Sulpicius Galba.
23	776	C. Asinius Pollio. C. Antistius Vetus.
24	777	Ser. Cornelius Cethegus. L. Visellius Varro.
25	778	Cossus Cornelius Lentulus. M. Asinius Agrippa.
26	779	Cn. Cornelius Lentulus Gaetulicus. C. Calvisius Sabinus.
27	780	L. Calpurnius Piso. M. Licinius Crassus Frugi.
28	781	C. Appius Iunius Silanus. P. Silius Nerva.
29	782	C. Fufius Geminus. L. Rubellius Geminus.
30	783	M. Vinicius. L. Cassius Longinus.
31	784	Ti. Caesar V. L. Aelius Seianus.
32	785	Cn. Domitius Ahenobarbus. L. Arruntius (Furius) Camillus Scribonianus.
33	786	L. Livius Ocella Sulpicius Galba. L. Cornelius Sulla Felix.
34	787	Paullus Fabius Persicus. L. Vitellius.
35	788	C. Cestius Gallus. M. Servilius Nonianus.
36	789	Sex. Papinius Allenius. Q. Plautius.
37	790	Cn. Acerronius Proculus. C. Petronius Pontius Nigrinus.
38	791	M. Aquila Iulianus. P. Nonius Asprenas.
39	792	C. Caesar Augustus Germanicus II. L. Apronius Caesianus.
40	793	C. Caesar III. C. Laecanius Bassus.
41	794	C. Caesar IV. Cn. Sentius Saturninus.
42	795	Ti. Claudius Caesar Augustus Germanicus II. C. Caecina Largus
43	796	Ti. Claudius III. L. Vitellius II.
44	797	T. Statilius Taurus. C. (Sallustius) Passienus Crispus II.
45	798	M. Vinicius II. T. Statilius Taurus Corvinus.
46	799	D. Valerius Asiaticus II. M. Iunius Silanus.
47	800	Ti. Claudius IV. L. Vitellius III
48	801	A. Vitellius. L. Vipstanus Publicola Messalla
49	802	Q. Veranius. C. Pompeius Longinus Gallus.
50	803	C. Antistius Vetus II. M. Suillius Nerullinus
51	804	Ti. Claudius V. Ser. Cornelius (Scipio) Salvidienus Orfitus
52	805	Faustus Cornelius Sulla Felix. L. Salvius Otho Titianus
53	806	D. Iunius Silanus Torquatus. Q. Haterus Antoninus

AD	a.u.c.	
54	807	M'. Acilius Aviola. M. Asinius Marcellus
55	808	Nero Claudius Caesar Augustus Germanicus. L. Antistius Vetus
56	809	Q. Volusius Saturninus. P. Cornelius (Lentulus?) Scipio
57	810	Nero II. L. Calpurnius Piso
58	811	Nero III. M. Valerius Messalla Corvinus
59	812	C. Vipstanus Apronianus. C. Fonteius Capito
60	813	Nero IV. Cossus Cornelius Lentulus
61	814	P. Petronius Turpilianus. L. Caesennius Paetus
62	815	P. Marius Celsus. L. Asinius Gallus
63	816	C. Memmius Regulus. L. Verginius Rufus
64	817	C. Laecanius Bassus. M. Licinius Crassus Frugi
65	818	A. Licinius Nerva Silianus Firmus Pasidienus. M. (Iulius) Vestinus Atticus
66	819	C. Luccius Telesinus. C. Suetonius Paullinus II?
67	820	L. Iulius Rufus. Fonteius Capito
68	821	Ti. Catius Asconius Silius Italicus. P. Galerius Trachalus
69	822	Ser. Sulpicius Galba Imperator Caesar Augustus II. T. Vinius (Rufinus?)
70	823	Imp. Caesar Vespasianus Augustus II. Titus Caesar Vespasianus
71	824	Imp. Vespasianus III. M. Cocceius Nerva
72	825	Imp. Vespasianus IV. Titus Caesar II
73	826	Caesar Domitianus II. L. Valerius Catullus Messallinus
74	827	Imp. Vespasianus V. Titus Caesar III
75	828	Imp. Vespasianus VI. Titus Caesar IV
76	829	Imp. Vespasianus VII. Titus Caesar V
77	830	Imp. Vespasianus VIII. Titus Caesar VI
78	831	D. Iunius Novius Priscus (Rufus?). L. Ceionius Commodus
79	832	Imp. Vespasianus IX. Titus Caesar VII
80	833	Imp. Titus Caesar Vespasianus Augustus VIII. Caesar Domitianus VII
81	834	L. Flavius Silva Nonius Bassus. L.? Asinius Pollio Verrucosus
82	835	Imp. Domitianus VIII. T. Flavius Sabinus
83	836	Imp. Domitianus IX. Q. Petillius Rufus II
84	837	Imp. Domitianus X. C. Oppius Sabinus
85	838	Imp. Domitianus XI
86	839	Imp. Domitianus XII. Ser. Cornelius Dolabella Petronianus
87	840	Imp. Domitianus XIII. L. Volusius Saturninus
88	841	Imp. Domitianus XIV. L. Minucius Rufus
89	842	T. Aurelius Fulvus. M. Asinius Atratinus
90	843	Imp. Domitianus XV. M. Cocceius Nerva II
91	844	M'. Acilius Glabrio. M. Ulpius Traianus
92	845	Imp. Domitianus XVI. Q. Volusius Saturninus
93	846	Sex. Pompeius Collega. Q. Peducaeus Priscinus
94	847	L. Nonius Calpurnius Asprenas Torquatus. T. Sextius Magius Lateranus

AD	*a.u.c.*	
95	848	Imp. Domitianus XVII. T. Flavius Clemens
96	849	C. Manlius Valens. C. Antistius Vetus
97	850	Imp. Nerva Caesar Augustus III. L. Verginius Rufus III
98	851	Imp. Nerva IIII. Imp. Caesar Nerva Traianus Augustus II
99	852	A. Cornelius Palma Frontonianus. Q. Sosius Senecio
100	853	Imp. Traianus III. Sex. Iulius Frontinus III
101	854	Imp. Traianus IIII. Q. Articuleius Paetus
102	855	L. Iulius Ursus Servianus II. L. Licinius Sura II
103	856	Imp. Traianus V. M'. Laberius Maximus II
104	857	Sex. Attius Suburanus Aemilianus II. M. Asinius Marcellus
105	858	Ti. Iulius Candidus Marius Celsus II. C. Antius A. Iulius Quadratus II
106	859	L. Ceionius Commodus. Sex. Vettulenus Civica Cerialis
107	860	L. Licinius Sura III. Q. Sosius Senecio II
108	861	Ap. Annius Trebonius Gallus. M. Atilius Metilius Bradua.
109	862	A. Cornelius Palma Frontonianus II. P. Calvisius Tullus Ruso
110	863	M. Peducaeus Priscinus. Ser. (Cornelius) Scipio Salvidienus Orfitus
111	864	C. Calpurnius Piso. M. Vettius Bolanus
112	865	Imp. Traianus VI. T. Sextius Africanus
113	866	L. Publilius Celsus II. C. Clodius Crispinus
114	867	Q. Ninnius Hasta. P. Manilius Vopiscus Vicinillianus
115	868	L. Vipstanus Messalla. M. Pedo Vergilianus
116	869	L. Fundanius Lamia Aelianus. Sex. Carminius Vetus.
117	870	Q. Aquilius Niger. M. Rebilus Apronianus.
118	871	Imp. Caesar Traianus Hadrianus Augustus II. Cn. Pedanius Fuscus Salinator
119	872	Imp. Hadrianus III. P. Dasumius Rusticus.
120	873	L. Catilius Severus Iulianus Claudius Reginus II. T. Aurelius Fulvus Boionius Arrius Antoninus
121	874	M. Annius Verus II. Cn. Arrius Augur
122	875	M'. Acilius Aviola. Corellius Pansa
123	876	Q. Articuleius Paetinus. L. Venuleius Apronianus Octavius Priscus
124	877	M'. Acilius Glabrio. C. Bellicius Flaccus Torquatus Tebanianus
125	878	M. Lollius Paullinus D. Valerius Asiaticus Saturninus II. L. Epidius Titius Aquilinus
126	879	M. Annius Verus III. C. Eggius Ambibulus
127	880	T. Atilius Rufus Titianus. M. Gavius (Claudius) Squilla Gallicanus
128	881	L. Nonius Calpurnius Asprenas Torquatus II. M. Annius Libo
129	882	P. Iuventius Celsus T. Aufidius Hoenius Severianus II. L. Neratius Marcellus II
130	883	Q. Fabius Catullinus. M. Flavius Aper
131	884	M. Ser. Octavius Laenas Pontianus. M. Antonius Rufinus
132	885	C. Iunius Serius Augurinus. Trebius Sergianus

D	a.u.c.	
3	886	M. Antonius Hiberus. P. Mummius Sisenna
4	887	L. Iulius Ursus Servianus III. T. Vibius Varus
5	888	L. Tutilius Lupercus Pontianus. P. Calpurnius Atilianus (Atticus Rufus?)
6	889	L. Ceionius Commodus. Sex. Vet(t)ulenus Civica Pompeianus
7	890	L. Aelius Caesar II. P. Coelius Balbinus Vibullius Pius
8	891	Canus Iunius Niger. C. Pomponius Camerinus
9	892	Imp. Caesar T. Aelius Hadrianus Antonius Augustus Pius II. C. Bruttius Praesens L. Fulvius Rusticus II
0	893	Imp. Antoninus Pius III. M. Aelius Aurelius Verus Caesar
1	894	T. Hoenius Severus. M. Peducaeus Stloga Priscinus
2	895	L. Cuspius Pactumeius Rufinus. L. Statius Quadratus
3	896	C. Bellicius Flaccus? Torquatus. L. Vibullius Hipparchus Ti. Claudius Atticus Herodes
4	897	L. Lollianus Avitus. T. Statilius Maximus
5	898	Imp. Antoninus Pius IIII. M. Aurelius Caesar II
6	899	Sex. Erucius Clarus II. Cn. Claudius Severus Arabianus
7	900	C. Prastina Pacatus Messallinus. L. Annius Largus
8	901	L. Octavius Cornelius P. Salvius Iulianus Aemilianus. C. Bellicius Calpurnius Torquatus
9	902	Ser. Cornelius Scipio L.? Salvidienus Orfitus. Q. (Pompeius) Sosius Priscus
50	903	M. Gavius Squilla Gallicanus. Sex. Carminius Vetus
51	904	Sex. Quintilius Condianus. Sex. Quintilius Valerius Maximus
52	905	M'. Acilius Glabrio Cn. Cornelius Severus. M. Valerius Homullus
53	906	L. Fulvius C. Bruttius Praesens. A. Iunius Rufinus
54	907	L. Aelius Aurelius Commodus. T. Sextius Lateranus
55	908	C. Iulius Severus. M. Iunius Rufinus Sabinianus
56	909	M. Ceionius Silvanus. C. Serius Augurinus
57	910	M. (Ceionius) Civica Barbarus. M. Metilius Aquillius Regulus Nepos Volusius Torquatus Fronto
58	911	Sex. Sulpicius Tertullus. Q. Tineius Sacerdos Clemens
59	912	Plautius Quintillus (Quintilius). M. Statius Priscus Licinius Italicus
50	913	Appius Annius Atilius Bradua. T. Clodius Vibius Varus
51	914	M. Aurelius Caesar III (from 7 Mar.: Imp. Caesar M. Aurelius Antoninus Augustus III). L. Aelius Aurelius Commodus II (from 7 Mar.: Imp. Caesar L. Aurelius Verus Augustus II)
52	915	Q. Iunius Rusticus II. L. Titius Plautius Aquilinus
53	916	M. Pontius Laelianus. A. Iunius Pastor Caesennius Sospes
54	917	M. Pompeius Macrinus. P. Iuventius Celsus
55	918	M. Gavius Orfitus. L. Arrius Pudens
56	919	Q. Servilius Pudens. L. (A.) Fufidius Pollio
57	920	Imp. L. Aurelius Verus III. M. Ummidius Quadratus

AD	a.u.c.	
168	921	L. Venuleius Apronianus Octavius II. L. Sergius Paullus II
169	922	Q. Pompeius Senecio Roscius Murena Coelius, etc. M. Aqu(iliu) P. Coelius Apollinaris
170	923	C. (Sex.) Erucius Clarus. M. Gavius Cornelius Cethegus
171	924	T. Statilius Severus. L. Alfidius Herennianus
172	925	Ser. (Calpurnius) Scipio Orfitus. Quintilius Maximus
173	926	Cn. Claudius Severus II. Ti. Claudius Pompeianus II
174	927	L. Aurelius Gallus. Q. Volusius Flaccus Cornelianus
175	928	L. Calpurnius Piso. P. Salvius Iulianus
176	929	T. Pomponius Proculus Vitrasius Pollio II. M. Flavius Aper
177	930	Imp. Caesar L. Aelius Aurelius Commodus Augustus. M. Pedu caeus Plautius Quintillus
178	931	Ser. (Cornelius) Scipio (Salvidienus) Orfitus. D. Velius Ruf (Iulianus)
179	932	Imp. Commodus II. P. Martius Verus II
180	933	L. Fulvius C. Bruttius Praesens, etc. Sex. Quintilius Condien
181	934	Imp. Caesar M. Aurelius Commodus Antoninus Augustus II L. Antistius Burrus
182	935	M. Petronius Sura Mamertinus. Q. Tineius Rufus
183	936	Imp. Commodus IIII. C. Av[f]idius Victorinus
184	937	L. Cossonius Eggius Marullus. Cn. Papirius Aelianus
185	938	Maternus. Ti. Claudius M. Appius Atilius Bradua Regillus Atticu
186	939	Imp. Commodus V. M'. Acilius Glabrio II
187	940	L. Bruttius Quintius Crispinus. L. Roscius Aelianus Paculus
188	941	P.? Seius Fuscianus II. M. Servilius Silanus II
189	942	Dulius Silanus. Q. Servilius Silanus
190	943	Imp. Commodus VI. M. Petronius Sura Septimianus
191	944	Opilius Pedo Apronianus. M. Valerius Bradua Mauricus
192	945	Imp. Commodus VII. P. Helvius Pertinax II
193	946	Q. Pompeius Sosius Falco. C. Iulius Erucius Clarus Vibianus
194	947	Imp. Caesar L. Septimius Severus Pertinax Augustus II. D Clodius Septimius Albinus Caesar II
195	948	P. Iulius Scapula Tertullus Priscus. Q. Tineius Clemens
196	949	C. Domitius Dexter II. L. Valerius Messalla Thrasea Priscus
197	950	T. Sextius Lateranus. L. Cuspius Rufinus
198	951	P. Martius Sergius Saturninus. L. Aurelius Gallus
199	952	P. Cornelius Anullinus II. M. Aufidius Fronto
200	953	Ti. Claudius Severus Proculus. C. Aufidius Victorinus
201	954	L. Annius Fabianus. M. Nonius Arrius Mucianus
202	955	Imp. Severus III. Imp. Caesar M. Aurelius Severus Antoninu Augustus
203	956	C. Fulvius Plautianus II. P. Septimius Geta II
204	957	L. Fabius Cilo Septiminus Catinius Acilianus Lepidus Fulcinianu II. M. Annius Flavius Libo
205	958	Imp. Antoninus II. P. Septimius Geta Caesar

AD	a.u.c.	
206	959	M. Nummius Umbrius Primus Senecio Albinus. Fulvius (Gavius Numisius Petronius?) Aemilianus
207	960	(L.?) Annius Maximus. L. Septimius Aper
208	961	Imp. Antoninus III. Geta Caesar II
209	962	Pompeianus. Avitus
210	963	M'. Acilius Faustinus. A. Triarius Rufinus
211	964	Terentius Gentianus. Bassus
212	965	C. Iulius Asper II. C. Iulius Galerius Asper
213	966	Imp. Antoninus IIII. D. Caelius (Calvinus) Balbinus II
214	967	L. Valerius Messalla (Apollinaris?). C. Octavius Appius Suetrius Sabinus
215	968	(Q.) Maecius Laetus II. M. Munatius Sulla Cerialis
216	969	P. Catius Sabinus II. P. Cornelius Anullinus
217	970	C. Bruttius Praesens. T. Messius Extricatus II
218	971	Imp. Caesar M. Opellius Severus Macrinus Augustus Oclatinius Adventus. From 8 June: Imp. Caesar M. Aurelius Antoninus Augustus (Elagabalus)
219	972	Imp. Antoninus II. Q. Tineius Sacerdos II
220	973	Imp. Antoninus III. P. Valerius Comazon Eutychianus
221	974	C. Vettius Gratus Sabinianus. M. Flavius Vitellius Seleucus
222	975	Imp. Antoninus IIII. M. Aurelius Severus Alexander Caesar
223	976	L. Marius Maximus Perpetuus Aurelianus II. L. Roscius Aelianus Paculus Salvius Iulianus
224	977	Ap. Claudius Iulianus II. C. Bruttius Crispinus
225	978	Ti. Manilius Fuscus II. Ser. Calpurnius Domitius Dexter
226	979	Imp. Severus Alexander II. C. Aufidius Marcellus II
227	980	M. Nummius Senecio Albinus. M. Laelius (Fulvius?) Maximus Aemilianus
228	981	Q. Aiacius Modestus Crescentianus II. M. (Pomponius?) Maecius Probus
229	982	Imp. Severus Alexander III. Cassius Dio Cocceianus II
230	983	L. Virius Agricola. Sex. Catius Clementinus Priscillianus
231	984	Claudius Pompeianus. T. Flavius Sallustius Paelignianus
232	985	L. Virius Lupus (Iulianus?). L. Marius Maximus
233	986	L. Valerius Maximus. Cn. Cornelius Paternus
234	987	M. Clodius Pupienus Maximus II. [Su?]lla Urbanus
235	988	Cn. Claudius Severus. L. Ti. Claudius Aurelius Quintianus
236	989	Imp. Caesar C. Iulius Verus Maximinus Augustus. M. Pupienius Africanus
237	990	L. Marius Perpetuus. L. Mummius Felix Cornelianus
238	991	(C.?) Fulvius Pius. Pontius Proculus Pontianus
239	992	Imp. Caesar M. Antonius Gordianus Augustus. M'. Acilius Aviola
240	993	Sabinus II. Se[ius?] Venustus
241	994	Imp. Gordianus II. (Clodius) Pompeianus

AD	a.u.c.	
242	995	C. Vettius Gratus Atticus Sabinianus. C. Asinius Lepidus Praetextatus
243	996	L. Annius Arrianus. C. Cervonius Papus
244	997	Ti. Pollenius Armenius Peregrinus. Fulvius Aemilianus
245	998	Imp. Caesar M. Iulius Philippus Augustus. C. Maesius Titianus
246	999	C. Bruttius Praesens. C. All[– –] Albinus
247	1000	Imp. Philippus II. Imp. Caesar M. Iulius Severus Philippus
248	1001	Imp. Philippus III. Imp. Philippus II
249	1002	Fulvius Aemilianus II. L. Naevius Aquilinus
250	1003	Imp. Caesar C. Messius Quintus Traianus Decius II. Vettius Gratus
251	1004	Imp. Decius (Divus Decius) III. Q. Herennius Etruscus Messius Decius Caesar
252	1005	Imp. Caesar C. Vibius Trebonianus Gallus Augustus II. Imp Caesar C. Vibius Afinius Gallus Veldumnianus Volusianus Augustus
253	1006	Imp. Volusianus II. Valerius Maximus
254	1007	Imp. Caesar P. Licinius Valerianus Augustus. Imp. Caesar P. Licinius Egnatius Gallienus Augustus
255	1008	Imp. Valerianus III. Imp. Gallienus II
256	1009	L. Valerius Maximus II. M. Acilius Glabrio
257	1010	Imp. Valerianus IIII. Imp. Gallienus III
258	1011	M. Nummius Tuscus. Mummius Bassus
259	1012	(Nummius) Aemilianus (Dexter). (Ti. Pomponius) Bassus
260	1013	P. Cornelius Saecularis II. C. Iunius Donatus II
261	1014	Imp. Gallienus IIII. L. Petronius Taurus Volusianus. In Gaul: Imp. Caesar M. Cassianius Latinius Postumus Augustus II
262	1015	Imp. Gallienus V. Nummius Fausianus. In Gaul: Imp. Postumus II
263	1016	(M.) Nummius (Ceionius) Albinus II. Dexter (or Maximus)
264	1017	Imp. Gallienus VI. Saturninus
265	1018	(Licinius) Valerianus II. Lucillus
266	1019	Imp. Gallienus VII. Sabinillus
267	1020	Paternus. Arc(h)esilaus. In Gaul: Imp. Postumus IIII. M. Piavonius Victorinus
268	1021	(Aspasius?) Paternus II. (Egnatius?) Marinianus
269	1022	Imp. Caesar M. Aurelius Valerius Claudius Augustus. Paternus. In Gaul: Imp. Postumus V. Imp. Victorinus Augustus
270	1023	Flavius Antiochianus II. Virius Orfitus
271	1024	Imp. Caesar L. Domitius Aurelianus Augustus. (Ti.) Pomponius Bassus II. In Gaul: Imp. Caesar C. Pius Esuvius Tetricus Augustus
272	1025	Quietus. Iunius Veldumnianus. In Gaul: Imp. Tetricus II
273	1026	M. Claudius Tacitus. (Iulius) Placidianus
274	1027	Imp. Aurelianus II. Capitolinus. In Gaul: Imp. Tetricus III
275	1028	Imp. Aurelianus III. Marcellinus

AD	a.u.c.	
276	1029	Imp. Tacitus II. Aemilianus
277	1030	Imp. Caesar M. Aurelius Probus Augustus. Paulinus
278	1031	Imp. Probus II. Virius Lupus
279	1032	Imp. Probus III. Nonius Paternus II
280	1033	Messalla. Gratus
281	1034	Imp. Probus IIII. C. Iunius Tiberianus
282	1035	Imp. Probus V. Victorinus
283	1036	Imp. Caesar M. Aurelius Carus Augustus II. Imp. Caesar M. Aurelius Carinus
284	1037	Imp. Carinus II. Imp. Caesar M. Aurelius Numerius Numerianus Augustus
285	1038	Imp. Carinus III. T. Claudius M. Aurelius Aristobulus. After death of Carinus. Imp. Caesar C. Aurelius Valerius Diocletianus Augustus II
286	1039	M. Iunius Maximus II. Vettius Aquilinus
287	1040	Imp. Diocletianus III. Imp. Caesar M. Aurelius Valerius Maximianus Augustus
288	1041	Imp. Maximianus II. Pomponius Ianuarianus
289	1042	L. Ragonius Quintianus. M. Magrius Bassus
290	1043	Imp. Diocletianus IIII. Imp. Maximianus III
291	1044	C. Iunius Tiberianus II. Cassius Dio
292	1045	Afranius Hannibalianus. Iulius Asclepiodotus
293	1046	Imp. Diocletianus V. Imp. Maximianus IIII
294	1047	C. Flavius Valerius Constantius Nobilissimus Caesar. C. Galerius Valerius Maximianus Nobilissimus Caesar
295	1048	Nummius Tuscus. C. Annius Anullinus
296	1049	Imp. Diocletianus VI. Constantius Caesar II
297	1050	Imp. Maximianus V. Maximianus Caesar II
298	1051	(M. Iunius Caesonius Nicomachus) Anicius Faustus (Paulinus) II. Virius Gallus
299	1052	Imp. Diocletianus VII. Imp. Maximianus VI
300	1053	Constantius Caesar III. Maximianus Caesar III
301	1054	T. Flavius Postumius Titianus II. Virius Nepotianus
302	1055	Constantius Caesar IIII. Maximianus Caesar IIII
303	1056	Imp. Diocletianus VIII. Imp. Maximianus VII
304	1057	Imp. Diocletianus VIIII. Imp. Maximianus VIII
305	1058	Constantius Caesar V. Maximianus Caesar V
306	1059	Flavius Valerius Constantius Augustus VI. C. Galerius Valerius Maximianus Augustus VI
307	1060	West: Maximianus VIIII. Flavius Valerius Constantinus Nobilissimus Caesar Rome: Maximianus VIIII. C. Valerius Galerius Maximinus Nobilissimus Caesar East: Flavius Valerius Severus Augustus. C. Valerius Galerius Maximinus Nobilissimus Caesar

AD	a.u.c.	
308	1061	Diocletianus X. Galerius Maximianus VII.
		Rome: M. Aurelius Valerius Maxentius Augustus. M. Valerius Romulus
309	1062	Rome: Maxentius II. M. Valerius Romulus II.
		East: Valerius Licinianus Licinus Augustus. L. Flavius Valerius Constantinus Augustus
310	1063	Rome: Maxentius III
		East: Tatius Andronicus. Pompeius Probus
311	1064	Galerius Maximianus VIII. C. Valerius Galerius Maximinus Augustus II
312	1065	Constantinus II. Licinius II.
		Rome: Maxentius IIII
313	1066	Constantinus III. Licinius III
		Rome: Maximinus III
314	1067	C. Caeionius (Ceionius) Rufus Volusianus II. Petronius Annianus
315	1068	Constantinus IIII. Licinius IIII
316	1069	Antonius Caecina? Sabinus. Vettius Rufinus
317	1070	Ovinius Gallicanus. Caesonius Bassus★
318	1071	Licinius V. Flavius Iulius Valerius Crispus Nobilissimus Caesar
319	1072	Constantinus V. Valerius Licinianus Licinius Nobilissimus Caesar
320	1073	Constantinus VI. Fl. Claudius Constantinus Nobilissimus Caesar
321	1074	West: Crispus Caesar II. Constantinus Caesar II
		East: Licinius VI. Licinius Caesar II
322	1075	Petronius Probianus. Amnius Anicius Iulianus
323	1076	Acilius Severus. Vettius Rufinus
324	1077	Crispus Caesar III. Constantinus Caesar III
325	1078	Sex. Anicius (Faustus) Paulinus II. P. Caeionius Iulianus
326	1079	Constantinus VII. Flavius Iulius Constantius Nobilissimus Caesar
327	1080	Flavius Constantius. Valerius Maximus
328	1081	Flavius Ianuarinus. Vettius Iustus
329	1082	Constantinus VIII. Constantinus Caesar IIII
330	1083	Flavius Gallicanus. Valerius Tullianus Symmachus
331	1084	Iulius Annius Bassus. Flavius Ablabius
332	1085	L. Papinius (Fabius) Pacatianus. M(a)ecilius Hilarianus
333	1086	Flavius Iulius Delmatius. Domitius Zenofilus
334	1087	Flavius Optatus. Ammius Manius Caesonius Nicomachus Anicius Paulinus
335	1088	Flavius Iulius Constantius. Caeionius Rufius Albinus
336	1089	Virius Nepotianus. Tettius Facundus
337	1090	Flavius Felicianus. Fabius Titianus

★ *Cf.* J. F. Gilliam, *Historia* 1967, 252.

TABLE VIII

List of Emperors from Augustus to Constantine

Augustus (C. Octavius, *after his adoption by Caesar* C. Iulius C.f.
   Caesar, *but popularly called* Octavianus). Imp. Caesar Augustus 27 BC–AD 14

Tiberius (Ti. Claudius Nero, *after his adoption* Ti. Iulius Caesar).
   Ti. Caesar Augustus   A.D. 14–37

Caligula (C. Iulius Caesar). C. Caesar Augustus Germanicus   37–41

Claudius (Ti. Claudius Nero Drusus Germanicus). Ti. Claudius
   Caesar Augustus Germanicus   41–54

Nero (L. Domitius Ahenobarbus, *after his adoption* Ti. Claudius
   Drusus Germanicus Caesar). Nero (*later* Imp. Nero) Claudius
   Caesar Augustus Germanicus   54–68

Galba (Ser. Sulpicius). Ser (Sulpicius) Galba Imp. Caesar
   Augustus   68–69

Otho (M. Salvius Otho). Imp. M. Otho Caesar Augustus   69

Vitellius (A. Vitellius). A. Vitellius Imp. (*or* Germanicus Imp.)   69

Vespasian (T. Flavius Vespasianus). Imp. Caesar Vespasianus
   Augustus   69–79

Titus (T. Flavius Vespasianus). Imp. Titus Caesar Vespasianus
   Augustus   79–81

Domitian (T. Flavius Domitianus). Imp. Caesar Domitianus
   Augustus   81–96

Nerva (M. Cocceius Nerva). Imp. Caesar Nerva Augustus   96–98

Trajan (M. Ulpius Traianus). Imp. Caesar Nerva Traianus
   Augustus   98–117

Hadrian (P. Aelius Hadrianus). Imp. Caesar Traianus Hadrianus
   Augustus   117–138

Antoninus Pius (T. Aurelius Fulvus Boionius Arrius Antoninus,
   after his adoption T. Aelius Hadrianus Antoninus Pius). Imp.
   Caesar T. Aelius Hadrianus Antoninus Augustus Pius   138–161

Marcus Aurelius (M. Annius Catilius Severus, *after his adoption* M.
   Aelius Aurelius Verus Caesar). Imp. Caesar M. Aurelius
   Antoninus Augustus   161–180

Lucius Verus (L. Ceionius Commodus Verus, *after his adoption* L.
   Aelius Aurelius Commodus Verus). Imp. Caesar L. Aurelius
   Verus Augustus   161–169

Commodus (Imp. Caesar L. Aelius *or* L. (*or* M.) Aurelius Com-

Probus. Imp. Caesar M. Aurelius Probus Augustus	276–282
Carus. Imp. Caesar M. Aurelius Carus Augustus	282–283
Carinus. Imp. Caesar M. Aurelius Carinus Augustus	283–285
Numerianus. Imp. Caesar M. Aurelius Numerius Numerianus Augustus	283–284
Diocletian. Imp. Caesar C. Aurelius Valerius Diocletianus Augustus	284–305
Maximianus. Imp. Caesar M. Aurelius Valerius Maximianus Augustus	286–305
Constantius I. Imp. Caesar M. (or C.) Flavius Valerius Constantius Augustus	293–306
Galerius. Imp. Caesar C. Galerius Valerius Maximianus Augustus	293–311
Constantine I. Imp. Caesar Flavius Valerius Constantinus Augustus	306–337

(After M. Rostovtzeff, *Social and Economic History of The Roman Empire*[2], 1957, p. 752. By courtesy of Oxford University Press.)

TABLE IX

Comparative Chronological Table for Early Roman History

NOTE. This table is inserted to illustrate the schemes by which the chronology of early Roman history was reckoned. Where possible, events have been chosen which are dated in both the Varronian scheme and that followed by Diodorus.

(Reprinted from *Cambridge Ancient History* VIII, p. 321, by courtesy of Cambridge University Press).

Varronian dating a.u.c.	BC	Internal events	External events	Diodorus	Polybius
245	509	Fall of monarchy at Rome: institution of two annual consuls			
			First treaty with Carthage		508/7
259	495		Latin colony at Signia		
260	494	First secession of the Plebs: institution of tribunes	Latin colony at Velitrae		
261	493		Alliance with the Latins		
262	492		Latin colony at Norba		
268	486		Alliance with the Hernici		
269	485	Fall of Sp. Cassius		478	
277	477		Battle of the Cremera	471	
287	467		Latin colony at Antium		
303	451	The first Decemvirate, publication of XII Tables begun		443	
305	449	Second secession of Plebs: passing of the Valerio-Horatian laws		441	
309	445	Lex Canuleia			
312	442		Latin colony at Ardea	434	
323	431		Defeat of Volsci and Aequi at Mt Algidus, and decline of their power		
328	426		War with Fidenae	417	
348	406		Beginning of war with Veii	402	
358	396		Capture of Veii	392	
			Latin colony at Circeii	389	
364	390		Gallic victory at the Allia: sack of Rome	386	387/6
367	387	Creation of four tribes, Arnensis, Sabatina, Stellatina and Tromentina, on land taken from Veii			
369	385		Latin colony at Satricum		
371	383		Latin colonies at Sutrium and Nepete		
372	382		Latin colony at Setia		
387	367	Licinio-Sextian Rogations			
396	358		Renewal of treaty with the Latins		
397	357	Creation of two tribes: Pomptina, Poplilia			
400	354		Treaty with the Samnites	350	
406	348		Second treaty with Carthage	343 (Diodorus says *first* treaty)	
414	340		War with Latins	336	
415	339	Leges Publiliae			
416	338	Citizen colony sent to Antium	Rome dissolves Latin League		
420	334	Latin colony sent to Cales			
421	333	'Dictator year'		—	
422	332	Creation of two tribes: Maecia, Scaptia			
425	329	Citizen colony sent to Tarracina			
426	328	Latin colony sent to Fregellae			
427	327		Outbreak of great Samnite War		
430	324	'Dictator year'		—	
433	321		Roman disaster at Caudium		
436	318	Creation of two tribes: Falerna, Oufentina			
441	313	Latin colonies sent to Pontiae, Saticula and Suessa		311	
442	312	Latin colony sent to Interamna		310	
443	311	Appointment of *duoviri navales*			
445	309	'Dictator year'		—	
448	306		Third treaty with Carthage		
450	304	Latin colonies sent to Alba Fucens and Sora	Rome makes peace with the Samnites	303	
453	301	'Dictator year'		—	
454	300	Lex Ogulnia			
455	299	Creation of two tribes: Aniensis, Teretina. Latin colony sent to Narnia			

TABLE X

Chronological Tables of Greek and Roman History

(By courtesy of the Cambridge University Press these Tables are based on the Tables in the *Cambridge Ancient History*, vols V–XII.)

Most dates in Greek history before the end of the sixth century are only very approximate; traditional dates are given here for what they are worth. Roman Republican dates are given according to the Varronian system (for a comparison with other datings, see Table X): many of the early Republican dates are uncertain.

BC

776	The traditional date of the first recorded victor in the Olympic Games
c. 756	Foundation of Cyzicus and Trapezus by Miletus
754	The beginning of the Ephor list in Sparta
753	Varronian date of the foundation of Rome
c. 750	Greek colonization of Ischia. Foundation of Cumae by Chalcis. Greek trading factory at Al Mina, at the mouth of the Orontes (Syria)
c. 734	Foundation of Naxos by Chalcis
c. 733	Foundation of Syracuse by Corinth
c. 730	Foundation of Mende and Methone by Eretria
c. 729	Foundation of Catana and Leontini by Naxos
c. 728	Foundation of Megara Hyblaea by Megara
c. 720	Foundation of Sybaris by the Achaeans
c. 720	Spartan conquest of Messenia
711	A Greek lord of Ashdod (Palestine) defeated by the Assyrians
709	Sargon II receives the tribute of kings of Cyprus
c. 708	Foundation of Croton by Achaea
c. 706	Foundation of Taras by Sparta
c. 700	Foundation of Poseidonia (Paestum) by Sybaris
c. 688	Foundation of Gela by Rhodes and Crete
685	Foundation of Chalcedon by Megara
683	Beginning of the list of annual archons at Athens

c. 673	Foundation of Locri by Locris. Death of Numa at Rome
c. 669	Argives defeat Spartans at Hysiae
c. 660	Foundation of Byzantium by Megara
c. 660	Sea battle between Corinth and Corcyra
c. 654	Foundation of Acanthus by Andros, of Lampsacus by Phocaea and of Abdera by Clazomenae. Earliest Greek trading post in S. Russia
c. 650	Cypselus becomes tyrant at Corinth
c. 649	Foundation of Himera by Zancle
648	Eclipse of the sun (6 April). *Floruit* of Archilochus
c. 640	Theagenes becomes tyrant at Megara. Beginning of coinage in Asia Minor. Kolaios of Samos reaches the Straits of Gibraltar
c. 632	Cylon's attempted tyranny at Athens
c. 630	Foundation of Cyrene by Thera. Messenian revolt from Sparta
c. 629	Foundation of Sinope by Miletus
c. 628	Foundation of Selinus by Megara Hyblaea
c. 627	Foundation of Epidamnus by Corinth
c. 625	Periander tyrant at Corinth. Foundation of Ambracia, Anactorium and Leucas by Corinth
c. 621	Legislation of Draco at Athens
612	Fall of Nineveh, end of Assyrian empire
c. 610	Thrasybulus tyrant at Miletus. Foundation of Naucratis
c. 601	Foundation of Perinthus by Samos
c. 600	Cleisthenes becomes tyrant at Sicyon. Foundation of Massilia by Phocaea, Potidaea and Apollonia by Corinth, and Panticapaeum by Miletus. Sappho, Alcaeus and Pittacus flourish at Mytilene
c. 598	Foundation of Camarina by Syracuse
597	Capture of Jerusalem, 16 March
c. 594	Solon's reforms at Athens
585	Eclipse of the sun (28 May). Battle between Cyaxares of Media and Alyattes of Lydia
582	Damasias archon at Athens. The first Pythian Games
c. 582	End of tyranny at Corinth
c. 580	Foundation of Acragas by Gela
c. 575	Beginning of coinage in Athens
c. 571–55	Phalaris tyrant of Acragas
566	The first Panathenaea at Athens
c. 561/0	First tyranny of Peisistratus at Athens

c. 560	Croesus king of Lydia. Alalia founded by Phoceans. Sparta starts war with Tegea
c. 559	Miltiades tyrant in the Thracian Chersonese
556	Birth of Simonides
c. 556	Exile of Peisistratus
548	Temple at Delphi burnt
546	Cyrus, king of Persia, conquers Lydia and the Asiatic Greeks. Peisistratus returns to Athens
c. 540	Destruction of Siris
539	Cyrus conquers Babylon. Etruscan and Carthaginian fleets defeat Phocaeans off Alalia (Corsica)
c. 535	Thereafter Elea founded by Phocaeans
c. 534	Tarquinius Superbus king at Rome
c. 530	Pythagoras arrives in Croton
c. 528/7	Death of Peisistratus. Hippias and Hipparchus succeed him
525	Cambyses, king of Persia, conquers Egypt
524	Etruscans defeated at Cumae, where Aristodemus gains control
c. 523	Death of Polycrates, tyrant at Samos
522	Darius king of Persia
c. 519	Athens, allied to Plataea, defeats Thebes
514	Hipparchus assassinated by Harmodius and Aristogeiton
c. 512	Expedition of Darius, king of Persia, to Scythia: conquest of Thrace
511	Spartan expedition against Athens
510	Cleomenes leads second Spartan expedition against Athens. Fall of the Peisistratids. Sybaris destroyed by Croton
509	Fall of Tarquinius Superbus at Rome. First year of the Roman Republic. Treaty between Rome and Carthage. Dedication of the temple of Jupiter on Capitoline Hill
508/7	Reforms of Cleisthenes at Athens
506	Athenians defeat Boeotians and Chalcidians
499	Ionian revolt against Persia starts
499/8	Aristagoras at Sparta and Athens
498	Earliest extant poem of Pindar (*Pyth. X*)
c. 498	Ionians and allies take Sardes; Sardis burnt
c. 496	Battle of Lake Regillus fought by Rome against Latin League
c. 495	Latin colony at Signia
c. 494	Ionians defeated at battle of Lade; Persians capture Miletus. Spartans

defeat Argives at Sepeia. Anaxilas tyrant of Rhegium. First secession of the plebeians at Rome. Latin colony at Velitrae

493   Themistocles archon at Athens

c. 493   Treaty of Spurius Cassius with the Latins

492   Mardonius in Thrace

c. 492   Trial of Miltiades at Athens. Latin colony at Norba

c. 491   Gelon tyrant at Gela

490   Persian expedition against Greece. Destruction of Eretria. Battle of Marathon

c. 489   Expedition of Miltiades against Paros; his trial and condemnation

488   Gelon's Olympic victory

487   First election of archons by lot at Athens. Ostracism of Hipparchus

c. 487   War of Athens and Aegina

486   Ostracism of Megacles. Death of Darius. Treaty of Rome with the Hernici

484   Ostracism of Xanthippus. First victory of Aeschylus

c. 483   Discovery of fresh silver vein in Laurion mines: subsequent increase of Athenian navy

482   Ostracism of Aristeides. Pythian victory of Hieron in horse-race

481   Xerxes at Sardis. Greek congress at Isthmus

480   Xerxes' invasion of Greece. Battles of Artemisium, Thermopylae and Salamis. Anaxagoras at Athens. Carthaginians invade Sicily; defeated at Himera.

479   Mardonius in Attica. Battles of Plataea and Mycale. Ionians revolt from Persia. Athenians capture Sestos (winter)

c. 479   Defeat of the Romans and Fabian gens at the Cremera

479/8   Rebuilding of the walls of Athens

478   Pausanias' expedition to Cyprus and Byzantium. Death of Gelon. Hieron tyrant of Syracuse

477–6   Simonides' victory in dithyrambic competition

478/7   Foundation of the Confederacy of Delos

476   Death of Anaxilas of Rhegium

476/5   Cimon's campaign in Thrace

474   Defeat of the Etruscans off Cumae by Hieron of Syracuse

472   Death of Theron of Acragas. The *Persae* of Aeschylus

c. 471   Ostracism of Themistocles. *Lex Publilia Voleronis* at Rome

468   First victory of Sophocles

446 Revolt and reduction of Euboea. Athens loses Megara

446/5 Thirty Years Peace between Athens and the Peloponnesians. The latest datable poem by Pindar (*Pyth.* viii)

445 *Lex Canuleia* at Rome. Military tribunes with consular power instituted

444/3 Foundation of Thurii

443 Ostracism of Thucydides, son of Melesias. The censorship established at Rome

442 Latin colony at Ardea

442–1 First victory of Euripides

441/40 Revolt of Samos

439 Surrender of Samos

438 The *Alcestis* of Euripides. The consecration of Pheidias' statue of Athene Parthenos

437 Foundation of Amphipolis

c. 437 Pericles' expedition to the Euxine

436 Birth of Isocrates

435 Conflict between Corinth and Corcyra concerning Epidamnus: Corinthians defeated off Leucimme

433 Athenian alliance with Corcyra. Battle of Sybota

433/2 Renewal of Athenian treaties with Rhegium and Leontini

432 Revolt of Potidaea. 'Megarian decree' passed at Athens. Meton's calendar scheme

432/1 Conferences at Sparta

431 The Peloponnesian War begins. Theban attack on Plataea. First Peloponnesian invasion of Attica. The *Medea* of Euripides. Roman victory over the Aequi and Volsci on the Algidus

430 Second Peloponnesian invasion of Attica. Plague at Athens. Failure of Pericles' attack on Epidaurus. Pericles tried and fined. Phormio sent to Naupactus. Fall of Potidaea

429 Siege of Plataea begun. Death of Pericles. Successes of Phormio

428 Peloponnesian invasion of Attica. Revolt of Mitylene. Euripides' *Hippolytus*. Death of Anaxagoras. Birth of Plato

427 Peloponnesian invasion of Attica. Fall of Mitylene. Fall of Plataea. Stasis at Corcyra. Gorgias of Leontini comes to Athens with embassy. Expedition to Sicily under Laches

426 Operations of Demosthenes in north-west Greece. Battle of Olpae. Rome's war with Fidenae

425   Peloponnesian invasion of Attica. Fortification of Pylos. Cleon secures refusal of proposals for peace. Athenians capture Sphacteria. Re-assessment of tribute. Cleon raises jurymen's pay. Corcyrean oligarchs exterminated. *Acharnians* of Aristophanes. Congress at Gela

424   Athenian defeat at Delium. Brasidas captures Amphipolis and Torone. Exile of Thucydides. *Knights* of Aristophanes

423   One year armistice between Athens and Sparta. *Clouds* of Aristophanes

422   Cleon recaptures Torone. Cleon and Brasidas killed at Amphipolis. Negotiations for peace. *Wasps* of Aristophanes

421   Peace of Nicias. Fifty years alliance between Athens and Sparta. *Peace* of Aristophanes

421/0   The quaestorship at Rome opened to the plebeians. Alliance between Sparta and Boeotia.

420   Alliance between Athens, Argos, Mantinea and Elis. The Athenians introduce the cult of Asclepius

419   Nicias and Alcibiades generals

418   Spartan victory over Argos at Mantinea. Oligarchy established at Argos. Fifty years alliance between Sparta and Argos

417   Ostracism of Hyperbolus. Alliance between Athens and Argos renewed

416   Capitulation of Melos to Athens

415   Mutilation of the Hermae. Athenian expedition against Syracuse. Recall and flight to Sparta of Alcibiades. *Troades* of Euripides

414   Siege of Syracuse. *Birds* of Aristophanes

413   Spartans invade Attica and seize Decelea. Athenian disaster in Sicily

412   Revolt of Athenian allies. Agreements between Sparta and Persia. *Helen* and *Andromeda* of Euripides

412–11   Siege of Chios

411   The Revolution of the Four Hundred at Athens. The government of the Five Thousand. Army and fleet at Samos faithful to democracy. Athenian victories at Cynossema and Abydos. *Lysistrata* and *Thesmophoriazusae* of Aristophanes

410   Athenian victory at Cyzicus. Full democracy restored at Athens. Athenians refuse Spartan offers of peace

409   Founding of the city of Rhodes. Carthaginian expedition to Sicily; destruction of Selinus and Himera. *Philoctetes* of Sophocles

408   The Athenians regain Byzantium. *Orestes* of Euripides

174

389 Evagoras of Cyprus revolts from Persia in alliance with Athens. Dionysius besieges Caulonia, wins battle of Elleporus, and captures Caulonia

389/8 Plato visits western Greece

388 Plato returns to Athens from Sicily. *Plutus* of Aristophanes. *Olympiacus* of Gorgias

387 Antalcidas cuts off Athenian fleet in the Dardanelles. Dionysius captures Rhegium. Gauls capture Rome (Polybian date: see 390). Creation of four rustic tribes on the ager Veiens

386 The King's Peace (or Peace of Antalcidas)

386–5 Rome defeats Latins, Volsci and Hernici

385 Sparta reduces Mantinea. Latin colony at Satricum

385–3 Artaxerxes at war with Egypt

384 Birth of Aristotle and Demosthenes

383 Second war of Dionysius with Carthage begins

c. 383 Latin colony at Nepete

382 Spartan force sent against the Chalcidians; Phoebidas seizes the Cadmea at Thebes. Latin colony at Setia

381 Spartans besiege Phlius. Evagoras makes peace with Persia

380 The *Panegyricus* of Isocrates

379 Surrender of Phlius and of Olynthus to Sparta. Liberation of Thebes by Pelopidas. Dionysius captures Croton. Death of Lysias

378 Sphodrias' raid on Attica. Alliance between Athens and Thebes. Agesilaus' invasion of Boeotia

378/7 Formation of the Second Athenian League

376 Athenian naval victory over Sparta off Naxos

375 Timotheus defeats the Peloponnesian fleet off Acarnania. Chabrias operates in the northern Aegean

374 Peace between Athens and Sparta. Alliance between Athens and Jason of Pherae. Death of Evagoras

373 Spartan blockade of Corcyra. Thebans seize Plataea. Alliance of Jason and Amyntas of Macedon

371 Peace of Callias between Athens and Sparta. Thebans defeat the Spartans at the battle of Leuctra. Thebans, Euboeans and Chalcidians leave Athenian Naval League

370 Assassination of Jason. Formation of Arcadian League and alliance with Thebes. Epaminondas' first Peloponnesian campaign. Foundation of Messene

369 Iphicrates fails to capture Amphipolis. Thessaly appeals to Thebes for help. Epaminondas in Peloponnese. Dionysius helps Corinth against Thebes

c. 369 Foundation of Megalopolis

368 The Aleuadae of Larissa seek help from Alexander II of Macedon

c. 368 Third war of Dionysius with Carthage

367 The Tearless Battle. Alliance of Athens and Dionysius I. Death of Dionysius. Dionysius II succeeds. Plato visits Syracuse. Peace between Syracuse and Carthage. Aristotle joins the Academy. Licinian-Sextian rogations at Rome. Consulship restored; one consul must be a plebeian. Creation of curule aedileship

366 Epaminondas' third Peloponnesian campaign. Failure of congress at Thebes. Thebes recovers Oropus. Alliance between Athens and Arcadia. Corinthians make peace with Thebes. Exile of Dion. The *Archidamus* of Isocrates. First plebeian consul at Rome. Creation of praetorship

c. 366 Revolt of the satraps from Persia

365 War between Arcadia and Elis. Timotheus wins Samos; Athens settles cleruchs there. Dionysius II helps Sparta against Thebes

364 Destruction of Orchomenus by Thebes. Battle of Cynoscephalae against Alexander of Pherae; Pelopidas killed. Timotheus operates in Chalcidice. Epaminondas' fleet wins over Byzantium from Athenians

362 Battle of Mantinea. Epaminondas killed

362/1 General Peace (Koine Eirene) in Greece (except Sparta)

361 Alliance of the Thessalian Confederacy with Athens against Alexander. Agesilaus in Egypt. Plato revisits Syracuse with Speusippus

360 Persian authority re-established in Asia Minor. Death of Agesilaus

359 Death of Perdiccas and accession of Amyntas as king of Macedon under regency of Philip. Alexander of Pherae assassinated. Tarquinii revolts from Rome

358 Philip successful against Paeonians and Illyrians. Philip makes a formal peace with Athens. The Hernici re-admitted to Roman alliance. Renewal of treaty between Rome and the Latins

357 Athenian recovery of Euboea and the Chersonese. Philip captures Amphipolis. Chios, Rhodes, Byzantium and Cos revolt from the Athenian League (Social War). Eubulus in power at Athens. Roman tribes of Pomptina and Popilia created. Return of Dion to Syracuse

356 Philip captures Pydna and Potidaea, and founds Philippi. Birth of

Alexander. Battle of Embatum; Athenians defeated. Trial of Timotheus and Iphicrates. Chares helps Artabazus in revolt against Persia. Philip victorious against Illyrians and Paeonians. Dion besieges Ortygia. First plebeian dictator at Rome

355 Independence of Chios, Cos, Byzantium and Rhodes recognized by Athens. Phocians seize Delphi. Amphictyonic League declares Sacred War on Philomelus of Phocis. Isocrates' *On the Peace*. Demosthenes' *Against Leptines*

354 Battle of Neon; death of Philomelus. Dion murdered. Demosthenes' *On the Symmoriae*. Alliance of Rome and the Samnites

353 Onomarchus of Phocis captures Orchomenus. Athenian alliance with Cersobleptes of Thrace. Philip captures Methone. Successes of Onomarchus against Philip in Thessaly. Death of Mausolus of Caria; beginning of work on the Mausoleum. Demosthenes' *For the Freedom of the Rhodians*. Caere defeated by Rome

353/2 Demosthenes' *For the Megalopolitans*. Isocrates' *De Antidosi*

352 The Athenian Chares re-occupies Sestos. Onomarchus killed. Philip takes Pherae and Pagasae and marches to Thermopylae

352–1 Death of Phayllus. Charidemus sent to the Hellespont. First plebeian censor at Rome. Tarquinii and Falerii make forty-year truce with Rome

c. 352–1 Demosthenes' *First Philippic* (or 349)

350 Thebans obtain help from Artaxerxes. Demosthenes' *For Phormio*

349 Athenian alliance with Olynthus. Demosthenes' *Olynthiacs*

348 Phocion engaged in Euboea, whose independence Athens recognises. Philip captures Olynthus. Renewal of Rome's treaty with Carthage

347 Dionysius II recovers Syracuse. Death of Plato

346 Athenian embassy to Philip. Peace (of Philocrates) between Athens and Philip. Philip subdues Phocis and becomes a member of the Amphictyonic League, and presides at the Pythian Games. Demosthenes' *On the Peace*. Isocrates' *Philippus*

345 Syracuse appeals to Corinth. Hicetas intrigues with the Carthaginians. Revolt of Sidon from Persia. Aeschines' *Against Timarchus*

344 Demosthenes' mission in the Peloponese. Philip in Illyria; reorganizes Thessaly. Timoleon sails to Sicily and liberates Syracuse from Dionysius II. Demosthenes' *Second Philippic*. Isocrates' *Letter to Philip*

343 Alliance of Megara with Athens. Trial and acquittal of Aeschines. Demosthenes' *On the Embassy*. Aeschines' *On the Embassy*. Timoleon resettles Syracuse. Aristotle becomes tutor to Alexander

343–2   Persia reconquers Egypt. Speusippus' Letter to Philip

343–1   Rome's First Samnite War

342   Philip in Thrace. Timoleon's unsuccessful campaign against Hicetas. Archidamus helps Tarentines against Lucanians and Messapians. *Leges Genuciae* at Rome

342–1   Birth of Menander and Epicurus

341   Demosthenes at Byzantium. Formation of Euboean League. Carthaginian expedition against Syracuse. Timoleon's victory at the Crimisus. Demosthenes' *On the Chersonese* and *Third Philippic*

340   Philip besieges Perinthus and Byzantium. War declared by Athens on Philip. Demosthenes' *Fourth Philippic*

340–338   The Latin revolt against Rome

339   The siege of Byzantium raised. Thracian expedition of Philip. Outbreak of Amphissean War. Philip occupies Elatea. Peace between Timoleon and Carthage. Isocrates' *Panathenaicus*. Xenocrates succeeds Speusippus as head of the Academy. Leges Publiliae at Rome

338   Philip destroys Amphissa. Battle of Chaeronea. Philip forms a League of Greek states at Corinth. Beginning of Lycurgus' control of Athenian finances. Death of Isocrates. Latin League dissolved. Lanuvium, Aricia, Nomentum and Tusculum receive full Roman citizenship. Fundi, Formiae, Cumae and Capua receive *civitas sine suffragio*. Roman colony at Antium. Death of Archidamus III in Italy

337   Greek Confederacy under Philip declares war on Persia. First plebeian praetor at Rome

336   Assassination of Philip and accession of Alexander. Alexander elected general of the Greeks

335   Alexander in Thrace and Illyria. Destruction of Thebes. Aristotle settles in Athens

334   Alexander's Persian campaign started. Battle of Granicus. Democracies set up in Ionia. Sieges of Miletus and Halicarnassus. Alexander of Epirus in southern Italy. Latin colony at Cales

334–3   Alexander's conquest of Lycia, Pamphylia and western Pisidia. He winters in Gordium

333   Conquest of Cilicia. Battle of Issus; rout of Darius. Birth of Zeno. 'Dictator year' at Rome

332   Siege and capture of Tyre. Alexander's conquest of Egypt. Agis III of Sparta against Macedon. Two new Roman tribes created; Maecia and Scaptia

331 Foundation of Alexandria. Submission of Cyrene. Settlement of Syria. Battle of Gaugamela. Alexander occupies Babylon, Susa and Persepolis. Agis fails to secure an alliance with Athens. Battle of Megalopolis. Defeat and death of Agis

330 Alexander at Ecbatana. Death of Darius III. Execution of Philotas and Parmenion. Lycurgus' *Against Leocrates*. Aeschines' *Against Ctesiphon*. Demosthenes' *On the Crown*

329 Alexander at Bactria. Rome takes Privernum which receives *civitas sine suffragio*. Roman colony at Tarracina (Anxur)

328 Alexander conquers Bactria and Sogdiana. Alexander murders Cleitus. The Pages' Conspiracy and the execution of Callisthenes. Latin colony at Fregellae

327 Alexander's invasion of India

326–304 Rome's Second Samnite War

326 Alexander crosses the Indus and defeats Porus. Mutiny on the Beas. Voyage of Nearchus down the Jhelum. Conquest of the Malli. Philemon's first victory. First use of *prorogatio imperii* at Rome. Alliance of Rome with Neapolis, Nuceria and the Apulians

325 Alexander in Gedrosia. Nearchus returns to the Persian Gulf

324 Alexander rejoins Nearchus and reaches Susa. Restoration of Greek exiles. Mutiny of Macedonians at Opis. Death of Hephaestion. The Harpalus affair at Athens. Trial and exile of Demosthenes. Speeches of Hypereides and Deinarchus against Demosthenes. 'Dictator year' at Rome.

323 Alexander at Babylon. Death of Alexander (10 June). Perdiccas, regent, in power in Asia. Greek revolt against Antipater (Lamian War). Alliance of Athens and Aetolia. Return of Demosthenes to Athens. Antipater besieged in Lamia. Death of Leosthenes.

322 Perdiccas invades Cappadocia, establishes Eumenes as satrap, and invades Pisidia. Ophellas conquers Cyrene for Ptolemy. Athenian defeats. Lamian War ended by battle of Crannon. Change of constitution at Athens. Death of Aristotle, Demosthenes and Hypereides

321 Eumenes' victory over Craterus. Death of Perdiccas in Egypt. Antipater becomes regent of the Empire. Antigonus appointed commander against Eumenes. Eumenes and Alcetas defeated. First production of Menander. Roman defeat by Samnites at the Caudine Forks

319 Death of Antipater. Polyperchon regent. Syria annexed by Ptolemy. Execution of Demades by Cassander, son of Antipater

318 Polyperchon declares the Greeks free. Eumenes captures Babylon. Execution of Phocion. Two new Roman tribes created in northern Campania: Falerna and Oufentina

317 Demetrius of Phaleron established in power in Athens by Cassander. Agathocles seizes power at Syracuse

316 Defeat and execution of Eumenes by Antigonus. Cassander captures Pydna and kills Olympias. Thebes rebuilt by Cassander, now in control of Macedon. Menander's *Dyscolos*

315 The satraps (Seleucus, Ptolemy, Cassander and Lysimachus) start four years' war against Antigonus. Antigonus occupies Syria. Menander's first victory. Samnite victory over Romans at Lautulae

314 Freedom of Greek cities proclaimed by Antigonus. Roman victory at Tarracina. Capua and the Aurunci reduced. Latin colony at Luceria

313 (or /312) Latin colonies at Suessa Aurunca, Pontia, Saticula

312 Ptolemy defeats Demetrius Antigonus at Gaza. Seleucus regains Babylon. Carthaginian invasion of Sicily. Zeno comes to Athens. Censorship of Appius Claudius. Via Appia started. Latin colony at Interamna

311 The satraps, except Seleucus, make peace with Antigonus

310 Appointment of *duoviri navales* at Rome. Agathocles invades Africa. Roman advance into Etruria: treaties with Cortona, Perusia and Arretium

309 Dictator year at Rome

308 Magas seizes Cyrene. Roman alliance renewed with Tarquinii

307 Demetrius, son of Antigonus, frees Athens. Agathocles defeated and escapes to Sicily. Revolt of the Hernici from Rome

306 Naval victory of Demetrius over Ptolemy off Cyprus. Antigonus and Demetrius assume royal titles. Peace between Syracuse and Carthage. Epicurus opens his school at Athens. Anagnia stormed by Romans and granted *civitas sine suffragio*. Third treaty of Rome with Carthage

305 Demetrius besieges Rhodes. Ptolemy, Cassander, Lysimachus and Seleucus assume royal titles

304 Agathocles assumes title of king. Flavius publishes the *legis actones* at Rome. Aequi defeated. End of Samnite War. Roman alliance with Marsi, Paeligni, Marrucini and Frentani

303 Latin colonies at Alba Fucens and Sora. Arpinum receives *civitas sine suffragio*

302 Demetrius re-forms the League of Corinth. Latin colony at Carsioli (or 298). Roman alliance with the Vestini

301 Battle of Ipsus. Antigonus defeated and killed. Partition of Antigonus' kingdom by Seleucus and Lysimachus. Zeno founds the Stoa. 'Dictator year' at Rome.

300 Foundation of Antioch. *Lex Valeria de provocatione* and *Lex Ogulnia* at Rome

299 Alliance of Seleucus and Demetrius. Two new Roman tribes created; Aniensis and Terentina. Latin colony at Narnia. Alliance with Picentes. Gallic raid in Roman territory

298-90 Rome's Third Samnite War

297 Death of Cassander and his son Philip IV: division of Macedon between his younger sons

296 Coalition against Demetrius. Roman colonies at Minturnae and Sinuessa

295 Lachares seizes power in Athens. Ptolemy acquires Cyprus, Seleucus Cilicia, and Lysimachus (ultimately) Ionia. Roman victory at Sentinum over Samnites, Gauls and Umbrians

294 Demetrius Poliorcetes takes Athens and becomes king of Macedonia

293 Foundation of Demetrias. *Lex Maenia*

292 Death of Menander. Antiochus I joint king of the far East. Falerii reduced by Rome

291 Demetrius takes Thebes. Demetrius' wars with Aetolia and Pyrrhus. Latin colony at Venusia

290 End of Samnite War. Rome annexes Sabines as *cives sine suffragio*. Latin colony at Hadria and Roman (?) colony at Castrum Novum Piceni

289 Death of Agathocles. The Mamertines seize Messana. Demetrius prepares to invade Asia

288 Fall of Demetrius. Pyrrhus and Lysimachus partition Macedonia. Strato of Lampsacus succeeds Theophrastus as head of Peripatetic School

287 Demetrius crosses to Asia. *Lex Hortensia*

286 Ptolemy acquires Tyre, Sidon, the Island League and the command of the sea

285 Demetrius surrenders to Seleucus. Pyrrhus driven from Macedonia. Lysimachus king of all Macedonia. Ptolemy II joint king

284 Lysimachus conquers Paeonia. M'. Curius defeats the Senones. Roman colony at Sena

283 Death of Demetrius. His son, Antigonus Gonatas, takes the royal title. Death of Ptolemy I. Ptolemy II becomes sole king. Defeat of Boii and Etruscans at Lake Vadimo

282 Rome helps Thurii against the Lucanians

281 Lysimachus defeated and killed by Seleucus at Corupedion. Antigonus takes Athens. Death of Seleucus and accession of Antiochus I.

280 Ptolemy Ceraunus king of Macedonia. Beginning of the Achaean League. War between Ptolemy II and Antiochus. Pyrrhus lands in Italy: Roman defeat at Heraclea

279 Gauls invade Macedonia. Death of Ceraunus. Gallic invasion of Greece repulsed at Delphi. Treaty between Antigonus and Antiochus. Roman defeat at Asculum. Rome's treaty with Carthage

278 Pyrrhus crosses into Sicily. The Gauls cross to Asia. Miletus Egyptian

277 Anarchy in Macedonia. Antigonus defeats the Gauls at Lysimacheia. Gallic terror in Asia Minor

276 Antigonus Gonatas king of Macedonia; he marries Phila, sister of Antiochus I

275 Pyrrhus returns to Italy; is defeated near Beneventum: leaves Italy for Epirus. Hieron II appointed commander of Syracusan forces. Antiochus I defeats the Gauls

274 Pyrrhus overruns Macedonia. First Syrian War. Antiochus I defeats Ptolemy II in Syria

273 Latin colonies at Cosa and Paestum. Egyptian envoys received at Rome

272 Capture of Tarentum by Papirius Cursor. Livius Andronicus brought to Rome. Death of Pyrrhus at Argos

271 End of the First Syrian War

271/0 Ptolemy's victory parade in Alexandria

270 Capture of Rhegium. Death of Arsinoe II (9 July). Death of Epicurus. Theocritus' praise of Ptolemy II

269 Beginning of Roman silver coinage

c. 269 Hieron II king of Syracuse

268 Latin colonies Ariminum and Beneventum. Full citizenship granted to the Sabines

267 Coalition of Athens, Sparta, and Egypt against Antigonus. Chremonides moves the declaration of war

265 Battle of Corinth. Death of Areus II of Sparta

264   Latin colony at Firmum. Rome in alliance with the Mamertines. Appius Claudius dispatched to Sicily. First Punic War begins

263   Hieron becomes ally of Rome. Latin colony at Aesernia. Eumenes I succeeds Philetaerus as dynast of Pergamum

262   Warfare in Sicily, Roman capture of Agrigentum. Naval victory of Duilius off Mylae. Antigonus takes Athens. End of the *Atthis* of Philochorus

c. 262   Death of Zeno. He is succeeded by Cleanthes

262–1   (Between October and April) Death of Antiochus I and accession of Antiochus II. Peace between Ptolemy II and Antigonus.

260   Beginning of Second Syrian War. Ptolemy II against Antiochus II and Antigonus Gonatas

259   Death of Magas of Cyrene. Antiochus II recovers Ephesus

258   Demetrius the Fair king of Cyrene

257   Naval victory of Regulus off Tyndaris

256   Naval victory off Ecnomus. Regulus lands in Africa, defeats the Carthaginians, and winters at Tunis

255   Regulus' army defeated. Roman naval victory off Cape Hermaeum. Roman fleet wrecked off Pachynus. Peace between Ptolemy II and Antigonus

254   Romans capture Panormus.

253   Roman fleet wrecked off Palinurus. End of the Second Syrian War

252   Antiochus II marries Berenice II

251   Aratus frees Sicyon

250   Roman victory at Panormus. Siege of Lilybaeum. Insurrection of Parni (Parthians) in Bactria

249   Claudius' naval defeat at Drepana

248   Roman alliance with Hieron renewed

248–7   The Parthian era

247   Hamilcar Barca starts Carthaginian offensive in Sicily.

246   Death of Antiochus II and accession of Seleucus II. Death of Ptolemy II and accession of Ptolemy III. Third Syrian War begins (Ptolemy III against Seleucus II). Callimachus' *Coma Berenices*

245   Aratus' first generalship of the Achaean League

244   Latin colony at Brundisium. New fleet built by Rome. Agis IV becomes king of Sparta

243   Aratus takes Corinth

242   Institution of *praetor peregrinus*

241 Lutatius Catulus defeats Hanno in naval battle off Drepana (Aegates Insulae). Carthage asks for peace; end of the First Punic War. Latin colony at Spoletium in Umbria. Rome occupies Sicily. Peace between Seleucus II and Ptolemy III. Death of Eumenes I and accession of Attalus I at Pergamum. Death of Agis IV of Sparta

240 War of the Mercenaries ('Truceless War') against Carthage. First plays of Livius Andronicus

239 Death of Antigonus Gonatas of Macedon and accession of Demetrius II. Seleucus II defeated at Ancyra

238 Parthia invaded by Parni. Antiochus Hierax defeated by Attalus. Attalus proclaimed King. Occupation of Sardinia and (later) Corsica by Rome

237 End of War of the Mercenaries. Hamilcar goes to Spain. Cleomenes III becomes king of Sparta

235 Carthaginian conquests in Spain. Battle of Cleonae. Megalopolis joins the Achaean League. At Rome temple of Janus closed

232 Distribution of ager Gallicus in small lots carried by C. Flaminius

231 Roman envoys confer with Hamilcar. Seleucus' expedition against the Parthians. Chrysippus head of the Stoic schools

230 Death of Hamilcar. Hasdrubal becomes general in Spain

229 First Illyrian War. Corcyra, Dyrrahcium, Apollonia, and Issa become Roman allies. Death of Demetrius II; Antigonus Doson becomes king of Macedonia. Argos joins the Achaean League; great expansion of Aetolia. Athens recovers independence. Antiochus Hierax defeated at Coloe near Pergamum

228 Teuta of Illyria surrenders; Demetrius made ruler of Pharos. Roman protectorate on the Illyrian coast. War begins between Sparta and Achaean League (Cleomenic War). Roman envoys at Athens and Corinth

227 Four praetors elected annually. Sardinia and Corsica made a Roman province. Sicily and Sardinia under praetors. Revolution at Sparta. Antigonus Doson's expedition to Caria

226 Ebro Treaty between Rome and Hasdrubal. Battle of Hekatombaion near Dyme. Death of Seleucus II and accession of Seleucus III

225 Gauls invading Italy routed at Telamon. Argos and Corinth join Cleomenes of Sparta. Aratus negotiates with Antigonus

224 Aratus dictator: alliance with Antigonus. Antigonus takes Argos, and forms the Hellenic League

223 Flaminius defeats the Insubres. Antigonus and Aratus destroy Mantinea. Cleomenes razes Megalopolis. Death of Seleucus III and accession of Antiochus III

222 Battle of Clastidium. Insubres surrender to Rome. Antigonus defeats Cleomenes at Sellasia. Antigonus takes Sparta

221 Death of Hasdrubal: Hannibal becomes general in Spain. Death of Antigonus Doson and accession of Philip V (autumn). Death of Ptolemy III and accession of Ptolemy IV

220 Censorship of Flaminius. Construction of Via Flaminia. The War of the Allies (Social War) begins in Greece. Antiochus III subdues Molon's revolt. Revolt of Achaeus

219 Hannibal besieges and (Nov.) captures Saguntum. Second Illyrian War. Demetrius of Pharos flees to Philip V. Fourth Syrian War begins (Antiochus III against Ptolemy IV). Rhodes declares war on Byzantium. Death of Cleomenes in Egypt

218 War declared between Rome and Carthage. Hannibal's march to Italy. Hannibal wins battles of Ticinus and of Trebia (Dec.). Latin colonies at Placentia and Cremona. Victories of Philip V. Sack of Thermum by Philip V

217 Roman naval victory off the Ebro. Hannibal crosses the Apennines. Ludi Magni established. Carthaginian victory at Lake Trasimene. Fabius Maximus dictator. Peace of Naupactus between Philip and the Aetolians (Sept). Ptolemy IV defeats Antiochus III at Raphia (June 22); peace

216 Carthaginian victory at Cannae. Revolts in Central Italy, including Capua. Antiochus III and Attalus I against Achaeus. Native risings in Egypt start

215 Defeat of Hasdrubal near Dertosa by the two Scipios. Death of Hieron. Hannibal in S. Italy. Tributum doubled. Alliance of Syracuse with Carthage. Sumptuary measures at Rome (*Lex Oppia*). Philip in the Peloponnesus. Alliance of Philip with Hannibal. Achaeus blockaded at Sardes. Revolt of Syphax in Africa

214 Laevinus in Illyria. Philip attacks Messene. Birth of Carneades

213 Siege of Syracuse begun by Marcellus. Hannibal occupies Tarentum (except the citadel). Death of Aratus. Philip successful in Illyria; captures Lissus. Achaeus captured and killed

212 Carthage makes peace with Syphax. Siege of Capua. Laevinus negotiates treaty with the Aetolians. Antiochus recovers Armenia. Ludi Apollinares established

211 The Scipios defeated and killed in Spain. Hannibal's march on Rome. Fall of Capua. Capture and sack of Syracuse. Death of Archimedes. Sulpicius succeeds Laevinus in Greece

210 C. Claudius Nero holds the Ebro line. Scipio lands at Emporium. Twelve Latin colonies refuse contingents. Agrigentum taken. Machanidas of Sparta joins the Aetolians. Philip captures Echinus. Sulpicius captures Aegina. Antiochus in Media

209 Scipio captures Carthago Nova. Roman recapture of Tarentum. Vain peace-negotiations between Philip and the Aetolians. Attalus arrives at Pergamum. Campaign of Antiochus in Parthyene. Arsaces III makes peace. Birth of Ptolemy V (Oct.)

208 Scipio's victory at Baecula. Hasdrubal leaves Spain for Italy and winters in Gaul. Death of Marcellus. Naval victory of Laevinus. Naval campaign of Attalus and Sulpicius. Philip wins successes by land. Attalus returns to Asia. Antiochus attacks Bactria

207 Scipio's victory at Ilipa (or 206). Defeat of Hasdrubal at the Metaurus. Philipoemen, general of the Achaean League, defeats Sparta at Mantinea. Philip raids Aetolia. Hymn composed by Livius Andronicus

206 Gades surrender to Scipio. Foundation of Italica. Scipio leaves for Rome. Separate peace made by the Aetolians with Philip. Nabis king of Sparta. Antiochus makes peace with Euthydemus of Bactria

205 Scipio, consul, in Sicily, recaptures Locri. Mago in Liguria. Peace preliminaries in Phoenice with Philip. Peace ratified by Rome (or 204)

204 Scipio lands in Africa. The 'Black Stone' of Pessinus brought to Rome. Death of Livius Andronicus. Ennius brought to Rome by Cato. Beginning of the 'Cretan War'. Death of Ptolemy IV. Accession of Ptolemy V

203 Defeat of Syphax by Scipio. Scipio's victory at the Great Plains. An armistice agreed on, and broken. Defeat of Mago in Gaul. Hannibal recalled to Africa. Regency of Agathocles in Egypt. Antiochus III conquers Amyzus. Egyptian embassy to Philip

203/2 Alliance of Philip and Antiochus directed against Ptolemy

202 Victory of Scipio at Zama. Armistice. Antiochus invades southern Syria. Philip's conquests at the Straits. Rhodes declares war on Philip. Aetolian appeal to Rome for help rejected (aut.). Peace made with Carthage and triumph of Scipio

201 Masinissa made king of Greater Numidia. Carthage becomes a

client-state. Attalus and the Rhodians ask Rome's help against Philip. War between Sparta and the Achaeans. Antiochus takes Gaza. Philip in Asia Minor. Battles of Chios and Lade. Philip blockaded at Bargylia (winter 201/200)

200 Roman mission in Greece and the East. Insubres revolt, and sack Placentia. War declared on Philip, after he returns from Asia Minor and receives Roman ultimatum (Second Macedonian War). Sulpicius in Illyria. Philip on Thracian coast; takes Abydos. Victory of Antiochus at Panion. Roman envoys visit Antiochus

199 Sulpicius campaigns in Macedonia. The Aetolians join Rome

198 Cato in Sardinia. Praetors increased to six. Flamininus' victory at the Aous. Achaeans join Rome. Antiochus reduces all southern Syria

197 Cethegus defeats the Insubres. Defeat of Philip at Cynoscephalae. Peace between Rome and Macedonia. Antiochus moves on Asia Minor, occupies Ephesus. Dispute with Smyrna and Lampsacus. Accession of Eumenes II of Pergamum

196 Hannibal, as sufete at Carthage, begins democratic reforms. Smyrna and Lampsacus appeal to the Senate. Insubres defeated by Marcellus. Proclamation of 'Freedom of Greece' by Flamininus, at Isthmian Games. Settlement of Greek affairs. Antiochus reaches Thrace. Roman envoys meet him at Lysimacheia. Consecration of Ptolemy V as king at Memphis

195 Roman embassy at Carthage: Hannibal goes into exile. Masinissa begins his raids on Carthaginian territory. Cato sent to quell revolts in Spain. Repeal of the *Lex Oppia*. War against Nabis who submits. Peace between Antiochus and Egypt. Antiochus again in Thrace. Hannibal joins Antiochus at Ephesus. Death of Eratosthenes. He is succeeded by Aristophanes of Byzantium as librarian at Alexandria.

194 Lusitani at war with Rome. Latin colony at Buxentum. Temple of Juno Sospita dedicated in Forum Holitorium. Flamininus returns to Italy; evacuation of Greece. Antiochus again in Thrace. Ptolemy V marries Cleopatra. Antiochus re-opens negotiations with Rome

193 Masinissa raids Carthaginian territory. The Aetolians offer their support to Antiochus. Nabis breaks his treaty with Rome and attacks the Achaeans. Roman embassy to Antiochus. Breach between Antiochus and Rome

192 War declared by Rome on Antiochus (Nov.). Nabis' defeat and death. Sparta forced to join Achaean League. Aetolians surprise Demetrius. Antiochus, invited by the Aetolians, crosses to Greece (Oct.)

191 Rome refuses offer by Carthage to pay off whole indemnity. Defeat of the Boii by Scipio Nasica. Dedication of temple of Magna Mater. *Lex Acilia* alters the calendar. Acilius lands in Greece. Antiochus, defeated at Thermopylae, flees to Ephesus. War in Aetolia. Livius takes Roman fleet to Asia Minor. Eumenes and the Rhodians join Rome. Antiochus' fleet defeated off Corycus

190 Placentia and Cremona re-settled. The Scipios in Greece. Armistice with the Aetolians. Antiochus' fleets defeated at Side and Myonnesus. The Scipios land in Asia. Antiochus defeated at Magnesia

189 Latin colony at Bononia. Campanians enrolled as citizens. Libertini enrolled in rustic tribes. Siege and fall of Ambracia: the Aetolians submit. Sparta secedes from the Achaean League. Peace between Rome and Aetolia. Peace preliminaries at Sardis. Manlius raids the Galatians

188 Full citizenship granted to Arpinum, Formiae, and Fundi. Philopoemen and the Achaeans force submission of Sparta. Treaty of Apamaea with Antiochus. Settlement of Asiatic affairs

187 Building of the Via Aemilia. Temple of Hercules Musarum. Latins sent home from Rome. Political attacks on Scipio. Death of Antiochus: accession of Seleucus IV

186 The Ligurians defeat Marcius Philippus. *Senatus consultum de Bacchanalibus*. Roman envoys at court of Philip. Prusias I of Bithynia attacks Pergamum

184 Cato's censorship. Basilica Porcia. Demetrius, son of Philip, in Rome. Birth of Panaetius. Death of Plautus

184/3 Death of Scipio Africanus at Liternum

183 Citizen colonies at Parma and Mutina. Messenians revolt against the Achaeans: death of Philopoemen. War between Pontus and Pergamum

182 Masinissa raids Carthaginian territory. Death of Hannibal in Bithynia

181 Roman war with Celtiberians in Spain. Latin colony at Aquileia. Transplantation of 40,000 Ligurians to Samnium. *Lex Baebia de ambitu*. Expedition of Philip to the Balkans. Death of Ptolemy V. Accession of Ptolemy Philometor

180 Foundation of Gracchuris in Spain. Latin colony at Luca (last of the Latin colonies). *Lex Villia Annalis*. Philip puts his son Demetrius to death. End of war between Pontus and Pergamum. Birth of Lucilius

c. 180   Death of Aristophanes of Byzantium; he is succeeded by Aristarchus of Samothrace as librarian at Alexandria

179   Gracchus ends Celtiberian war by treaties. Basilica Aemilia begun. Death of Philip: accession of Perseus

178   Expedition against Istria

177   Annexation of Istria. Citizen colony at Luna. Gracchus subdues Sardinia. Latins sent home from Rome

175   Branch of Via Aemilia, connecting Aquileia with Bononia. Death of Seleucus IV (3 Sept.): accession of Antiochus IV Epiphanes

173   Latins struck off citizen rolls. Two Epicurean philosophers expelled from Rome

172   Two plebeian consuls in office for first time. Eumenes of Pergamum, at Rome, inveighs against Perseus. Roman mission in Greece

171   Latin colony at Carteia in Spain. War between Rome and Perseus (Third Macedonian War.) Success of Perseus in skirmishes

170   Basilica Sempronia. Indecisive campaigns: Perseus' success in Thessaly. Joint kingship of Ptolemy VI, Ptolemy VII and Cleopatra II (5 Oct.)

169   *Lex Voconia de mulierum hereditatibus.* Philippus marches into Macedonia. Rhodes, Pergamum, and Bithynia waver, Genthius of Illyria joins Perseus. War between Syria and Egypt. Death of Ennius

168   Foundation of Corduba in Spain. Aemilius Paullus defeats Perseus at Pydna (June). Romans in Illyria: capture of Scodra. Antiochus checked by Rome. Delos declared a free port. Weakening of Pergamum and Rhodes by Rome

167   Tributum discontinued. Epirus plundered and enslaved. Macedonia divided into four, Illyria into three protectorates. Achaeans deported to Italy. Polybius at Rome. Library of Perseus brought to Rome

166   Terence's first play, the *Andria*, produced. Risings in Palestine under Maccabees

165   Antiochus in the East; menace from Parthia. The Book of Daniel

164   Re-dedication of Temple at Jerusalem. Death of Antiochus Epiphanes

163   Roman mission to weaken Syria. Lysias as regent defeats Hasmonaeans. Demetrius Soter reaches Syria

161   *Lex Fannia sumptuaria.* Jewish embassy to Rome: treaty drawn up. Expulsion of Greek philosophers and teachers from Rome

160   Defeat and death of Judas Maccabaeus. Death of Eumenes II of Pergamum: accession of Attalus II

159	Law against bribery. Prusias driven to make peace with Pergamum
c. 159	Death of Terence
157	Roman campaigns in Dalmatia. Judaea begins to become an independent priestly state
156	Beginnings of dispute about Oropus and Athens
155	Carneades, Critolaus and Diogenes come to Rome as envoys and lecture on philosophy and rhetoric. The Dalmatians subdued
154	War with Lusitania (to 138). Massilia asks Rome for help against the Ligures Oxybii
153	Consuls enter office on Kalends of January. Celtiberian War (to 151)
152	Raids of Masinissa. Alexander Balas, rival of Demetrius, recognizes Jonathan as high-priest
151	Carthage declares war on Masinissa. Return of the Achaean exiles to Greece
150	Carthaginians defeated. Rome decides to intervene. Death of Demetrius Soter. Alexander Balas king, client of Egypt
149	Utica joins Rome: the Romans land in Africa. Third Punic War. Siege of Carthage begun. Establishment at Rome of permanent court *de repetundis* (*Lex Calpurnia*). Deaths of Cato and Masinissa. Rising in Macedonia under Andriscus (Fourth Macedonian War). Secession of Sparta from the Achaeans: Diaeus urges on war
148	Via Postumia connects Aquileia, Verona, Cremona, and Genuas
147	Temples of Jupiter Stator and Juno Regina at Rome. Viriathus wins successes against Romans (to 138). Scipio Aemilianus in command, presses siege of Carthage. L. Aurelius Orestes authorizes secessions from the Achaeans
146	Sack and destruction of Carthage. Establishment of Roman province of Africa. War between Rome and the Achaeans: defeat of Diaeus by Mummius. Sack of Corinth. Macedonia another Roman province
145	Egyptian intervention in Syria: victory at Oenoparus. Death of Ptolemy Philometor and Alexander Balas. Wars between Antiochus VI, supported by Tryphon, and Demetrius II
c. 145	Laelius' attempted agrarian law
144	Marcian aqueduct
143	Birth of the orator M. Antonius. Celtiberian revolt: the Numantine War

142 Censorship of Scipio Aemilianus. First stone bridge over the Tiber completed. Tryphon king of Syria. Independence for the Jews

141 Demetrius makes concessions to the Jews under Simon as High Priest. Parthia under Mithridates I annexes Babylonia

140 Birth of the orator L. Licinius Crassus

139 *Lex Gabinia* introduces ballot for elections. Defeat and capture of Demetrius by the Parthians. Antiochus Sidetes becomes king. Death of Attalus II of Pergamum; accession of Attalus III

138 Death of Viriathus in Lusitania. Death of Tryphon

137 D. Brutus advances through Lusitania. Defeat and surrender of Mancinus in Spain. Treaty made and broken. *Lex Cassia* introduces ballot in law-courts

135 First Sicilian Slave War, led by Eunus and Cleon; defeat of the praetor L. Hypsaeus

134 Death of Simon: John Hyrcanus High Priest. Syrian power restored in Judaea

133 Tiberius Gracchus, tribune, proposes *lex agraria*. Senatorial opposition. Tribune Octavius formally deposed: land-bill passed and land-commission instituted. Pergamum bequeathed to Rome under will of Attalus III. Gracchus murdered on eve of new election. Scipio Aemilianus captures Numantia and settles Spain

132 Consuls Popilius and Rupilius preside over *Quaestio* to punish Gracchans. Land commission continues. Victory of P. Rupilius at Enna in Slave War: Sicily re-organized under *Lex Rupilia*. Revolt of Aristonicus of Pergamum after Attalus' death

131 *Lex tabellaria* of tribune Papirius Carbo extends ballot to legislation. Civil war in Egypt. Ptolemy Physcon driven from Alexandria; Cleopatra II sole ruler

130 Consul Perperna defeats Aristonicus. Antiochus (VII) Sidetes of Syria perishes in war with Parthia

129 Scipio Aemilianus dies following popular disorder at Feriae Latinae. Defeat of Sempronius Tuditanus by the Iapudes in Illyria. Organization of province of Asia by Perperna and Manius Aquilius. Latter grants Phrygia to Mithridates (V) of Pontus, but Senate refuses confirmation. Ptolemy Physcon restored to Alexandria, but civil war continues. Death of Carneades, the Academic, founder of New Academy

126 Law of Junius Pennus (*de peregrinis*) forbids aliens access to Rome. Unrest in Sardinia: campaigns of L. Aurelius Orestes

125   M. Fulvius Flaccus, consul, proposes to enfranchise Latins, but is dissuaded by Senate. Latin colony of Fregellae revolts and is crushed

124   Inhabitants of Fregellae are moved to new colony of Fabrateria. First tribunate of C. Gracchus begins (10 Dec.). War in Gaul against Arverni and Allobroges

123   Many laws proposed by C. Gracchus who is re-elected tribune for 122. *Lex Rubria* (? 122) authorizes colony of Junonia at site of Carthage: subsequently repealed. Foundation of *castellum* at Aquae Sextiae near Massilia

122   Tribune M. Livius Drusus intervenes with counter-proposals. *Lex Acilia repetundarum. Lex Sempronia de sociis et nomine Latino* successfully opposed by Gracchus' opponents. Gracchus fails to gain re-election for 121. Conquest of the Balearic Isles by Q. Caecilius Metellus, who founds colonies at Palma and Pollentia

121   First use of *senatus consultum ultimum*. Gracchus is killed in civil disorder. Opimius executes Gracchan followers. Defeats of Arverni and Allobroges by Cn. Domitius Ahenobarbus and Q. Fabius Maximus. Construction of Via Domitia. Assassination of Mithridates V of Pontus at Sinope

120   Accusation and acquittal of Opimius for executing citizens *iniussu civium*

119   Marius, tribune, improves election procedure and carries law checking undue influence upon voters. Abolition of Gracchan commission. Birth of Sisenna, Roman historian

118   Colony at Narbo Martius in Transalpine Gaul. Death of Micipsa, successor of Masinissa: Adherbal, Hiempsal and Jugurtha joint-rulers of Numidia. Reconciliation of Ptolemy Physcon and first wife, Cleopatra II: general amnesty and restoration of order throughout Egypt

117   Death of Hiempsal, son of Micipsa

116   Jugurtha, adopted son of Micipsa, begins to consolidate his power. Senatorial commision sent to settle affairs in Numidia. Death of Ptolemy Physcon. Cyrene separated from Egypt under Ptolemy Apion. Continued dynastic conflicts. Birth of Terentius Varro, scholar and polymath

115   *Lex Aemilia* of Aemilius Scaurus, consul and princeps senatus, regulates distribution of freedmen among tribes. He campaigns against the Ligurians and Gauls. Mithridates VI seizes power in Pontus and initiates policy of territorial expansion

114 C. Marius in Spain. Defeat of C. Cato by Sordisci in Macedonia. Birth of Q. Hortensius the orator.

113 Cn. Carbo defeated by Cimbri at Noreia in Noricum. Jugurtha sacks Cirta, capital of Numidia: many Italian traders killed

112 Rome declares war on Jugurtha

111 *Lex agraria* at Rome. Temporary agreement with Jugurtha

110 Mamilian enquiry at Rome. War re-opened in Africa: surrender of Aulus Albinus

109 Successes of Metellus against Jugurtha. Death of Panaetius, Stoic philosopher. Birth of T. Pomponius Atticus

107 Marius, *cos*. I, begins enlistment of volunteers and *proletarii*. Marius, successor to Metellus, takes Capsa. Defeat of Cassius in Gaul by Tigurini

106 Marius advances through Western Numidia. Bocchus of Mauretania surrenders Jugurtha to Sulla. *Lex Caelia tabellaria* extends ballot to trials for *perduellio*. Birth of Cicero and of Pompey

105 Armies of Caepio and Mallius in Gaul destroyed by Cimbri and Teutoni at Arausio. Birth of Decimus Laberius, Italian mime-writer

104 Marius, *cos*. II, re-organizes the Roman army. *Lex Domitia de sacerdotiis* establishes election for priestly colleges. Second Sicilian Slave War

103 *Lex frumentaria* of L. Appuleius Saturninus, tribune. Lex Appuleia de maiestate establishes new *quaestio perpetua*. Saturninus provides land-allotments in Africa for Marius' veterans. Marius, *cos* III, trains his army in Gallia Transalpina. Jannaeus Alexander becomes priest-king of Judaea

102 Marius, *cos*. IV, defeats Teutoni near Aquae Sextiae. Rome at war with the pirates: M. Antonius sent to Cilicia. Death of Lucilius, Roman satirist

101 Marius, *cos* V, and Catulus defeat Cimbri near Vercellae in Gallia Cisalpina. Mithridates (VI) Eupator and Nicomedes II of Bithynia partition Paphlagonia and occupy Galatia

100 Marius, *cos*. VI. Saturnius' legislation. Marius' coalition with Glaucia Saturninus dissolves: rioting in Rome: Marius restores order under *ultimum decretum*. Death of Glaucia and Saturninus. Second Sicilian Slave War ended by M.' Aquilius. Colony at Eporedia in Gallia Cisalpina. Birth of C. Julius Caesar

99 Reaction in favour of Senate

98   Marius leaves Rome for Asia. *Lex Caecilia Didia* against 'tacking'. Revolts of Lusitani in Spain put down. Q. Mucius Scaevola and Rutilius Rufus govern in Asia

96   Sulla (praetor 97) ordered to install Ariobarzanes on throne of Cappadocia. Ptolemy Apion dies: will leaves Cyrene to Rome

95   *Lex Licinia Mucia* expells allies from Rome. Consulship of Q. Mucius Scaevola. Mithridates ordered out of Paphlagonia and Cappadocia by Rome. Tigranes becomes king of Armenia

94   Death of Nicomedes III (Euergetes) of Bithynia

92   Condemnation of Rutilius Rufus, *de repetundis*. Suppression of Latin *rhetores* by censors

91   Tribunate of M. Livius Drusus. His schemes of reform and in favour of the allies fail. Assassination of Drusus. Outbreak of the Social War: massacre of Romans at Asculum

90   Roman reverses in Social War. *Lex Julia* offers citizenship to all communities not in revolt. M. Aquilius urges on Nicomedes IV against Mithridates Eupator

89   *Lex Plautia Papiria* extends offer of citizenship. *Lex Pompeia* defines status of Transpadane Gaul. Capture of Asculum by Rome. Victory of Strabo and Sulla

88   Samnites alone remain in revolt and are gradually suppressed. Sulpicius Rufus, tribune, proposes to enrol new citizens in all 35 tribes and give command in Asia to Marius in place of Sulla. Sulla marches on Rome with his army. Repeals *Leges Sulpiciae*, and passes laws to strengthen Senate. Marius escapes. Mithridates VI overruns Asia Minor and orders general massacre of Romans and Italians. Athens joins Mithridates. Unsuccessful siege of Rhodes by Mithridates

87   Cinna's revolution. Marius returns to power: massacre in Rome of Sulla's supporters. Sulla lands in Greece: investment of Athens

86   Birth of Catullus. Marius (*cos.*) dies (Jan.). Cinna consul 87–84. Flaccus and C. Flavius Fimbria sent to Asia. Sulla takes Athens; battles of Chaeronea and Orchomenus. Birth of Sallust. Mithridates brought to terms by Sulla: Treaty of Dardanus (Aug.). Settlement of Asia: Nicomedes IV and Ariobarzanes restored, Rhodes rewarded

84   New citizens distributed through all tribes. Cinna killed by mutineers. Carbo remains sole consul

83   Sulla lands in Italy: is supported by Pompey. Murena begins Second Mithridatic War. Sulla brings the text of Aristotle's Works to Rome.

82   Civil War in Italy. Sulla destroys Marian and Samnite forces at the Colline Gate. Proscriptions. Sertorius leaves Italy for Spain. Pompey suppresses opponents of Sulla in Sicily. Murena is driven out of Cappadocia. Sulla orders cessation of hostilities

81   Sulla dictator *'legibus scribundis et rei publicae constituendae'*. Constitutional settlement by Sulla. Reforms in criminal law. Pompey successful in Africa against Marians. Annius Luscus drives Sertorius out of Spain. Cicero's *pro Quinctio*

80   Sertorius lands again in Spain to lead revolt of Lusitani and organizes an army; defeats Fufidius. Ptolemy XI Alexander II proclaimed king of Egypt on nomination of Sulla. He is murdered by Alexandrians. Ptolemy XII Auletes seizes the throne

c. 80   Cicero's *pro Sex. Roscio Amerino*

79   Sulla lays down the dictatorship. Metellus Pius defeated by Sertorius. Cicero in Athens and Rhodes

78   Sulla dies in Campania. Aemilius Lepidus aims at overthrow of Sullan constitution. P. Servilius campaigns for three years against pirates in Lycia, Pamphylia and Isauria

77   Lepidus defeated by Catulus and Pompey: dies in Sardinia. Caesar prosecutes Dolabella for extortion. Perperna joins Sertorius. Pompey appointed to Spain and on journey crushes revolt in Transalpine Gaul

76   Sicinius proposes to restore power to tribunes, frustrated by consuls. Successes of Sertorius against Metellus and Pompey: agreement between Sertorius and Mithridates. Death of Jannaeus Alexander: Salome Alexandra becomes Queen of Judaea

75   *Lex Aurelia* relieves tribunes of disability to hold other offices. Cicero quaestor in Sicily

74   Cyrene made a province. Reinforcements sent to Spain. M. Antonius, praetor, given *imperium infinitum aequum* to deal with pirates. Mithridates declares war on Rome and invades Bithynia: L. Lucullus given command against him. Death of Nicomedes IV of Bithynia: kingdom bequeathed to Rome

73   Agitation for reform by tribune Licinius Macer. *Lex Terentia Cassia* on supply and distribution of corn. Rising of Spartacus at Capua. Lucullus relieves Cyzicus and defeats Mithridates on the Rhyndacus

72   Continued successes of Spartacus: Cassius Longinus defeated at Mutina. Assassination of Sertorius by Perperna: Perperna defeated by Pompey and Spain settled. L. Lucullus wins victories over Mithridates in Pontus. M. Lucullus defeats Bessi and Dardani and ravages Thrace. M. Antonius defeated by pirates of Crete

71 Crassus crushes Spartacus' army in Lucania. Pompey returns from Spain. L. Lucullus winters in Asia and checks extortion: Amisus and last Pontic strongholds reduced. Mithridates, routed by Lucullus, takes refuge with Tigranes in Armenia

70 First consulship of Crassus and Pompey. Restoration of full tribunician powers; *Lex Aurelia* on re-constitution of *iudicia publica*. Trial of Verres, governor of Sicily; the Verrine orations of Cicero. Birth of Virgil

69 Lucullus invades Armenia: capture of Tigranocerta

68 Mithridates returns to Pontus. Discontent in Lucullus' army, but he captures Nisibis. Beginning of Cicero's correspondence

67 *Lex Cornelia* 'ut praetores ex edictis suis perpetuis ius dicant.' Tribunician legislation of Cornelius and Gabinius. *Lex Gabinia* gives Pompey extraordinary command against pirates whom he clears from Mediterranean. Death of Salome Alexandra: civil war in Judaea. Death of Sisenna in Crete

66 *Lex Manilia* gives Pompey command against Mithridates. First conspiracy of Catiline. Pompey supersedes Lucullus and enters into agreement with Phraates III of Parthia: Phraates attacks Tigranes. Final defeat of Mithridates. Cicero praetor. Cicero's *de imperio Cn. Pompei (Pro Lege Manilia)*, and *pro Cluentio*

65 Crassus censor: his intrigues for power in Spain and Egypt fail. Pompey's campaigns against Iberi and Albani between Caspian and Black Sea. Birth of Horace at Venusia in Apulia

64 *Lex Papia* evicts non-citizens from Rome. Pompey in Syria. End of Seleucid monarchy

63 Consulship of Cicero. *Lex agraria* of Rullus, tribune, defeated (Cicero's *de lege agraria*). Trial of Rabirius for *perduellio (pro C. Rabirio.)* Murena, consul-elect, successfully defended by Cicero (*pro Murena*). Caesar elected Pontifex Maximus. Birth of C. Octavius, later Augustus. Conspiracy of Catiline (Cicero's *in Catilinam*) betrayed by envoys of the Allobroges. Execution of the conspirators. Pompey in Damascus and Jerusalem (Spring). He winters at Amisus and organizes his conquests. Fall of Jerusalem and end of Hasmonaean power. Mithridates dies in Crimea

62 Defeat and death of Catiline at Pistoria (Jan.). The Concordia Ordinum. Clodius profanes Bona Dea festival. Pompey lands in Italy and disbands his army (Dec.). Bithynia and Cilicia definitely become provinces: Syria a province; Crete annexed. Pompey organizes these new provinces and sets up client-kings: Pharnaces II, Deiotarus, Brogitarus, Ariobarzanes and Antiochus (Com-

magene). He mediates between Tigranes and Phraates and gives Osrhoëne to Abgarus; makes Hyrcanus High Priest in Judaea: Aretas of Nabatea left independent

61 Pompey's '*acta*' opposed by Senate. Pompey's triumph (28 Sept.). Trial and acquittal of Clodius. Caesar governor of Further Spain. Revolt of Allobroges against extortion. Aedui, crushed by Sequani aided by Ariovistus, appeal to Rome

60 Land-law of Flavius, on behalf of Pompey's veterans, opposed and dropped. Caesar returns from Spain. Secret compact between Caesar, Pompey and Crassus: First Triumvirate. Helvetii decide to migrate westward

59 Caesar consul: his legislation. Pompey marries Julia, Caesar's daughter. *Lex Vatinia* gives Caesar Cisalpine Gaul and Illyricum; Senate adds Transalpine Gaul. Senate recognizes Ptolemy Auletes as king of Egypt

58 P. Clodius, tribune, beats down opposition to Triumvirate: Cicero exiled, M. Porcius Cato sent to take over Cyprus. Cyprus annexed. Clodius' corn law. Caesar's victories over Helvetii and Ariovistus; Roman army winters at Vesontio. Ptolemy driven out of Alexandria

57 Rioting in Rome between Clodius and Milo. Return of Cicero secured (Sept.). Pompey provides for Roman food supply. The Egyptian question re-opened by flight of Ptolemy Auletes to Rome. Caesar defeats Belgae and Nervii: P. Crassus in Normandy. Catullus on the staff of C. Memmius in Bithynia with C. Helvius Cinna. Civil War in Parthia between Mithridates III and Orodes II.

56 Signs of dissension in Triumvirate. Cicero attacks Caesar's Campanian land-law. Conference at Luca (April). Cicero's speeches *pro Sestio* and *de provinciis consularibus*. Return of Cato from Cyprus. Caesar's campaigns against Veneti and Morini

55 Crassus and Pompey, *coss.* II. *Lex Trebonia* and *Lex Pompeia Licinia* assign commands to the three partners. Caesar massacres Usipetes and Tencteri: the Rhine bridged: first expedition to Britain. Dedication of first stone theatre in Rome by Pompey. Cicero's *de Oratore* and *in Pisonem*

54 Pompey, near Rome, governs Spain through *legati*. Death of Julia (Sept.). Rioting prevents consular elections. Caesar's second expedition to Britain. Widespread revolt in N.E. Gaul; defeat of Sabinus and Cotta (Winter). Crassus, in Syria, prepares for Parthian campaign. Gabinius, governor of Syria, restores Ptolemy. Mithridates III surrendered by Seleuceia and put to death by Orodes II. War with Rome

53   Consuls not elected till July 53. Continued rioting between gangs of Clodius and Milo. Crassus defeated and killed by Parthians at Carrhae (May): Cassius reorganizes remnants of the army. General unrest in Gaul: Caesar pacifies Senones, Carnutes and Nervii. Second bridging of the Rhine. Devastation of country of Eburones. Caesar's *de Analogia*

52   Murder of Clodius by Milo (Jan.). Pompey sole consul till August. Milo prosecuted, exile in Massilia. *Leges Pompeiae*. Law of the Ten Tribunes. General rising in Central Gaul under Vercingetorix. Repulse of Caesar from Gergovia. Siege of Alesia: surrender of Vercingetorix. Caesar winters in Gaul. Cicero's *pro Milone* (never delivered).

51   Optimate moves against Caesar. Caesar wins over Curio. Revolt of Bellovaci and siege of Uxellodunum. Parthian invasion of Syria: Bibulus sent as governor to Syria and Cicero to Cilicia. Death of Ptolemy Auletes. Pompey XIII marries sister Cleopatra VII: joint rulers. Publication of Cicero's *de Re publica*, and of Caesar's *Commentarii de Bello Gallico*. Posidonius in Rome

50   Question of successor to Caesar: Curio uses tribunician veto to prevent decision. Illness of Pompey during summer. Curio's proposal for both Caesar and Pompey to lay down commands is passed, but vetoed. The consul Marcellus bids Pompey save the State (mid-Nov.). Tribunes leave Rome. Caesar organizes Gaul and moves into North Italy. Caesar crosses the Rubicon into Italy. Death of Hortensius

49   Civil War.[1] Pompey leaves Italy for Greece (Jan.). Caesar, dictator for eleven days, passes emergency legislation. Caesar defeats the Pompeian forces in Spain at Ilerda. Siege and surrender of Massilia. Curio, sent to take charge of Sicily and Africa, is defeated and killed in Africa while attacking relief force sent by Juba to aid Pompeian commander Varus. Cleopatra and Ptolemy XIII at war

48   Caesar, *cos.* II. Caelius and Milo cause disturbances in Italy: Caelius dies, Milo is executed. Caesar lands in Greece. The campaign of Dyrrhachium: Caesar defeats Pompey at Pharsalus (6 June). Pompey murdered in Egypt (28 Sept.). Caesar arrives in Egypt: the Alexandrine War; death of Ptolemy XIII; Caesar sets up Cleopatra and brother Ptolemy XIV as rulers. Pharnaces of Bosporus defeats Domitius Calvinus at Nicopolis in Pontus

47   Caesar declared dictator II (in absence); M. Antonius as *magister*

[1] Dates according to the Julian calendar following the calculation of Ginzel. The calculation of Le Verrier gives somewhat different Julian dates. *Cf.* J. Carcopino, *César* (1936) 696. *Cf.* n. 43.

equitum. Antony tries to maintain order in Italy. Caesar leaves Egypt, defeats Pharnaces at Zela, and settles affairs in Syria and Asia Minor. Caesar arrives in Italy and quells mutiny in Campania. Emergency measure to cope with debt. Caesar sails for Africa (Oct.) against Pompeian forces there. Birth of Propertius

46 Caesar's campaigns in Africa; victory at Thapsus (6 Feb.). Suicide of Cato. Roman province of Africa Nova. Caesar, dictator II and III, *cos.* III, returns from Africa: celebration of triumph for Gaul, Egypt, Pontus and Africa (Summer). Domestic legislation. Reform of calendar. Caesar leaves for Spain (Nov.). Cicero's *pro Marcello* and *pro Q. Ligario*; *Brutus* and *Orator*

45 Caesar, dictator III and IV, *cos.* IV, defeats the Pompeians at Munda (17 March); exceptional honours voted to Caesar at home. Return from Spain; triumphs of Caesar, Fabius, and Pedius. Cicero's *pro rege Deiotaro*, *de finibus*, *Academica* and *Cato*. Caesar's *Anti-Cato*

44 Caesar, dictator IV (for life) and *cos.* V. Conspiracy against Caesar. Tribunician opposition. Caesar publicly refuses the crown (15 Feb.). Assassination of Caesar (15 March). Return of Octavian from Apollonia. Antony given by the People five years' command in Cisalpine and Transalpine Gaul. Cicero's *de natura deorum*, *de officiis*, *Tusculans:* first *Philippic* (2 Sept.), third *Philippic* (20 Dec.).

43 Antony's siege of Mutina raised: deaths of consuls Hirtius and Pansa. D. Brutus killed in Gaul on Antony's order. Octavian declared consul (Aug.). Triumvirate of Antony, Octavian and Lepidus (Nov.). The proscription-lists: death of Cicero at Formiae. Birth of Ovid at Sulmo. M. Brutus in Macedonia, Cassius in Syria

42 Julius Caesar included among the gods of the State. Sextus Pompeius in control of Sicily. Battle of Philippi: suicides of Cassius and M. Brutus (Oct.). Ariarathes X succeeds to the throne of Cappadocia. Birth of Tiberius

41 Perusine War in Italy. Antony in Asia Minor: meets Cleopatra at Tarsus and visits Alexandria

40 L. Antonius surrenders Perusia to Octavian. Pact of Brundisium divides Roman world (Oct.). Antony marries Octavia. Illyrian Parthini expelled from Macedonia by Censorinus. Death of Deiotarus, king of Galatia. Parthian invasion of Syria. Herod formally made king of Judaea by Roman Senate. Virgil's Fourth *Eclogue*

39 Concordat of Misenum between Antony, Octavian and Sextus Pompeius (Spring). Pollio recaptures Salona in Dalmatia. Agrippa campaigns in Gaul. Antony and Octavia winter in Athens. Ventidius' victory over the Parthians at Mt. Amanus

BC

38 Octavian marries Livia (Jan.). Success of Sextus Pompeius against Octavian in the Straits of Messina. Second victory of Ventidius and death of Pacorus at Gindarus. Antony captures Samosata

37 Pact of Tarentum; Triumvirate probably renewed. Capture of Jerusalem by Herod and Sosius (July). Antony marries Cleopatra at Antioch. Antigonus executed by Antony (Winter). Ariarathes executed and succeeded by Archelaus in Cappadocia. Amyntas made king of Galatia. Polemo made king of Pontus. Varro's *de Re Rustica*

36 Tribunician right of sacrosanctity conferred on Octavian. Renewed offensive against Sextus Pompeius. Octavian defeated at Tauromenium (Aug.). Pompeius defeated off Naulochus in Sicily (Sept.). Lepidus ceases to be Triumvir. Antony joins Canidius at Carana (May). Antony's failure at Phraaspa and retreat through Armenia

35 Octavian campaigns against the Iapudes. Sextus Pompeius killed in Asia by Titius

34 Octavian in Dalmatia. Antony invades Armenia and captures Artavasdes. Antony celebrates a triumph at Alexandria followed by the 'Donations of Alexandria'. Death of Sallust

33 Octavian, *cos.* II: Agrippa aedile. Death of Bocchus II and lapse of all Mauretania to Rome. Antony again in Armenia (Spring) and legions left there until the autumn.

33/2 Antony and Cleopatra winter at Ephesus

32 Octavian defends his acts before the Senate. Octavia divorced by Antony. Antony's will published by Octavian at Rome. Restoration of the Theatre of Pompey

32/1 Antony and Cleopatra winter in Greece

31 Octavian's third consulship followed by successive consulships to 23. Agrippa storms Methone in the Peloponnese; Octavian lands in Epirus. Antony defeated at battle of Actium (2nd Sept.). Octavian winters in Asia

30 Tribunician power conferred on Octavian for life. M. Licinius Crassus consul. Phraates captures Media and restores Artaxes to the Armenian throne. Suicide of Antony. Octavian enters Alexandria. Suicide of Cleopatra

30/29 Cornelius Gallus crushes a revolt in the Thebaid

29 Triple triumph of Octavian (13–15 Aug.). Revolt of the Morini and Treveri. Successes of Crassus in Balkans (and in 28). Dedication of the Temple of Divus Julius

28　Census held by Octavian and Agrippa: *lectio senatus*. Dedication of the Temple of Apollo on Palatine (9 Oct.). Mausoleum of Augustus begun. Messalla wins successes in Aquitania

27　The Act of Settlement. Provincial *imperium* for ten years conferred on Octavian who is now called Augustus (Jan.). Division of senatorial and imperial provinces. Triumph of Crassus (July). Augustus in Gaul and Spain until 25. Death of Varro. First Pantheon erected by Agrippa

26　Disgrace and suicide of Cornelius Gallus

25　Marriage of Julia and Marcellus. Antistius and Carisius subjugate Asturia. Augustus makes Juba king of Mauretania. Terentius Varro crushes the Salassi of the Val d'Aosta. Tarraconensis organized as a province. Annexation of Galatia on the death of Amyntas. Successes of C. Petronius in the Ethiopian war. Aelius Gallus' two year expedition to Arabia Felix.

23　Augustus ill. Conspiracy of Caepio and Murena. Constitutional resettlement. Augustus resigns the consulship and receives *proconsulare imperium maius* and full *tribunicia potestas*. Death of Marcellus. Agrippa sent out as viceregent in the East. Publication of the first three books of Horace's *Odes*.

22　Augustus refuses dictatorship, and consulship for life, but accepts the *cura annonae*. Augustus in Greece and Asia for three years

21　Marriage of Agrippa and Julia

20　Agrippa quells disturbances in Gaul and on the Rhine. Parthia restores Roman standards and prisoners. Tiberius enters Armenia and, on the murder of Artaxes, crowns Tigranes. Rebuilding of the Temple at Jerusalem begun. Erection of the Temple of Mars Ultor on the Capitol

19　Augustus returns to Rome. Agrippa pacifies Spain. Expedition of Cornelius Balbus against the Garamantes. Arch of Augustus set up over the Via Sacra. Death of Virgil (21 Sept.). Death of Tibullus

18　Augustus' *imperium* extended for five years. Agrippa co-regent with *imperium maius* and *tribunicia potestas*. *Leges Juliae*. *Lectio Senatus*

17　Augustus adopts his grandsons, Gaius and Lucius. Celebration of the *ludi saeculares*. Horace's *Carmen Saeculare*

16　The kingdom of Noricum incorporated by P. Silius Nerva. Agrippa sent out to the East. Augustus in Gaul four years

15　Tiberius and Drusus defeat Raeti and Vindelici, and reach the Danube. Agrippa visits Jerusalem

14 Agrippa gives the Bosporan kingdom to Polemo. Restoration of the *Basilica Aemilia*

13 Tiberius consul. Return of Augustus, his *imperium* extended for five years. Return of Agrippa. Death of Lepidus. Vinicius operates in Pannonia. Rising in Thrace quelled by Calpurnius Piso (13–11). Dedication of the Theatre of Marcellus

12 Augustus becomes Pontifex Maximus. Death of Agrippa. Tiberius in command in Pannonia. Drusus dedicates an altar to *Roma et Augustus* near Lugdunum, and campaigns in Germany till 9. Dedication of the Temple of Vesta on the Palatine

11 Tiberius divorces Agrippina to marry Agrippa's widow, Julia

10 Herod's inauguration of Caesarea

9 Death of Drusus near Elbe. Herod's punitive invasion of Nabataea. Dedication of the *Ara Pacis Augustae*

8 Augustus' *imperium* extended for ten years. Census held. Tiberius operates against the Sugambri in Germany. Polemo captured and put to death by his queen Dynamis. Deaths of Horace and Maecenas

7 Tiberius' triumph over Sugambri. Rome divided into fourteen *regiones*, subdivided into *vici*, for local administration

6 *Tribunicia potestas* granted to Tiberius for five years. He retires to Rhodes. Paphlagonia added to Galatia

5 Augustus's twelfth consulship. C. Caesar introduced to public life

4 Execution of Antipater. Death of Herod

2 Augustus's thirteenth consulship. L. Caesar introduced to public life. Augustus receives title of *Pater Patriae*. Exile of Julia. Lex Fufia Caninia. Murder of Parthian king Phraates IV who is succeeded by Phraataces. Dedication of the Temple of Mars Ultor

1 C. Caesar in Syria

2 Return of Tiberius from Rhodes. Death of L. Caesar at Massilia. C. Caesar's agreement with Phraataces. Armenian throne given by C. Caesar to Ariobarzanes, king of Media, who dies soon afterwards

3 Augustus' *imperium* extended for ten years

4 Death of C. Caesar in Lycia. Tiberius adopted by Augustus and invested with *tribunicia potestas* for ten years. Tiberius required to adopt Germanicus. *Lex Aelia Sentia*. Germanicus sent to Germany, invades as far as the Weser

5   Tiberius reaches the Elbe

6   Creation of the *aerarium militare* and of the office of the *praefectura vigilum*. Revolt in Pannonia and Illyricum. Maroboduus recognized as king of the Marcomanni. Judaea made a province; Sulpicius Quirinius, legate of Syria, superintends its assessment. Temple of the Castores rebuilt by Tiberius

8   Claudius made augur. Capitulation of the Pannonians. Ovid banished, leaves for Tomis on the Black Sea

9   *Lex Papia Poppaea.* Revolt finally crushed in Dalmatia. Defeat of Varus by Arminius in Germany and loss of three legions

10 *Senatus consultum Silanianum.* Temple of Concord restored by Tiberius and dedicated to the *Concordia Augusta*

12 Tiberius' triumph *ex Illyrico*

13 Augustus' *imperium* extended for ten years. Tiberius receives *tribunicia potestas* for ten years and proconsular *imperium* equal to that of Augustus

14 *Lustrum* held. Death of Augustus (19 Aug.). Accession of Tiberius to the Principate. Sejanus appointed to the Prefecture of the Praetorians. Revolt of legions in Pannonia and Germany. Drusus sent to put down mutiny in Pannonia. Germanicus crosses the Rhine against the Marsi

15 Germanicus invades the territory of the Chatti and Lower Germany. Achaea and Macedonia transferred from the Senate to the *princeps* and attached to Moesia

16 Accusation and suicide of Libo Drusus. Germanicus again invades Germany; he is recalled

17 Triumph of Germanicus. Cn. Piso appointed legate of Syria. Earthquake in Asia Minor. Germanicus in the East. Cappadocia and Commagene organized as imperial provinces. Rising of Tacfarinas in Africa. Death of Livy at Padua

18 Consulship of Tiberius (III) and Germanicus. Germanicus in Asia Minor and Syria. Artaxias set on the throne of Armenia. Germanicus' unauthorized visit to Egypt (18–19)

19 Jews banished from Rome. Arminius killed by his own kinsmen. Piso leaves Syria. Death of Germanicus at Antioch (10 Oct.)

20 Trial and suicide of Piso

21 Consulship of Tiberius (IV) and his son Drusus. Tiberius retires for a time to Campania. Rising of Julius Florus and Julius Sacrovir in Gaul. Disturbances in Thrace

21/22 Castra Praetoria built at Rome

22 *Tribunicia potestas* conferred on Drusus

23 Death of Drusus (14 Sept.)

24 Defeat (and death) of Tacfarinas at Auzia in Mauretania by Cornelius Dolabella

25 Accusation and suicide of Cremutius Cordus, the historian

26 Insurrection in Thrace quelled by Poppaeus Sabinus. Pontius Pilate appointed governor of Judaea

27 Tiberius withdraws to Capreae

28 Titius Sabinus put to death on a charge of *maiestas*. Revolt of the Frisii in Germany

29 Death of Livia. Banishment of Agrippina the elder and her son Nero

30 Suicide of Nero in Pontia. Velleius Paterculus publishes his *History*

31 Consulship of Tiberius (V) and Sejanus. Gaius given the *toga virilis* and priesthood. Sejanus put to death. Macro appointed Prefect of the Praetorians

33 Death of Agrippina on island of Pandateria (Oct.). Quaestorship of Gaius. Financial crisis in Rome

34 Death of Philip; his tetrarchy incorporated into the province of Syria. Death of Artaxias of Armenia. Interference of Artabanus in Armenia

36 Pontius Pilate sent to Rome on charge of maladministration by L. Vitellius, governor of Syria.

37 Death of Tiberius (16 March). Accession of Gaius (Caligula) and consulship with Claudius. Commagene re-established as a client-kingdom under Antiochus. Agrippa I given a kingdom in Syria. Temple of Divus Augustus consecrated

38 Death and deification of Drusilla. Disturbances against the Jews in Alexandria. Deposition of Avillius Flaccus. Pontic kingdom given to Polemo II. Cotys made king of Armenia Minor

39 Gaius leaves Rome (Sept.) for Gaul (Oct.), raids German tribes. Lepidus and Gaetulicus executed; Julia and Agrippina exiled

40 Gaius' expedition to the Channel; returns to Rome (31 Aug.). Murder in Rome of Ptolemy, king of Mauretania. Revolt of Aedemon in Mauretania. Jewish embassy to Rome from Alexandria. Agrippa I receives the dominions of Antipas. Disturbances in Judaea against Gaius

41 Gaius murdered (24 Jan.). Claudius made emperor. The Chauci in Germany defeated by Gabinius. Claudius' settlement of Greek and

Jewish disputes in Alexandria. Judaea and Samaria added to the dominion of Agrippa I. Kingdom of Chalcis given to Herod. Recognition of the sovereignty of Mithridates in the Bosporan kingdom. The Cilician kingdom given to Polemo II. Exile of Seneca to Corsica

42 Revolt of Furius Camillus Scribonianus in Dalmatia followed by his suicide. Mauretania organized as two provinces, Caesariensis and Tingitana

43 Expedition to Britain under Aulus Plautius. Claudius comes to Britain for final victory. Lycia made an imperial province

44 Claudius' triumph for Britain. Achaea and Macedonia transferred to the Senate. Death of Agrippa I; Judaea made a province again

46 On the murder of Rhoemetalces III, Thrace is made an imperial province

47 Triumph of Aulus Plautius. Censorship of Claudius and L. Vitellius. *Ludi saeculares* held. Corbulo reasserts Roman authority over the Frisii. Plautius succeeded in Britain by Ostorius Scapula

48 Messallina and her paramour C. Silius put to death. Claudius marries Agrippina. Ventidius Cumanus procurator of Judaea till 52

49 Seneca recalled from Corsica and made praetor and tutor to Domitius (Nero)

50 Nero adopted by Claudius as guardian for Britannicus. Pomponius Secundus checks an incursion of Chatti in Germany. Agrippa II sent to rule Chalcis on the death of Herod

51 Burrus made Prefect of the Praetorians. Consulship of Vespasian. Defeat of Caractacus in Wales. Death of Gotarzes of Parthia, succeeded by Venones for a short while and then by Vologases

51–52 Gallio proconsul in Achaea

53 Marriage of Nero and Octavia. Imperial procurators in the provinces given the right of jurisdiction. Parthians re-occupy Armenia and Tiridates recovers the throne

54 Claudius poisoned by Agrippina. Accession of Nero. Claudius deified. Seneca's *Apocolocyntosis*

55 Consulship of Nero and L. Antistius Vetus. Pallas removed from office of financial secretary. Britannicus poisoned. Corbulo takes up his command against Armenia and Parthia with Ummidius Quadratus. Seneca's *de Clementia* dedicated to Nero

56 *Quaestores aerarii* replaced by *praefecti aerarii*

57 Nero orders the participation of senators and knights in the games

58 Nero refuses perpetual consulship. Nero's proposal to abolish all indirect taxes. Tiridates attacked by Corbulo and client-kings. Corbulo captures Artaxata

59 Murder of Agrippina on Nero's orders. Nero introduces Greek games in Rome. Establishment of *Augustiani*. Fall of Tigranocerta to Corbulo

60 Puteoli raised to the rank of a colony. Institution of the *Neronia*. Corbulo completes the subjugation of Armenia. Tigranes, nephew of Tigranes IV, placed on the throne. Festus succeeds Felix in Judaea. Corbulo governor of Syria

61 Death of Prasutagus, king of Iceni in Britain. Revolt of the Iceni under Boudicca, and of the Trinovantes. Tigranes invades Adiabene. Vologases gives help to Tiridates and threatens Syria. Armistice arranged between Corbulo and Vologases

62 Death of Burrus. Tigellinus made Prefect of the Praetorians with Faenius Rufus. Fall of Seneca. Nero divorces Octavia and marries Poppaea. Octavia banished and murdered. Paetus arrives in Cappadocia on his task of annexing Armenia. Paetus surrenders to Vologases at Rhandeia. Death of Persius

64 Fire in Rome (18 July) for nine days. Persecution of Christians. Canal from Ostia to Lake Avernus begun. Exploratory mission to Ethiopia. Gessius Florus procurator of Judaea until 66.

65 *Neronia* held again. Conspiracy of Piso (April). Suicides of Seneca and the poet Lucan. Banishment of the Stoic Musonius Rufus. C. Nymphidius Sabinus becomes Prefect of the Praetorians with Tigellinus and holds office until 68. Death of Poppaea

66 Tiridates crowned king of Armenia by Nero at Rome. Nero goes to Greece and orders death of Scribonius Rufus and Scribonius Proculus. Thrasea Paetus condemned by Senate at Nero's order; his son-in-law Helvidius Priscus exiled. 'The freedom' of Greece proclaimed by Nero. Vinician conspiracy at Beneventum. Nero marries Statilia Messallina. Temple of Janus closed. Rebellion spreads all over Palestine. Suicide of Petronius. The 'Column of Nero' at Mainz

67 Nero inaugurates work on a canal at Corinth. Corbulo ordered by Nero to kill himself. Vespasian appointed with the rank of *legatus* to carry on the war in Judaea (Feb.). Fall of Jotapata; Josephus surrenders to Vespasian

68 Return to Nero to Italy. Death of Nero (6 June). The Senate and Praetorians accept Galba as princeps. Nymphidius Sabinus succeeded by Cornelius Laco and killed by the Praetorians. Galba enters Rome

(Autumn). Rebellion of Vindex in Gaul opposed by Verginius Rufus at Vesontio. Suicide of Vindex after defeat of his troops. Verginius Rufus succeeded in Upper Germany by Hordeonius Flaccus. Vespasian begins an attack on Jerusalem, but suspends operations on hearing of the death of Nero

69 Two legions at Mainz refuse to renew the oath of allegiance to Galba (1 Jan.): Galba killed and Otho hailed as emperor by the Praetorians (15 Jan.). A. Vitellius hailed as emperor in Lower Germany and later in Upper Germany and elsewhere. Caecina and Valens join forces at Cremona on behalf of Vitellius. Otho's forces defeated at Bedriacum. Suicide of Otho (16 April). Vitellius reaches Rome. Mucianus repels an attack on Moesia by the Dacians. Rising of Civilis on the Rhine. Murder of Hordeonius. Vespasian declared Emperor in Alexandria, Judaea and Syria (1–3 July) and soon accepted on the Danube. Vespasian's forces under Antonius sack Cremona (end of Oct.). Antonius captures Rome. Death of Vitellius (20 Dec.)

70 Arrival of Mucianus at Rome (Jan.). Arrival of Vespasian at Rome (Summer). Conspiracy of Julius Classicus and Julius Tutor with Julius Sabinus to create an 'Imperium Galliarum'. Operations of Petilius Cerialis and Annius Gallus in Lower and Upper Germany. Cerialis forces Civilis to submission. Titus begins operations against Jerusalem (Spring) and captures it (Sept.). Laying of foundation stone of the restored Capitoline Temple (21 June) which is completed in 71.

71 Titus returns from the East (Spring), receives proconsular imperium and shares tribunician power with Vespasian. Temple of Janus closed. Banishment from Rome of the *astrologi* and *philosophi*

72 Deposition of Antiochus IV of Commagene. Armenia Minor added to Cappadocia

73–74 Censorship of Vespasian and Titus. Roman operations in Upper Germany

75 Visit of M. Julius Agrippa II and Berenice to Rome. Invasion of Media and Armenia by the Alani

76 Birth of Hadrian

78 Conspiracy of A. Caecina Alienus and Eprius Marcellus. Agricola governor of Britain (until 85)

79 Death of Vespasian (June 24). Accession of Titus. Eruption of Vesuvius (24 Aug.); destruction of Pompeii and Herculaneum; death of the Elder Pliny

116 Revolt against Rome in the East. Jewish revolt spreads to Egypt and Cyprus

117 Death of Trajan in Cilicia: accession of Hadrian. Birth of Aelius Aristides, the Sophist

118 Hadrian reaches Rome (9 July)

120 Antoninus consul

121 Hadrian travels in western provinces. Birth of M. Aurelius (26 April)

122 Hadrian visits Britain. Second Moorish revolt

124 Hadrian in Asia Minor

129 Hadrian at Athens. Birth of Galen at Pergamum

130 Antinoöpolis founded by Hadrian in Middle Egypt (30 Oct.). Aelia Capitolina founded on site of Jerusalem

131 Jewish revolt under Bar Cocheba

134 Invasion of Parthia by the Alani

135 Hadrian's final victory over the Jews followed by the reorganization of Syria Palaestina

136 Hadrian adopts L. Aelius as Caesar

138 Death of L. Aelius Caesar (1st Jan.). Antoninus adopted as co-regent (25 Feb.). Death of Hadrian (10 July). Accession of Antoninus Pius

138–9 Defeat of Brigantes by Lollius Urbicus

139 Dedication of Mausoleum of Hadrian

140 First consulship of Marcus Aurelius

143 Herodes Atticus and Fronto, Marcus' tutors, consuls

145 Temple dedicated to Divus Hadrianus. M. Aurelius marries Faustina, daughter of Pius

148 900th anniversary of founding of Rome

152 Peace re-established in Mauretania Caesariensis and Tingitana

157–158 Operations against Dacian tribes

159 Dacia divided into three provinces

160 Marcus Aurelius and L. Verus appointed consuls designate. Risings in Africa suppressed

161 Death of Antoninus Pius (7 March). Accession of Marcus Aurelius. L. Verus given the title Augustus

162 Parthia declares war on Rome and invades Armenia. L. Verus dispatched from Rome to the East

163 Armenia regained

164 Defeat of the Parthians and destruction of Seleucia and Ctesiphon

165 Plague spreads from Seleucia to Asia Minor, Egypt, Italy and the Rhine

166 Roman successes in Media. L. Verus returns to north Italy. Marcus Aurelius and L. Verus celebrate a joint triumph (12 Oct.)

167 Plague in Rome. Outbreak of war in Upper Pannonia and invasion of N. Italy

168 M. Aurelius and L. Verus successful against the Germans

169 Death of L. Verus (Jan.). War continued against the Germans and Sarmatae until 175

173 Revolt in Egypt

174 Marcus Aurelius begins his *Meditations*

175 Revolt of Avidius Cassius, governor of Syria (April). Cassius killed (July). M. Aurelius and his son Commodus go to the East

176 M. Aurelius and Commodus return to Rome and hold triumph (23 Dec.)

177 Consulship of Commodus, who is named Augustus. Roman victory over the Mauretanians

178 Unrest of the Marcomanni and other tribes on the Danube. Marcus and Commodus go north (3 August)

180 Death of Marcus Aurelius (17 March). Accession of Commodus. Pacification of Daci, Quadi, Iazyges, Vandali. Perennis is Prefect of Praetorians

182 Conspiracy of Lucilla, sister of Commodus; she and Crispina executed

185 Perennis executed; Cleander Prefect of the Praetorians

186 Pertinax suppresses mutiny of the armies in Britain

188 Roman victory against revolt in Germany

190 Fall and execution of Cleander. Pertinax crushes disorders in Africa

192 Murder of Commodus (31 Dec.)

193 Pertinax proclaimed Emperor (1 Jan.). Murdered by Praetorians (28 March). Didius Julianus emperor; (13 April) he is put to death on 1 June. Accession of Septimius Severus; who gives D. Clodius Albinus, governor of Britain, the position of Caesar, and marches against C. Pescennius Niger, governor of Syria, already proclaimed emperor by Syrian legions. Siege of Byzantium begun

194 Defeat of Niger by Severus on the plain of Issus and his subsequent death at Antioch. Severus crosses the Euphrates

196 Caracalla, son of Severus, proclaimed Caesar. Fall of Byzantium

197 Caracalla proclaimed joint Augustus with Severus. Defeat of Albinus near Lyons (19 Feb.) followed by his suicide. Britain divided into two provinces. Severus returns to Rome (June). Resumption of Severus' Eastern campaign, which is concluded two years later. Tertullian's *Apologeticum*

199–200 Severus in Egypt

202 Severus returns to Rome

203 Consulship of C. Fulvius Plautianus and P. Septimius Geta. Dedication of the Arch of Septimius Severus at Rome. Origen succeeds Clement as head of the Catechetical School. The *Passion* of Perpetua

203–4 Severus in Africa

205 Consulship of Caracalla and Geta. Murder of Plautianus. Birth of Plotinus in Egypt

206 Brigandage of Bulla Felix in Italy

208 Severus leaves Rome for Britain

211 Death of Severus at York (4 Feb.). Return of Geta and Caracalla to Rome

212 Geta killed by Caracalla, who becomes sole emperor (Feb.). The 'Constitutio Antoniana'. Accession of Artabanus V

213 Caracalla successful against the Alemanni

214 Edessa becomes Roman colony

215 Caracalla winters at Antioch and subsequently advances to the eastern borders of Adiabene

216 Birth of Mani

217 Assassination of Caracalla near Carrhae (8 April). Macrinus becomes emperor, meets with a reverse near Nisibis (Summer)

218 Elagabalus proclaimed emperor at Raphaneae (16 May), after his supporters defeat Macrinus, who is put to death. Elagabalus winters at Nicomedia

219 Elagabalus arrives at Rome (late Summer)

220 Consulship of Elagabalus and Comazon

222 Elagabalus adopts his cousin, Alexianus, as Caesar under the name of Marcus Aurelius Alexander. Murder of Elagabalus and his mother Julia Soaemia. Severus Alexander becomes emperor (13 March)

223 Praetorian prefect and jurist Ulpianus murdered by his soldiers

226 Ardashir is crowned and becomes King of Kings of Iran

229 Consulship of Severus Alexander and Cassius Dio

230 The Persians invade Mesopotamia and besiege Nisibis

231   Severus Alexander leaves Rome for the East (Spring).

232   Failure of Roman offensive against Persia. Origen, banished from Alexandria, resettles in Caesarea

233   Alexander returns to Rome

234   Campaign against the Alemanni. Maximinus, a Thracian, proclaimed emperor by Pannonian soldiers

235   Death of Severus Alexander near Mainz (mid-March). Maximinus, confirmed as Emperor by the Senate, successful in battle against the Alemanni. Enforcement of regulations against Christians

236   Campaigns against the Sarmatians and the Dacians

238* M. Antonius Gordianus, proconsul of Africa, declared emperor: he rules with his son. They are killed by the legate of Numidia, Capellianus. The Senate appoints two new emperors, M. Clodius Pupienus Maximus to command the legions and D. Caelius Balbinus to administer civil affairs (16 April). Maximinus is murdered while besieging Aquileia (10 May). The Praetorians kill Pupienus and Balbinus and raise the third Gordianus (aged 13) to the throne (9 July). Attacks by the Goths across the Danube and by the Dacian Carpi. M. Tullius Menophilus governor of Lower Moesia till 241

240   Mani begins to preach in Persia. Shapur I succeeds Ardashir on the Persian throne

242   Inauguration of a campaign against the Persians by the Praetorian Prefect, Timostheus

243   Successes of Timesitheus against the Persians

244   Murder of Gordian III in Mesopotamia. Philip the Arabian recognized as emperor. Philip makes peace with the Persians and goes to Rome. Birth of Diocletian (22 Dec.)

245   Wars on the Danube frontier until 247

247   Philip, the Emperor's son, given the rank of Augustus. Millennary celebrations at Rome

248   Decius re-establishes order in Moesia and Pannonia. Origen's *Contra Celsum*

249   Decius compelled by his troops to assume the purple (June). Philip and his son are killed in battle against Decius near Verona (September). Renewed attacks by the Goths. Persecution of the Christians by Decius until 251

* The dates for 238–275 are often uncertain. *Cf.* G. Walser, T. Pekary, *Die Krisis des römischen Reiches* (1962).

251 Decius' two sons proclaimed Augusti (May). Defeat and death of Decius and his son Herennius Etruscus on the Danube. Trebonianus Gallus proclaimed second emperor with Decius' second son, Hostilianus, who is still a child and soon afterward dies. Cyprian's *De Lapsis* and *De catholicae ecclesiae unitate*. Volusianus, son of Gallus, proclaimed Augustus

252 European provinces invaded by Goths and other barbarians. Tiridates is driven from his throne in Armenia by the Persians, who proceed to attack Mesopotamia

253 Aemilianus is proclaimed emperor, but three or four months later, after killing Gallus, he is murdered by his own troops following the proclamation of Valerian as emperor by the Rhine legions in Moesia. Valerian reaches Rome and his son Gallienus is appointed second Augustus by the Senate. First Gothic expedition by sea to Asia Minor. Death of Origen at Tyre

254 The Marcomanni penetrate Pannonia and make a raid as far as Ravenna. The Goths lay waste Thrace. Shapur captures Nisibis

256 Gothic expedition by sea to Asia Minor

257 New persecution of the Christians launched by Valerian. Renewed Persian invasion

258 Martyrdom of Cyprian (14 Sept.); (or 259) Gallienus defeats Alemanni

259 Dionysius I Bishop of Rome

260 (or 259?) Valerian captured by Shapur. Gallienus ends the persecution of the Christians. Macrianus and Quietus proclaimed emperors by the army in the East, Postumus in Gaul. (or 258?) Revolts of Ingenuus and then of Regalianus in Pannonia

261 Macrianus killed in battle against Aureolus. Quietus executed at Emesa

262 Odenathus of Palmyra is successful against Shapur and the Persians. Dedication of the Arch of Gallienus

267 The Goths invade Asia Minor. Odenathus of Palmyra assassinated; his widow Zenobia secures power in the name of her infant son Vaballathus

268 Large Gothic forces by sea and land active in Thrace, Greece and elsewhere. Gallienus wins a victory at Naissus in Moesia. Gallienus murdered at the siege of Milan (Aug.). Claudius becomes emperor;

has Aureolus put to death. A synod at Antioch pronounces Paul of Samosata a heretic

268/9 Postumus killed

269 Further Roman successes against the Goths

270 Claudius dies of the plague at Sirmium in Pannonia (Jan.). Quintillus, his brother, is chosen emperor by the Senate, but Aurelian successfully rises against him. Aurelian's successes against the Juthungi. Palmyrene troops enter Alexandria. Death of Plotinus

271 Aurelian begins the construction of new walls around Rome. Organized migration of Romans from Dacia to the south side of the Danube. Aurelian takes the offensive against Zenobia

272(?)Death of Shapur I who is succeeded by Hormizd I

273 Destruction of Palmyra by Aurelian. Death of Hormizd I, who is succeeded by Vahram I

274 Tetricus comes over to Aurelian, who recovers the allegiance of Gaul. Aurelian triumphs in Rome and reforms the coinage. Aurelian's temple to the Sun-God at Rome

275 Aurelian is murdered in Thrace. Tacitus is made emperor (Sept.)

276 Tacitus dies at Tyana; his brother Florian seizes power, but is killed at Tarsus and is succeeded by Probus. Vahram II ascends the throne of Persia

277 Probus delivers Gaul from Germans and Goths

278 Probus is occupied with work of pacification in Asia Minor

282 Murder of Probus, who is succeeded by Carus (early Autumn)

283 Death of Carus near Ctesiphon: he is succeeded by his sons, Carinus in the West and by Numerian in the East. Vahram II makes peace with Rome. The *Cynegetica* of Nemesianus

284 Numerian is killed at Perinthus and Diocles succeeds (20 Nov.)

285 Diocles meets Carinus in battle at Margus; Carinus is killed by one of his own officers. Diocles takes the name of Diocletian

286 Maximian is given the rank of Augustus, after defeating the Bagaudae in Gaul

286–7 Revolt of Carausius

288 Diocletian makes an agreement with Vahram II and sets up Tiridates III in Armenia. Diocletian suppresses a revolt in Egypt

289 Diocletian campaigns against the Sarmatians. Maximian defeated by Carausius

292 Diocletian campaigns against the Sarmatians

293 Constantius and Galerius appointed Caesars in the West and East respectively. Constantius captures Boulogne from Carausius, who is killed by his minister, Allectus, who continues to hold Britain. Death of Vahram II. Vahram III, King of Persia, succeeded by Narses I

296 Constantius recovers Britain from Allectus. Settlement of Galerius with Narses

297 Diocletian's Edict against the Manicheans (31 March). Rebellion of Domitius Domitianus in Egypt. Galerius' war against Persia

298 Diocletian in Egypt

301 Diocletian's Edict *de maximis pretiis*

302 Death of Narses who is succeeded by Hormizd II

303 Diocletian celebrates his *Vicennalia* in Rome (20 Nov.). Persecution of the Christians begins at Nicomedia

304 Death of Pope Marcellinus

305 Abdication of Diocletian and Maximian, who are succeeded by Constantius and Galerius as Augusti: Severus and Maximinus Daia are appointed Caesars

306 Death of Constantius at York (25 July). His son Constantine proclaimed emperor of the West by Constantius' soldiers. Maxentius proclaimed *princeps* at Rome and supported by his father Maximian. Invasion of Italy by Severus

307 Constantine marries Fausta, Maximian's daughter, and acknowledges Maxentius as Augustus. Defeat and death of Severus. Galerius reappears in Italy but withdraws to Pannonia

308 Licinius declared Augustus. Conference of emperors at Carnuntum on the Danube (Diocletian, Galerius, and Maximian)

309 Death of Hormizd II

310 Maximian, captured at Massilia, takes his own life. Pamphilus executed

311 Galerius issues an edict at Nicomedia giving Christians legal recognition (30 April). Death of Galerius. Persecution resumed (Oct.–Nov.). Rebellion in Africa put down. Martyrdom of Peter, Bishop of Alexandria. Miltiades Bishop of Rome

312 Constantine's victory over Maxentius at the Mulvian Bridge (28 Oct.). Death of Maxentius

313 Meeting of Constantine and Licinius at Milan; they agree to partition the Roman world. Licinius defeats Maximinus at Tzirallum (1 May). Licinius issues at Nicomedia a grant of freedom of belief (June). Death of Maximinus at Tarsus. Council in Rome condemns Donatists

INDEX